THE ROAD
TO REUNION
1865 – 1900

BY

PAUL H. BUCK

*Assistant Professor of History at
Harvard University*

BOSTON
LITTLE, BROWN AND COMPANY
1937

TO

ARTHUR MEIER SCHLESINGER

PREFACE

WHEN the colors of the Confederacy were furled in surrender at Appomattox the United States confronted a problem new to American statecraft. For the first time in its history the country was called upon to deal with a disaffected people who had aspired to independence and failed. The situation was a perplexing one. The restored Union rested frankly upon force. The North was arrogant in victory and inclined to be assertive in the realization of newly found power. The South lay spent and exhausted, yet ready to offer stolid resistance to the unfriendly gestures of its assailant. Certainly he who essayed to rejoin the disrupted fabric of national life would learn in full measure how strong and unyielding is the hatred of brothers.

Victors in a civil strife are prone to consider themselves as constituting the nation. The defeated tend as readily to resent the implied inferiority of their humiliating position. The misunderstanding of the Reconstruction period arose naturally from these conditions. For twelve years the North endeavored to build a policy upon force. The South in resistance rejected good and bad indiscriminately. In the process the sectional division persisted and perhaps intensified.

And yet the central theme of American life after the war, even in the years of political radicalism, is not to be found in a narrative of sectional divergence. It was national integration which triumphed at Appomattox. It was national integration which marked every important development in the years that followed. The period of Reconstruction, as usually defined, it is true, gave rise to an abnormal political condition which in its divisive influence ran counter to the basic theme. But

political Reconstruction was not fundamental. Seemingly regardless of the political clamor that so filled the public ear,
the formation of American character continued. The sturdy
barriers of sectional antipathy and distrust crumbled one by
one. Not all the misunderstanding disappeared. And certainly
as should be expected the normal differences in economic and
sociological regionalism persisted and will persist. But within
a generation after the close of the Civil War the particularistic aspirations of North and South had lost their bitter edge
and an American nationalism existed which derived its elements indiscriminately from both the erstwhile foes. A union
of sentiment based upon integrated interests had become a
fact.

This speedy reconciliation was a striking illustration of the
dynamic force exerted by nationalism in the Nineteenth Century. There had been a distinctive American character as early
as dwellers in a new world had interests and ways of looking
at things peculiar to themselves. It had developed rapidly in
the common work of the Revolution until the Constitution of
1787 gave it perfected form by establishing an effective central
government. But no sooner had the early republic entered
upon its career than the bases of national life shifted profoundly. The energies of new forces found an easy lodgment
in the fluid state of an unformed society and made of America
a laboratory of contending currents. In time the pattern of a
new and stronger nationalism emerged.

It was in the North that the potent influence of this new
agency was first introduced. There it was that the common
man came earliest into his own, where means of transportation were more revolutionized and communication of ideas
facilitated, where immigration left a greater non-English element in the population, where industry was transformed and
cities grew to mammoth size, where the scientific and humanitarian thought of the new century made provincials susceptible
to world influences, where the older and stabler trilogy of
aristocracy, decentralization, and agriculture were sacrificed
to the newer and more experimental trilogy of democracy,
nationalism, and industrialism, where in short the centripetal
process triumphed in producing a united society conscious of

its kinship. The North was on the march toward new and yet untested objectives.

One might also find considerable sentiment for the nation in the South on the eve of the Civil War. There, too, men took pride in recalling the common traditions of the past. Southerners had taken a major rôle in the winning of independence and the framing of the Constitution. For the greater portion of the period from 1789 to 1860 it was the South which controlled the government at Washington and directed the national destinies. But meanwhile the transformation of Northern society was being paralleled by a peculiar development in the South. The slave plantation system drew the cotton states apart until men in 1860 rightly spoke of a distinct Southern nationality. The Southern trend, it must be emphasized, was truer to the older traits of American character than was the Northern revolution, although both were tending toward new creations. Patriotism of locality, loyalty to agriculture and to an aristocratic structure of society, and adherence to stability in folkways were imperative concomitants of a slave society.

Here then was rivalry. Out of common Americanism had developed divergent nationalisms. When Lincoln's election gave evidence that the social organization of the North was winning a permanent victory in the race for supremacy within the Union the minority read aright the future. Outside alone would it be possible, if possible there, to create a Southern nation.

The not inhumane institution of slavery both made and destroyed the hope of Southern nationalism. Certainly it was the most formidable barrier that the developing American nationalism had to overcome. In fostering a society peculiar to its own economy it had sheltered the South from influences which had revolutionized life in the North, and, in fact, in the European world at large. In this sense alone can the South be said to have been retarded in its development. The common man with whom seemed to rest the future was, in the South of slavery, largely a "forgotten man" and the vast resources of the South were in the main left unexploited. But much as large areas of the ante-bellum South seemed waiting to be aroused from a lethargy of undevelopment; society was far from being static. The "slave power" was dynamic in its growth and held the section united in its defense. That the system was essentially unsound and outworn should not disguise the fact that for a brief space of time it shaped the course of Southern nationalism. But its disharmony with conditions in the world at large gave to the Southern cause the forlorn appearance of an heroic people endeavoring to check the inevitable sweep of the century. The elements in Southern life which a later generation has learned to respect might have had a chance to survive by themselves, but intertwined as they were in slavery the entire cause seemed destined to defeat.

The Civil War brought an end to Southern dreams of independence. The system which had built a society was completely destroyed and lay in ruins. Over all stalked the spirit of the triumphant North. Yet what had won? Did the outcome mean that the Northern pattern of nationalism was to be the Americanism of the future to which the South must conform? To an extent this was true, for with the Northern troops came also the revolutionary forces which had remade and were remaking Northern life. But the old problem of harmonizing the rival structures of the two societies remained. Much in Southern life was far too stubborn and far too vital, if not too valuable, to disappear. In time the nationalism that emerged was a mixture in which victors and vanquished alike were subjugated to a common amalgam which was not completely the choice or the will of either, but to which both had learned to conform in common patriotism.

The history of how two bitter foes were reconciled, two rival societies harmonized, therefore, leads to the core of American life since the Civil War. The task of tracing and evaluating the various influences which bear upon the theme is not an easy one. Virtually every activity of the American people in the years between 1865 and 1900 left some mark great or small, which must be deciphered and appraised. It has been my endeavor to describe and correlate the many themes, political, social, economic, cultural, and emotional, which figured in the complexity of postwar life.

Consequently the materials used in the preparation of this

work were both comprehensive and extensive. My complete bibliography included sixteen hundred items of manuscripts, Federal and State documents, newspapers, periodical articles, published books, and pamphlets. Because I have been chiefly interested in giving to the reader a clear account of the narrative of reconciliation I have reduced to a minimum the apparatus of scholarship. Notes have been used only to indicate the variety of materials and to establish responsibility for conclusions that may possibly be disputed.

Many friends, North and South, have made valuable suggestions and given me aid in the course of my researches. Specifically I wish to thank Professor Frederick Merk and Mr. Bernard De Voto for reading and criticizing the manuscript. I am indebted to Mr. Donald Born for substantial help in reading the proofs. I owe much to courteous assistance given me by the officers of the following libraries: the Harvard College Library, the Charleston (S. C.) Public Library, the State Libraries of Virginia, North Carolina, South Carolina, and Georgia, the New York Public Library, and the Library of Congress.

Above all I wish to express my gratitude to Professor Arthur Meier Schlesinger, without whose constant criticism and stimulating advice this book would not have been possible.

CONTENTS

THE ROAD TO REUNION

CHAPTER I

VICTORY

JOHN ANDERSON had fought with Grant at Shiloh and later had marched with Sherman's bummers. All parts of the South he had seen. He thought mostly of his feet, being a veteran, how they had been coated with the dust of Kentucky, soaked in the muddy lowlands along the Mississippi, and colored with the red clay of Georgia. He remembered the Tennessee family of friendly enemies who had found him ill and had nursed him back to health. But also he recalled how it had felt in the Carolinas to have people with tired and worn expressions on their faces look at him with dread and repugnance. Even the triumphal march down Pennsylvania Avenue had seemed empty after that.

But now he was home. Home to John Anderson was a farm which nestled safely in the pleasant hills of Southern Ohio with Paint Creek running placidly nearby. He sat evenings smoking on his porch, thinking that he wanted nothing more than to spend the remainder of his life watching the orderly way in which season followed season, crops were planted, grew, and were harvested. He would like to grow old in that routine with his wife and growing children around him. True he would like occasionally to indulge in reminiscences about those four romantic years which contained all the great hardships and great adventures his life would know. But he wanted his memories to mellow dreamlike and not come surging forth in tragic nightmares. He was the Northern veteran and for him the Civil War was over.

Yet as he thought of that April in 1865 he could not escape a sense of elation. It had been a victor's peace. Something had been won, something which had cost more than three hundred and fifty thousand lives, great treasure, and four years of anxiety; something, therefore, to be guarded in the future. A persistent undertone of stern determination had crept unconsciously into his song of rejoicing. He had not intended to phrase the hallelujahs of Julia Ward Howe's stirring anthem other than as an expression of thanksgiving. Yet they had sounded as a fateful augury of a crusade still incomplete. And when he had joined boisterously in the refrain, "We'll hang Jeff Davis on a sour apple tree," it had seemed as though he had been carried beyond himself into a wild demand for vengeance.

Nevertheless John Anderson normally was not much concerned with the fruits of victory. To him the finest fruit would be the quiet enjoyment of his farm. Not all, however, were like John Anderson. Many not having fought as he had fought, still felt an unexpressed hatred in them seeking an outlet. Some were more ambitious than he and realized that even John Anderson had certain apprehensions which might be exploited until ends were reached which were not altogether what Anderson might desire. Some again were better bargainers and believed a thing so dearly purchased should be made the most of. And still others were unfortunately more righteous than he. The God who had presided over the tribunal of arms had given a mandate to his chosen ones which it would be sinful to disobey. And consequently those who in times of war had been less heroic than John Anderson, those who had selfish ends in view, and those who sought the reformation of a Southern society which Anderson had not altogether disliked, came to him and told him that he must fight on and on.

As the last winter of the Civil War was drawing to a close and the promise of victory grew momentarily brighter, the Northern public began to speculate as to the sequel of the bitter conflict. For the first time it occurred to some that the hostility which existed between the sections would be an embarrassment if not a danger now that it was about to be decreed the two must live together in one union. The Civil War like all modern wars had been waged as much by propaganda as by armies in the field. The morale of each section had been maintained largely by emphasizing the so-styled irrepressible antagonisms of the respective rivals. As a consequence the war had left not only the necessity of rebuilding an exhausted and impoverished South, but also the unfamiliar task of reforming habits of thought that had been fixed in strife.

The ending of hostilities gave birth to great emotions in the North. It was a period of abnormal adjustment in which rational conduct could not be premised. The drums beat and the flags waved as long files of blue-clad veterans marched in triumph through the streets of Northern cities on their return to civilian life. Beneath the rejoicing lay an ill-concealed eagerness to resume the interrupted course of private concerns. Civilians as well as soldiers were prone to turn aside from the suffering of the past. The discipline and trials of war pressed too heavily upon the memory to permit of unrelieved joy. To the end of the decade there persisted an aversion toward all that related to the struggle, making unwelcome "everything that brought back those days and nights of suffering and anxiety." Editors suiting their columns to the public taste, and publishers with an eye to the market, offered little encouragement to the few writers who in these early months and years sought to use the war as a fictional background. An emotion-wearied public reacted against that which recalled the tragedy of war.

Lincoln was among the first to appreciate the necessity of removing the war psychosis. In the cabinet meeting of April 14, 1865, he uttered the well remembered words, "We must extinguish our resentments if we expect harmony and union." Both Lincoln and his successor in the presidency, Andrew Johnson, believed that if the heart of the North could be reached there would be found a desire to be magnanimous to the defeated South. Possibly the majority of Northerners would not go so far as Johnson in welcoming the Southerners as "our brethren," but he was not alone when he asserted, "I do not want them to come back into this Union a degraded and debased people." To hold that the Presidents misread the popular attitude in assuming a desire for leniency is saying that Lincoln and Johnson had now lost the uncanny faculty of instinctively sharing the innermost aspirations of their constituents which had so marked both their careers.

As a matter of record the two leaders were not unsupported. Behind them there existed a far-reaching if inchoate public opinion seeking surcease from continued strife. Partly it arose from the soldiers, who, having done their job, entertained little patience with the politician who showed a propensity for endless conflict.[1] Partly it came from men like Governor John Andrew, of Massachusetts, who, having worked effectively for the cause of union during the war, now felt that charity to the South would best serve the same cause in time of peace.[2] There were business men urging, like the leading business journal of the day, *The Commercial and Financial Chronicle,* a policy of rapid conciliation as the most efficacious means of restoring trade between the sections.[3] A group of clergymen, notably Henry Ward Beecher and the young Washington Gladden, advised forgiveness and gentleness.[4] Nor should it be forgotten that the conservatives of the fifties, men like Robert C. Winthrop, while no longer active in politics, were for the most part quietly in support of a good will program.[5] Even some of the later radicals had not yet hardened their hearts, as is indicated by Senator Henry Wilson writing to a colleague, "I do not consider it either generous, manly, or Christian, to nourish or cherish or express feelings of wrath or hatred toward them" of the South.[6] Finally among intellectuals one could find the belief that the country's salvation depended upon an attitude of leniency toward the South.[7]

But wars are not discarded as easily as an outworn garment. When Governor Andrew declared after Lee's surrender that "there ought now to be a vigorous prosecution of the Peace, — just as vigorous as our recent prosecution of the war," he was perhaps appreciating the tremendous difficulties in the way of a policy of magnanimity. The North, as one Southerner

[1] Well exemplified by General W. T. Sherman, Rachel Sherman Thorndike (ed.), "The Sherman Letters" (New York, 1894), 247, 262, 295.
[2] *Sumner Mss.* (Harvard College Library) ; John A. Andrew, *Valedictory Address, January 4, 1866* (Boston, 1866).
[3] *Commercial and Financial Chronicle* (New York), July 29, Sept. 23, and Dec. 9, 1865; *Hunt's Merchants' Magazine* (New York), LIII (1865), 134–135.
[4] Henry Ward Beecher, *Conditions of a Restored Union,* a sermon preached in Plymouth Church, Brooklyn, Oct. 29, 1865; Washington Gladden, "Recollections" (Boston, 1909), 146–156.
[5] Robert C. Winthrop, Jr., "Memoir of Robert C. Winthrop," 269, 287.
[6] Letter to Senator Nye, published in the *American Historical Review,* XV (1910), 574.
[7] W. C. Ford, "Letters of Henry Adams" (Boston, 1930), II, 284.

was disconsolately to observe, seemed mastered by "some mysterious spell" which silenced her better impulses. Magnanimous as the majority of Northerners might well have wished to be in the spring months of 1865, the war itself had left conflicting emotions to block the free expression of leniency.

Basic was the all pervading sense of responsibility arising from the tremendous sacrifices of wartime. The exulting "Glory, Glory, Hallelujah," of the triumph song passed quickly into grim appreciation of the half million lives and the three billion dollars the war had cost.[8] The period of rejoicing was brief. The mind harked back to the graves of "the patriot hosts that had fallen on fearful battle fields," and the query on every lip was, in the Lincolnian phrase, have these honored dead died in vain?[9] Apprehension came with victory. "From fearful trip the victor's ship comes in with object won," wrote the poet Whitman, not realizing that the safeguarding of the "object won" was to be a venture as arduous as that by which it had been gained.

A young Frenchman sojourning in the United States, himself destined in later years to fight ardently, if not vindictively, to garner the fruits of an even greater struggle, saw the reaction as a simple phenomenon. "When anyone," wrote Clemenceau, "has for four successive years joined in such a struggle as that which the United States has seen, one thing stands out to which a man clings all the more in proportion as he is ready to forget personal animosities, and that is his desire not to lose the dearly bought fruits of so many personal sacrifices. When the war ended, the North was concerned not to let itself be tricked out of what it had spent so much trouble and perseverance to win."[10] To the same effect the moderate Winthrop observed in midsummer 1865 that his New England neighbors were "full of apprehension" that the Union was to be restored too soon, and that the Southern states were about to reorganize themselves upon their old principles.[11]

[8] Actually a contemporary over-statement, *Atlantic Monthly* (Boston), XVII (1865), 238–247.
[9] See as typical, John T. Trowbridge, "The South" (Hartford, 1866), 143.
[10] Georges Clemenceau, "American Reconstruction, 1865–1870" (New York, 1928), 296.
[11] Letter, quoted in "Memoir," 268.

This was the first step in the process that transformed magnanimity into vindictiveness. The fruits of victory must be preserved — a sobering and disquieting assumption. No treaty of peace ended the Civil War, defining in clearly worded articles the rewards of victory and the penalties of defeat. The defeated were brought back within the Union to share as Americans in the enjoyment of the fruits of victory. At most the erstwhile Confederates could be kept only temporarily in a state of probation. Eventually, unless the American system of government were to be radically altered, the day must come when the results of the Civil War should in part be entrusted to those who had been inimical to the very existence of the Union. Consequently those who had won the war came to feel as one of them wrote, "the war will not be over until we have *secured* the safety for which we fought." Not until after "we have absolutely established our ideas," affirmed a second, "which must pervade and be incorporated into their system of public policy," could the nation turn itself to healing the wounds of war. The "magnanimous" peace was thus converted into the "just" peace, which when unilaterally applied is mere euphony for a "victor's" peace.

The problem was made more perplexing by the lack of unanimity in defining both why the war had been fought and what should be the terms of settlement. All the disputes of a conference of peace were multiplied a thousand fold when the settlement of the Civil War was precipitated out of the hands of Congress and thence into the arena of public opinion at large. Into the prolonged discussion there came every range of emotion, every political interest in the nation, religion, business, the welfare of the Negro, — apparently every source of cantankerous rivalry the nation could produce. Well-meaning people of generous impulses were again made partisans, and hardened their hearts to play the rôle of even if somewhat grim justice.

But what were the fruits of victory? All recognized three general positions as logical consequences of the war. First, the doctrine of secession was renounced and the Union was recognized, in Webster's phrase, to be one and indissoluble. Secondly, the institution of slavery was forever destroyed.

And thirdly, it was more or less tacitly recognized that the prewar leadership of the Southern slavocrat in national politics was permanently to be replaced in favor of Northern direction. But each of these general positions had in itself logical consequences, and it was in the unraveling that disputes arose.

The Union was preserved, but how could the tension and conflict within the Union be removed? The Negro was a freeman, but what was necessary to safeguard him in his new estate and to whom was the safeguarding to be entrusted? The Southern oligarchy had been overthrown, but how could the destruction be made complete and what was to take its place? These were not easy questions as they cut through so many old established ways of thought and activity. Yet a society accustomed to the discipline of wartime action and prodded by deep-seated apprehension might move impulsively to ends which would require a generation of adaptation in more normal times. "Half the North," wrote one who favored a policy of leniency, "is persuaded that you [Southerners] have the power to jockey them out of what cost them so dear." Many had learned to distrust halfway measures — "the spirit of compromise which plunged the United States [so it was held] step by step into the Civil War." Moderation, it was argued, "will once again obscure the issues, veiling the appearance of the danger spots until they grow deep and ineradicable." The Northerner, jealous of the fruits of victory, came easily to reason that inasmuch as the South was now prostrate here was the opportunity for a radical operation. All the halfway cures could be discarded. Doctor Compromise had been a quack. The knife with its clean penetrating cut would do a better job. The cancers in the South (and how well the North knew those cancers were in the South!), the cancers which had long vexed the body politic, could now be removed. It was an attractive prospect for a war-trained generation that had been taught to believe in thorough measures. The emotional relief, for it was basically that, with which large numbers of Northerners turned to the twin solution of the radicals — the enfranchisement of the Negro and the mortgaging of the nation's future to the Republican party — is evidence

of the widespread neurosis of a people who had emerged
from war.

To accept such a program the North must necessarily subscribe to an orthodox interpretation of war guilt. A man
could exclaim "Let justice be our only retribution," only if
he entertained no doubts as to the correctness of his position.
Clemenceau, always to be trusted to mirror the advancing
views of the radicals, likewise affirmed that "any postponement
of justice is postponement of peace." [12]

God's hand was seen in the outcome. Nothing had been
commoner in both sections than references to the war as a
grand arbitrament of the deity. Lincoln had done much to
popularize the mechanistic view of the struggle as one in
which human pawns worked out the implacable will of a
righteous God. Behind the lyric beauty of his inaugurals, the
Gettysburg Address, and his other wartime utterances, is the
calm philosophy that God is willing this tragic tribulation to
make right triumph on the earth. Whatever solace Lincoln
derived from this conception unquestionably contributed to
sustaining him through his arduous trial. It cannot be neglected,
however, that he with others was implanting in his people a
smug assumption that they had been chosen as God's agents
first in overthrowing and then in chastising an iniquitous opponent. The gentle Lincoln had no suspicion of becoming another Cromwell. He merely saw God's hand in the conflict.
But his people took the added step and visioned themselves as
a new Ironsides, the instrumentality for the application of stern
policy cloaked as God's directing and righteous will.

The idea appealed strongly to a religious age. The people
were ingrained with the conception, approximating fatalism,
that the divine intention explained all the mysteries of life.
When victory came, not superior force but God's will had
made right triumph over evil. Pæans of praise were sung to

[12] Clemenceau, "American Reconstruction," 84. Samplings of Northern
opinion are best found in newspapers like the *Boston Daily Advertiser,* the
Chicago Tribune, the *New York Herald,* the *New York Times,* and the
New York Tribune; from weeklies like *Harper's Weekly Magazine* (New
York), IX (1865), and the *Nation* (New York), I (1865); and from
periodicals like the *Atlantic Monthly* (Boston), XVI (1865), *Harper's
Monthly Magazine* (New York), XXX (1865), and the *North American
Review* (New York), C (1865).

a God as exclusively a Northern God as the God of the Hebrews had been a Hebrew God. "We thank Thee, O God," prayed the eloquent Phillips Brooks in a thanksgiving service for the capture of Richmond, "for the power of Thy right arm which has broken for us a way, and set the banners of our Union in the central city of treason and rebellion. We thank Thee for the triumph of right over wrong. We thank Thee for the loyal soldiers planted in the streets of wickedness. We thank Thee for the wisdom and bravery and devotion which Thou hast anointed for Thy work and crowned with glorious victory. . . . Thou hast led us, O God, by wondrous ways. . . . And now, O God, we pray Thee to complete Thy work." [13]

God had still another reminder that His work was not yet complete. The assassination of Abraham Lincoln at the very moment of national rejoicing was interpreted generally as a divine caution. Lincoln had been known to advocate a policy of tenderness to the defeated "Rebels." Those who had restlessly chafed under his moderation, compromising opportunism, and gentle conservatism during the war itself, now welcomed the freedom his removal gave to emotional unrestraint. "Was," queried the *Boston Journal* in an editorial on April 15, "the loyal country in danger of losing sight of this [Southern] cancer of wickedness and becoming disposed, out of regard to the cheering future, to heal it over with misjudged leniency?" A "merciful God" had let fall this awful blow on "docile hearts" to teach His purpose and to cause obedience to His will.

The tragedy consisted largely in that it further directed the Northern postwar neurosis into radical outlets. It appeared to the *Cincinnati Daily Gazette* that the "olive branchers" were routed and "stones" not "grass" were to be thrown at the defeated "rebels" who lived to see Lincoln dead. Deep into rustic Concord the impression penetrated and Emerson confided to his journal: "And what if it should turn out in the unfolding of the web, that he [Lincoln] had reached the term; that the heroic deliverer could no longer serve us; that

[13] A. V. G. Allen, "Life and Letters of Phillips Brooks" (New York, 1900), I, 531.

the rebellion had touched its natural conclusion, and what remained to be done required new and uncommitted hands?" Actually there was no question in the philosopher's mind, for a week earlier he had asserted, " 'Tis far the best that the rebels be pounded into a peace," and expressed fear that Grant's "easy" terms of surrender to Lee might soften "the high tragic justice which the nation should execute." [14] It remained for Booth's unhappy bullet to make God a part of the Emersonian logic.

It so happened in this "unfolding web" of history that because Lincoln was shot on Good Friday and died on Saturday morning, the clergymen in Sunday sermons had first opportunity to express and mold public opinion, and the newspapers on Monday, in widely spreading the preachers' gospel, let themselves be guided by the men of God.[15] It was Easter Sunday the sermons were preached, the great feast day of the Christian calendar. Never did pulpits consecrated to the Prince of Peace take on grimmer aspect than on this Easter Day of 1865. Not the Christ of sacrifice and forgiveness but the God of righteousness and vengeance was preached to a saddened people. In the great church of the Trinity in New York City the Reverend Doctor Vincent assured his congregation that the martyred President had been "unfitted, by the natural gentleness and humanity of his disposition to execute the stern justice of Christ's vicegerent." For Christ's vicegerent, the President of the United States, was "to hew the rebels in pieces before the Lord," and cast them out of the Kingdom of God. "So let us say, God's will be done." Uptown in the Madison Avenue Presbyterian Church, the Reverend Doctor William Adams was reviewing the "atrocities" perpetrated during the war by the "barbarous spirit of slavery" so as to convince

[14] E. W. Emerson and W. E. Forbes, "Journals of Ralph Waldo Emerson" (Boston, 1914), X, 93; Emerson, "Miscellanies," 313–314.

[15] Virtually every Northern newspaper between the 17th and 20th of April devoted much space to reporting the sermons. I have scrutinized the newspapers of Boston, Chicago, Cincinnati, Cleveland, Indianapolis, New York, and Philadelphia. I have also read a large number of the sermons in pamphlet form. Some of these reveal what was preached in the smaller cities and villages. The New York sermons from which I quote in the text are reported in the *New York Herald*, April 17; the Cincinnati sermon in the *Cincinnati Gazette*, April 20.

his flock that the South must be punished. In Cincinnati the
lesson was the same. "We faltered with God's eternal laws of
retribution," a Baptist clergyman asserted. "We thought we
might be more merciful than God. . . . We seemed to feel
that we had a right to show our fellowship of philanthropy,
even at the expense of fidelity to the demands of God." So
throughout the North the general trend was as summarized in
the *National Anti-Slavery Standard,* "We believe that this cruel
calamity will be blest by a sterner line of treatment of the
slaveholding rebels than the humane and generous heart of
Lincoln liked to present."

Not all the clergymen shared the extreme views of the
majority. In the Roman Catholic Cathedral of St. Patrick in
New York City Archbishop McClosky reminded his people of
"the sentiments of mercy and conciliation that so filled the
heart" of Lincoln, and prayed that they would continue to
actuate and guide the nation through the desperate crisis the
assassination had precipitated. So also Washington Gladden
was touched by grief that permitted no thought of vengeance,
and wisely cautioned his congregation that "stern and severe
measures, instead of preventing the repetition of such acts,
will have a tendency to multiply them."

The great body of Northern clergymen passed through the
experience to a result disastrous to any hope of reconciliation.
The defeat of the South came more than ever to signify a
moral victory. The ability to understand, much less to sym-
pathize, with the problems of Southern life grew more impossible. The feeling that a moral crusade for the regenera-
tion of "rebeldom" was necessary became henceforth a fixed
article in the creed of the Northern churches. The lenient
element of religious men, as Gladden and Lyman Abbot sadly
confessed, was silenced. "Seeds of distrust and ill will were
widely and deeply sown." [16]

So grew and became transcendent the belief in the righteousness of a thorough policy. Lyman Abbott could despairingly
wish that the words "right" and "wrong" be erased from our
political vocabulary. They stood in uncompromising starkness.

[16] Gladden, "Recollections," 156; **Lyman Abbott, "Reminiscences"** (Boston, 1915), 180.

And for a moment, the most critical of all, the voice of charity was unheard while the cry of vengeance rose unchallenged. Adding to its increasing volume came the politician. In words that penetrated the bedrock of national hatred, the temporarily unbalanced Johnson vehemently shouted upon his accession to the presidency, "I hold that robbery is a crime; rape is a crime; murder is a crime; treason is a crime and crime must be punished. Treason must be made infamous, and traitors must be impoverished." So likewise John Sherman, Senator from Ohio, hardened into radicalism. "We should not only brand the leading rebels with infamy, but the whole rebellion should wear the badge of the penitentiary, so that for this generation at least, no man who has taken part in it would dare to justify or palliate it." As a consequence there arose a determined cry of the pack for the punishment of the Confederate leaders. It must be shown that "treason leaves a stain." Julian, in Indianapolis, was among those who demanded that Jefferson Davis be hanged "in the name of God." [17]

The temper of the North in this respect was clearly revealed by an incident of late summer of 1865. The great hero of the South, Robert E. Lee, was chosen by the trustees of Washington College president of that institution. The appointment was received with universal satisfaction throughout the South, and Lee entered the office in a spirit highly conducive to the best interests of the reunited country. But throughout the North it appeared as though the South in general and Lee in particular were guilty of an unpardonable offense. Godkin in the *Nation* put it mildly when he asserted that Lee was unfit to train the youth of Virginia.[18] Again, because of the abnormal state of nerves, the extremists set the pitch, and Wendell Phillips came nearest to expressing the uncontrolled judgment of the North, — "If Lee is fit to be president of a college,

<hr/>

[17] For typical comment by politicians see George W. Julian, "Speeches on Political Questions" (New York, 1872), 262–290, and "Political Recollections, 1840–1872" (Chicago, 1884), 257; F. Moore, "Speeches of Andrew Johnson" (Boston, 1866), 470–479; G. C. Gorham, "Life and Public Services of Edwin M. Stanton" (Boston, 1872), II, 195; John Sherman, "Recollections" (Chicago, 1895), I, 355.

[18] *Nation*, Sept. 14, 1865.

then for Heaven's sake pardon Wirz and make him professor of what the Scots call the humanities." [19]

The seed that had been planted produced its harvest. In the Antietam cemetery it was an issue whether Confederate dead deserved decent burial. Sanitary considerations ended the discussion by compelling interment of "skeletons, rooted up by hogs, and blanching in the open fields." [20] So also when Memorial Day was observed in Arlington Cemetery the hatred of righteousness was in command. Soldiers in Federal blue were stationed around the graves of Confederate dead to prevent flowers being placed upon them. "Treason must be made infamous."

The nerves of the North were nerves that had borne too heavy a strain. And still they were being burdened by complex emotional loads. Given such a situation a radical reaction was almost certain. What other legacy could a Civil War bequeath? It had aroused hatreds. It had closed the mental processes of the people and enthroned prejudice in the place of reason. "Our hearts were touched with fire," wrote a thoughtful veteran of the conflict.[21] A fire, indeed, had burnt out the softer element of mercy and forged a rod of steel. The radically intentioned well knew how to apply the rod thus shaped. But whatever motivated the radicals, and in a sense they were only the sickest of the nerve-shot age, they could never have marched to triumph in 1866 and 1867 had it not been for the emotional conflicts that prevented a normal reaction among the mass of people.

The misunderstanding and distrust engendered in the war lived on in part because the reporting of Southern conditions to the Northern reading public continued bad. It is possible to explain this reporting largely in terms of directed propaganda on the part of radical Republicans. Unquestionably the North was flooded with speeches unfavorably describing conditions in the South; men like Carl Schurz were sent South

[19] *Ibid.*, Nov. 2, 1865. Henry Wirz, Confederate commander of Andersonville Prison, had been condemned by a military court for alleged brutalities to Union prisoners and was awaiting execution.

[20] Trowbridge, "The South," 55.

[21] Oliver Wendell Holmes, Jr., "Dead Yet Living" (Boston, 1884), 11–12, pamphlet reprinted from the *Boston Advertiser.*

especially to bring back inspired reports; and Northern newspapers were supplied with an endless source of "news articles"
illustrating Southern recalcitrance. All this, be it remembered, was in part countered by the propaganda activity of
conservatives and Democrats. What needs to be pointed out
is that, had there been no villain in the plot seeking to cap-
italize for party advantage the unfortunate state of sectional
relation, the result would have been much the same. Again
it was the peculiar postwar conditions which delivered the
situation into radical hands. The North had a natural appe-
tite for news from the South. The newspapers in wartime
had developed a new journalism of special articles prepared
by a new type of trained correspondents. The correspondents
were now available to enter the heart of the opened territory
of the Confederacy and the reading public eagerly awaited their
descriptions of the people and the places that had been so prominent in the news of war years. The South itself did nothing,
possibly could do nothing to assist in shaping the publicity so
vitally affecting its welfare. The North had only Northerners
to do the reporting. And these men possessed in common with
their reading public the biased views in regard to the South
that had been shaped in time of war. The result was inevitable.
The predilections of the North in regard to the South were
strengthened, and again the consequence was increased misunderstanding.

It would be gratuitous to seek hidden and possibly villainous
motives beneath the work of the majority of these Northern
reporters. Sidney Andrews, special correspondent for the *Chicago Tribune* and the *Boston Advertiser,* and possibly the
ablest Northerner to report Southern conditions in 1865 and
1866, was a gentleman with the highest professional standards governing his work. His book, "The South since the
War," however, based as it was upon the honest observation
of an intelligent man, was pronouncedly anti-Southern in effect. Andrews conceived of the South as a PROBLEM, and
distrusted any share the white South might be given in the
solution of it. As if drawn by magnetic force the book reached
every issue that inflamed the day and always presented the
Northern view with little capacity for seeing the other side.

The fundamental implications of a society in process of revolution were not understood, and sympathy with the people forced to undergo what Southerners were undergoing was completely absent. Especially did Andrews measure certain deep-rooted resentments of the North against the South. Not least important among the factors which rankled in the Northern psychology was the oft repeated Southern boast of a civilization superior to the North. Andrews had heard "a great deal about the superior civilization of the South." Perhaps his reaction was only a natural one, and one which his reading public in the North would readily applaud. He collected evidence of as much of the unfavorable aspects of Southern life as he could to reach the conclusion that Southern civilization was in reality "Southern barbarism."

The book which best measured the mental content of the ordinary Northerner was possibly J. T. Trowbridge's "The South," which was published in 1866, the result of two trips in eight of the Confederate states during the summer of 1865 and the winter of 1865–1866. Trowbridge had done his share in maintaining Northern morale during the war by writing popular war novels, most notable of which was "Cudjo's Cave." His reporting is certainly not the most accurate or the most trustworthy. His significance is quite otherwise. He shared the opinions and the emotions of a wide reading public, giving to his readers a language they understood because it was their own. His narrative in addition was interesting and effective.

Apparently Trowbridge went South much as Herodotus went to the Persians. He sought out the battlefields and he saw the ruined cities. He talked with the officers and the soldiers and conversed "with all sorts of people from high state officials to low down whites and negroes." He sought "correct impressions of the country, of its inhabitants, of the great contest of arms just closed, and [significantly] of the still greater contest of principles not yet terminated." He planned a record built upon facts free from fictitious coloring and an understanding based upon the "broad grounds of Truth and Eternal Right."

The book has a central theme, vigorously and effectively presented, and that theme is that the South was barbarous. The "spirit of slavery" had debased the Southern mind, destroyed liberty and law, and vitiated all white elements upon which a restored union might be erected. The men who had been active in the Confederacy could not be trusted. Their loyalty was "simply disloyalty subdued." They acquiesced in what they could not alter, but their aims, which "command the sympathy of the Southern people," were "to obtain the exclusive control of the freedmen, and to make such laws as shall embody the prejudices of a late slaveholding society." Even the whites of the non-slaveholding class, whom Trowbridge portrayed as the victims of exploitation in the old régime and who would be, he predicted, greatly benefited by free society, could not at the moment be trusted as a stable foundation for society. They had been rendered too ignorant by slavery. The smug sense of superiority so prevalent in Trowbridge was sharply revealed in the language he used to describe his contact with a young yeoman of Virginia. "What a gulf betwixt his mind and mine! Sitting side by side there [on the buggy seat] we were as far asunder as the great globe's poles." "He was," Trowbridge later added in his reminiscences, "a common product of Southern institutions."

There remained only the emancipated Negro, and he emerged as the hero of Trowbridge's pages. He was pictured as a self-reliant character, eager for advancement and deserving impartial enjoyment of his "rights as a freedman." In contrast to him stood the white people who, "well-educated or illiterate, . . . detested the negroes and wished every one of them driven out of the State." Trowbridge concluded therefore that some protection on the part of the Federal government was necessary to the black man in his new condition.

That the propaganda of war days, the stories of atrocities and the recriminations that embitter, were not to be dismissed is pathetically apparent in the anecdotes of sectional strife which are strewn through the pages of Trowbridge's book. The brutality of a war-barbarized society is there. Andersonville and Libby are visited and horrendously described. "You think of what they suffered [the prisoners at Libby], as you walk the pavements of the conquered capital; and something swells within you, which is not exultation, nor rage, nor grief, but a strange mingling of all these." And still there persists that Northern rankling at the assumed superiority of Southerners. Trowbridge never forgot a conversation with W. G. Simms in Charleston in which the novelist had asserted "South Carolina, sir, was the flower of modern civilization."

Three other reports of Southern conditions were made by prominent journalists in the year following the surrenders. Thomas W. Knox had made a creditable record as a war correspondent on the *New York Herald*. His book, "Camp Fire and Cotton Field," touched the postwar South only in its concluding chapters, where the burning topic of Northern emigration to the South was discussed. Knox's bias was apparent in the caution that not until Southerners were taught that "there is no possible hope for them to control the national policy" could conciliation be accomplished. Most penetrating of all the journalists and most sympathetic to the Southern point of view was the New Englander, Benjamin C. Truman. He placed implicit trust in the disbanded Confederate veterans as the best material for worthy citizenship and as the safest basis for the erection of a Reconstruction policy. In his opinion the Negro's future would be most secure in the understanding and friendly hands of the former master class. "Stories and rumors" of Southern outrages he assailed as overdrawn. Few reporters spent as much time in the South as he. None had a better technique of investigation. But whereas other journalists presented their material in readable books, Truman's report was in the nature of an official governmental document of fourteen pages. In such form it was a mere bundle of conclusions with none of the vivid anecdotes, personal encounters, or circumstantial intimacies that conveyed so effectively the message of his rivals.[22] Mere assurances of Southern loyalty and good intentions were not enough to allay the apprehensions of the North. Truman exerted little influence. Whitelaw Reid,

[22] *Report on the Condition of the South, 39 Cong., 1 Sess., Sen. Exec. Doc. No. 43.* More directly partisan were the reports of two men not journalists. U. S. Grant's *Letter Concerning Affairs in the South,* was appended by President Johnson to Carl Schurz's *Report on the States of South Carolina, Alabama, Mississippi, and Louisiana,* to counteract the inspired radicalism of the latter. Both are contained in *39 Cong., 1 Sess., Sen. Exec. Doc. No. 2.* These two reports figured large in the partisan debate, Schurz probably affecting a greater influence.

on the other hand, put in his book, "After the War: a Southern Tour," all that Truman missed.

Reid because of his later prominence in Republican ranks has sometimes been dismissed as one of the inspired propagandists. But Reid in 1865 was in contact with the most enterprising journalism of the day. During the war an avid public had read his earnest and patriotic presentation of news from Washington and the front. Could it be expected that the same public would now desert him when he published his animated, highly circumstantial recital of experiences in the South? "After the War," whatever it may be as evidence in a strict historical sense, was a masterpiece of journalism and elevated Reid to the top of his profession. Reid was never dull, and his swift-running narrative had an answer to every question that the North was raising. The message he transmitted was that the Southern people were arrogant and defiant, still nursing the embers of the "rebellion" and cherishing its ashes.

The work of these men was supplemented by the activity of newspapers and periodicals. During the summer and fall of 1865 the Nation published a series of unsigned letters from the South written by J. R. Dennett, whose point of view approximated that of Sidney Andrews. The *New York Tribune* and the *New York Times* printed significant contributions describing conditions in the conquered area. *Harper's Weekly* took the lead among periodicals. To a large extent, especially in the lesser journals of the West, this material came from Northern sojourners in the South. As a class this group had aggravated conceptions of Southern failings, and was inclined to urge a policy of sternness, vigilance, and repression. Yet being Northerners they had the ear of the North, and gave a tone of unrelaxing severity to Northern journalism.

If the reporting of Southern affairs was conditioned by habits of thought that carried over from war, much the same was true of the great machinery of propaganda that had been used to maintain the popular morale. "The Struggles of Petroleum V. Nasby," for example, had begun in 1861.[23] The letters which serially described the escapades, principles, and ambitions of a burlesqued "Copperhead" settled in "Con-

[23] The creation of David Ross Locke.

federit X Roads," Kentucky, filled columns of many Northern newspapers, and became in time, together with General Grant, the blockade, and Great Britain's refusal to recognize the independence of the Confederacy, a major force in winning the war. The picture of President Lincoln reading to his cabinet the latest "Nasby" comment is one of our popular traditions. "Nasby" did not stop writing when Lee surrendered. Nor did he lose his appeal to Northern taste. Here is no hidden, invidious motivation for the rising tide of radicalism. "Nasby" was a wartime habit carrying on. He became one of the most powerful as well as vitriolic influences in making conciliation appear ridiculous.

The great Juggernaut of propaganda ran easily into radicalism because that was the line of least resistance, where war emotions found readiest outlet. It was indicated to President Johnson in October that the radicals were flooding the country with partisan accounts, and that it was "wrong for us to wait until prejudices and passions, and hate of the South, and avarice, and ambition shall all be joined together hand in hand, before wise statesmanship, magnanimity and returning affection and loyalty can have a fair chance." [24] But actually it was Johnson who was acting in the field of Reconstruction. In the face of growing apprehension over his moderation the radicals had one effective plea. Why should the process move so fast? Why hurry when haste might jeopardize the future? Why reconcile at the expense of sacrificing the security of the fruits of victory?

The reaction was governed by the legacy of hatred bequeathed by war. What Lord Grey wrote in reference to the world of 1919 could be applied to the United States of 1865.

War has stirred passion, enlisted sympathies, and aroused hatreds; many of the war generation have formed opinions that nothing will modify, and are dominated by predilections or prejudices that have become an inseparable part of their lives. With such people mental digestion ceases to be able to assimilate anything except what nourishes convictions already formed; all else is rejected or resented; and new material or reflections about the

[24] Senator J. R. Doolittle to A. Johnson, Oct. 10, 1865, as quoted in H. K. Beale, "The Critical Year" (New York, 1930), 115.

war are searched not for the truth, but for fuel to feed the flame of preconceived opinion.[25]

The men who had lived through the strife-torn years of the fifties into the war itself had come to believe that the normal condition of mankind was to be in a state of violent agitation over some fundamental question of right and wrong. It seemed inconceivable that men on the other side of the issue could be honorable or in any way capable of trust. "I remember the thrill of horror that shook my small person," wrote Maud Howe Elliott, "on hearing my father say, 'The Rebels have sent a box of live copperheads and rattlesnakes to Governor Andrew.'. . . On another occasion I was shocked at hearing of a case of clothing or bedding, infected with yellow-fever germs, that had been sent to Mr. Lincoln at the White House." [26] Children of 1863 were given novels like "Cudjo's Cave," bitterly partisan, "frankly designed," as its author later confessed, "to fire the Northern heart. . . . The most sensational incidents had their counterpart in the reign of wrath and wrong I was endeavoring to hold up to all lovers of the Union." [27] There was reason, then, for the balanced mind of Oliver Wendell Holmes, later Justice of the United States Supreme Court, to reflect that his generation had "been set apart by its experience. . . . It was given us to learn at the outset that life is a profound and passionate thing." [28]

The conquered South remained the enemy of right as the North conceived the right. The South of so many sins — the sin of causing the war, the sin of slavery, the sin of seeking the life of the Union — was still a South in which the evil consequences of wrong exerted a baneful influence. Henry Ward Beecher, who considered himself a moderate, expressed a common belief when he wrote in April, 1865, that communities in which slavery had existed could not be trusted. "Its products are rotten. No timber grown in its cursed soil is fit for the ribs of our ship of state or for our household homes. The people are selfish . . . brittle, and whoever leans on them for

[25] Lord Grey, "Twenty Five Years" (London, 1925), introduction, xv-xvi.
[26] Maud Howe Elliott, "Three Generations" (Boston, 1923), 19.
[27] J. T. Trowbridge, "My Own Story" (Boston, 1903), 262.
[28] Holmes, "Dead Yet Living," 11-12.

support is pierced in his hands. Their honor is not honor, but a bastard quality, . . . and for all times the honor of the supporters of slavery will be throughout the world a byword and a hissing." [29] In its later years of moderation the *Nation* was compelled to observe that many Northerners thought of Southerners as "a wild set of murderous savages." If so, the *Nation* of 1865 had contributed its share in implanting the notion in Northern minds.

To some Northerners it therefore appeared essential that a conquest of the Southern spirit must follow the conquest of arms. "Is it not time," argued James Russell Lowell, "that these men [Southerners] be transplanted at least into the nineteenth century, and, if they cannot be suddenly Americanized, made to understand something of the country which was too good for them, even though at the cost of a rude shock to their childish self-conceit?" To Lowell "Americanization" was the planting of schools, roads, churches, printing presses, industry, thrift, intelligence, security of life (Northern virtues it is to be assumed!) in the South, where there had been "no public libraries, no colleges worthy of the name, . . . no art, no science, still worse no literature but Simms' — there was no desire for them." For Lowell the great ideal of the war had been the "Americanization of all America." That ideal must not now be surrendered. "When men talk of generosity toward a suppliant foe, they entirely forget what that foe really was. To the people of the South no one thinks of being unmerciful. But they were only the blind force wielded by our real enemy, — an enemy, prophesy what smooth things you will, with whom we can never be reconciled and whom it would be madness to spare." [30]

The exigencies of the political situation proved an added hindrance to conciliatory influences. Just as in the crisis of 1860–1861 the political chieftains found it impossible to retreat from the extreme positions they had assumed, so now in the crisis of 1865–1866 the idea of partisan supremacy dictated intrenchment deep in the divisions of the period. The major parties acted not as unifying forces, but as divisive forces.

[29] As reported in the *Boston Transcript*, April 25, 1865.
[30] *North American Review*, CIII (1866), 536, 537, 540, 542.

The Democratic *New York World* asserted with much truth that the "real leaders" of the Republican party "see that unless the South can be trodden down and kept under foot for long years, or unless they can give the negroes the ballot, and control it in their hands, their present political supremacy is gone forever." [31] What the *World* failed to acknowledge was that the ill-concealed desire to gain Democratic votes from the white South was pushing its own party into extremes of early Reconstruction just as party necessity was precipitating the Republicans into the opposite extremes of radicalism. Moderate Northerners had natural apprehensions of the future. Something concrete was needed for their assurance. The one party assumed a false position when it seemed prone to underestimate the difficulties of the problem, and this came with especially bad grace from a party that had offered organized resistance to the war administration. The other party exaggerated the fears, and offered too much a program of "thorough." But the better emotional appeal was with the latter. For when the alternative is between too little and too much the timid man is apt to choose the second.

The unlaid ghosts of old disputes thus stalked the stage. The drama began in confusion and proceeded unplanned through perplexing shifts until the unintentioned climax of vindictiveness triumphing over magnanimity was reached. Reconciliation was to come only after the Northern program was firmly implanted in the South. "We cannot dream of conciliation until resistance ceases," was not merely the cry of the politician. There was a dominant public response to Lowell's assertion, "We have the same right to impose terms and to demand guarantees . . . that the victor always has." At last, a victor's peace could be unblushingly demanded. To many, it remains to be said, the decision brought relief, if only the relief of permitting fears and doubts to find outlets in action.

So again the North sent its armies into the South, this time to overthrow the moderate Reconstruction governments established under the auspices of Lincoln and Johnson, and to rule by martial law until new structures based upon Negro rule and directed by Republican chieftains might make a con-

[31] *New York World*, Sept. 11, 1865.

quest of the Southern spirit. The result was disorder worse than war, and oppression unequaled in American annals.

Yet the North continued to cherish a belief in its own supposed leniency. The record of having taken no lives in execution and virtually no property in confiscation as punishment for the "crimes of treason and rebellion" was pointed to with pride. It seemed to men so different in their backgrounds as Thomas Wentworth Higginson, General Sherman, and the historian Rhodes, "the mildest punishment ever inflicted after an unsuccessful civil war." Nor could the ordinary Northerner realize how any one could charge him with hatred toward the South. In his own mind he acted out of charity. A final way in which the sectional conscience might be cleared was to maintain, as Beecher did, that the evils suffered by the South were her own responsibility. "She willed the conflict and must abide the consequences." [32]

It would seem the part of wisdom to understand rather than to blame. The victorious are as deserving of pity as the defeated. Few in the America of 1865 could have envisioned the arduous road that must be traversed before true peace and brotherhood could be achieved.

[32] *Cf.* Henry Ward Beecher, *Centennial Address,* "Patriotic Addresses" (New York, 1887), 779.

CHAPTER II

DEFEAT

THE defeated South stretched more than twelve hundred miles from the ancient settlement of Jamestown to the open frontier in Texas. In the Northern mind this South of majestic distances was generalized as a formula or idea that must be combated and destroyed. The South did in fact assume a unity in face of Northern hostility. But in reality the situation was not so simple. The South was a vast congeries in which geographic variations, cultural deviations, and conflicting currents of historical development rested in yet imperfect adjustment. The assimilation of such complexity was a problem of far greater scope than the nationalists of 1865 appreciated.

Physically the South was far from a unit. The eleven states of the defunct Confederacy, in size alone, had been a vaster land than all the empire Napoleon had ever ruled. Central in the South, separating the eastern portion from the western was the mountain and hill country of the Appalachian highlands. Here was a region as large as a kingdom of western Europe, one occupied in 1865 by more than a million whites, isolated from and almost untouched by the dominant trends in Southern life. Along the eastern and southern coast stretched a sandy plain from fifty to two hundred miles in width — a land of dense pine forests and impassable swamps, with now and then a seaport or a village breaking the monotony. Fertile river bottoms penetrated the normal unproductiveness of this plain from the Potomac to the Rio Grande. Along these rich alluvial bottoms the plantations throve in a prosperity that stood in stark contrast to the impoverished life of the piney woods. The Piedmont uplands constituted still another region, a favored area where farm and plantation met in mute conflict for the better soils. Beyond the Mississippi was Texas, whose great open spaces offered opportunities of booming prosperity to both cotton planter and cattle raiser.

From yet another point of view there was the South of the Old Dominion and her western daughter, Kentucky, land of tobacco, established ways, and partially exhausted soils. There was the deep South, land of cotton, a newer and more aggressive type, that pressed westward into the frontier regions across the Mississippi. Thus the South of tobacco, corn, cotton, sugar, and rice, the South of primitive backwoods and bluegrass refinement, the South of plains, rolling uplands, mountains, and great rivers, was a South of striking contrasts. But mostly it was a rural South where four out of five people lived not in cities or on plantations or on barrens but on farms.

The most notable characteristic affecting life in the Old South was its isolation. The typical Southerner that the observant Olmsted met on his travels in Dixie was a farmer living remote from neighbors and hungry for human contacts. The typical county had less than ten thousand inhabitants with its only "city" a central village where court house, inn, and a few places of business clustered in lonely contrast to the unyielding countryside. No part of America had a larger percentage of self-sufficing farms. A feeling of "magnificent solitude" pervaded even the plantations where social activity was most highly organized. In the South at large there was little to relieve the monotony of stern routine on isolated farms. Frontier conditions had lingered, leaving traces that long affected Southern modes of life and thought.

Slavery and the semifeudal state it fostered proved another factor in determining the character of the South. The presence of the Negro conditioned every Southern reaction. It gave to the Southerner the basic premise of his creed, — the inferiority of the black man and the absolute need of discipline to keep society in proper adjustment. To the Southerner of all classes slavery was the most satisfactory discipline, and to its maintenance planter, yeoman, and poor white were all willing to make considerable sacrifices.

From the action and interaction of these influences, the

lingering frontier and the slave plantation, were derived most of
the qualities that characterized the Southerner who faced the
problems of 1865. His virtues and his vices were not those of
crowded places. Nor were they typical of a society free from
the shadow of race division. Plantation and frontier combined
to give to the South much personal kindness, hospitality, loyalty to home, and patriotism of locality. But they also produced a society in which violence was prevalent, with crudity
of living conditions general outside a restricted few, and an
alarmingly great degree of social wastage existing in the form
of ignorant, unskilled blacks and impoverished whites. On the
one hand there were manliness and womanliness, high standards of personal conduct, bravery, and the capacity for great
sacrifice. On the other hand there were few books of modern
literature, few newspapers of wide influence, little music, and
almost no theater. And finally there was an unyielding stability
of opinion, the twin product of isolation and the need of defending slavery, that served the South so well in war and was
to be its chief resistance to what was to follow.

In many respects the South embodied a survival of older
folkways into the modernity of the Nineteenth Century. It
did not welcome the "spirit" of the new age with its experimental isms, its energies, and its remakings. Southern life
was on simpler terms, conservatively adjusted to agriculture
and quiet aloofness. Even its problems it preferred to let alone,
like the poor whites who were permitted to lie basking in the
sunlight of indifference. Its folkways were near the soil and
for that reason seemed to Southerners to be more sincere than
the modernism that they believed was sweeping the North into
the maelstrom of European change. Southerners took pride
in their provincial culture. The familiar, homely ways were
preferred to foreign ways, and the poorest felt as keenly
as the richest the pride of being of the South.

Much has been written of Southern pride, especially by
Northerners who were galled by what they considered the
arrogance of Southern boasting. Whatever the cause, whether
it was the reflex of Southern provincialism, the defense reaction of a slave society in a world of freedom, or inherent
justification, the South did firmly believe in its own superi-

ority. Few people have carried self-respect and self-pride to so sensitive a degree. It was a complete identification of the individual with the section. To praise one was to justify the other. To attack the South was an insult to the Southerner, and vice versa.

The clash of Southern and Northern societies in the political arena of the fifties and on the battlefields of the Civil War accentuated Southern pride and focused its expression in growing disdain for the North. The South, like the North, built its morale upon a propaganda of hatred. "I do believe," wrote a Southern lady of rare refinement in 1866, "that the words which passed from North to South, and back again did more to set us against each other than the bullets. . . . I look back aghast now to think what lies we swallowed about you . . . the poisoned minié-balls our papers said you shot at us — the poisoned drugs they said you smuggled into our hospitals, the starved, rat-eating prisoners they said you abused, the murderous emissaries they said you sent among our slaves." [1] The influence such stories had upon the growing youth of the South is revealed in the case of Walter Hines Page, who, born in 1855 and raised in the lonesome rural life of wartime North Carolina, entered early manhood with all the beliefs of his environment. "Indeed," he wrote as late as the middle seventies, "however much the Southern race (I say race intentionally: Yankeedom is the home of another race from us) however much the Southern race owes its strength to Anglo-Saxon blood, it owes its beauty and gracefulness to the Southern climate and culture. Who says that we are not an improvement on the English? An improvement in a happy combination of mental graces and Saxon force." [2]

The full force of Southern character reached its peak of development in the effort to secure independence. Few wars more thoroughly enlisted the hearts of an entire people than the struggle for Southern nationalism. "To us," wrote the scientist, Joseph Le Conte, "it was literally a life and death struggle for national existence." Le Conte, like many thought-

[1] H. S. Chamberlain, "Old Days in Chapel Hill, Being the Life and Letters of Cornelia Phillips Spencer" (Chapel Hill, 1926), 128–129.
[2] B. J. Hendrick, "Life and Letters of Walter Hines Page" (New York, 1922), I, 28.

ful men, had originally opposed secession, but "gradually a change came about — how, who can say? It was in the atmosphere; we breathed it in the air; it reverberated from heart to heart; it was like a spiritual contagion. . . . The final result was enthusiastic unanimity of sentiment throughout the South." [3] Even after due allowance is made for the fatal division of opinion within the Confederacy as to the conduct of the war, there remains an essential truth in the assertion of Judah P. Benjamin, the Southern Secretary of State, that, "No people have ever poured out their blood more freely in defense of their liberties and independence, nor have endured with greater cheerfulness than have the men and women of these Confederate States." [4]

The Civil War was no war of professional soldiers who made a business of fighting. Men went into the army as amateurs. Each felt "the fate of the nation resting on his shoulders. . . . It was [the burden of responsibility] which killed — killed and weakened — more than shot and shell and frost and heat together." [5] Back of the soldier stood a nation socialized for purposes of waging war. To maintain the morale of such an army and such a society the motives for fighting had to be translated into ideals. The Southern cause was preached as a soul-absorbing aspiration for an independent existence. Consequently defeat when it came was more than merely the loss of an armed contest. It was a crushing of the spirit. Desertion from the army and loss of the will to fight at home evidenced a people robbed of faith in themselves as their nation sank beneath the power of Northern force.

The Southern veteran came back to no such scenes of jubilation as brightened the return of his adversary. Wearied in body, exhausted in spirit, he passed through wasted countrysides until he found retreat in a home that had been saddened by loss and impoverished by sacrifice. His was the retreat of a wounded stag seeking nothing better than the peace of solitude where the hounds of his enemy could not follow and the

[3] W. D. Armes, "The Autobiography of Joseph Le Conte" (New York, 1903), 179, 181.
[4] *Messages and Papers of the Confederacy*, II, 694.
[5] Le Moyne, a Confederate veteran, in A. W. Tourgee, "Bricks without Straw" (New York, 1880), 303.

taunting cries of the victorious chase could not penetrate. As
the stag in the depths of its forest had been lord, so also the
South in its aloofness had felt supreme. The brief emergence of
the nation in the brilliant enthusiasm of the early war years had
brought it dire exposure to the great, unsuspected strength of
the North. Force had undeceived the Southerner. What was
left but to retire deep again into the shadows of isolation?
But even there must now be felt the dread of pursuit.

The first and unforgettable impression of humiliating defeat
was the dispersion of the Southern armies. Not in columns of
marching men proud in bearing and strong in spirit did the
Southern veterans return. Singly or in pairs they straggled
into all parts of the South. They sat down in ragged gray to
no fatted calf but begged a crust from people who had little
more than crusts to share. They heard no music of fife and
drum but met the silence of exhaustion that better harmonized with their own despair. Few who underwent this experience ever erased the memory of the inglorious humiliation it
engraved upon their hearts.

It was not merely the ruin of war in a physical sense. The
utter prostration of the South was only in part a story of
devastation, burnt cities, bankrupt financial institutions, torn-up
railways, depleted farms, and a disrupted labor force. More
disastrous was the impoverishment of spirit that came with
defeat and continued in the depressed standard of living that
followed the war. "The flower of [our] labors," lamented a
veteran of the conflict, "and those of [our] fathers for cen-
turies had been trampled in the dust." [6] A stagnation of the
soul was as noticeable in 1865 as the opposite extreme of
enthusiasm in 1861. It was, as one observed, "a mute consent
to almost any misfortune which might happen." [7]

Yet these exhausted people confronted a sequel to war of
even greater import than their impoverishment. "Our people,"
wrote Sidney Lanier, "have failed to perceive the deeper movements under-running the times; they lie wholly off, out of
the stream of thought, and whirl their poor dead leaves of

[6] Edward Mayes, "Lucius Q. C. Lamar, His Life, Times, and Speeches"
(Nashville, 1896), 118–119.
[7] Edward King, "The Great South" (New York, 1875), 333.

recollection round and round, in a piteous eddy that has all the wear and tear of motion without any of the rewards of progress." The armies of the Union had penetrated the Southern aloofness. How much the imponderables of Southern life would continue to resist change from outside remained for the future to decide. But it was obvious even in 1865 that defeat involved a certain revolution of Southern life.

The forced remaking of a society is never pleasant to envision. The South faced a prospect made grimmer still by the heritage of hate and bitterness. Little sympathy could be expected from the North. Too many there thought of Southerners as rebels who had "framed iniquity into universal law." Northern hatred was met by Southern hatred. Conquest taught the South not respect for Northern ways but sullen dread of Northern strength. A writer in the recalcitrant *Southern Review* saw nothing in his survey of the war poetry more striking than "the expression of hate, . . . intense, unquenchable personal hate of Northerners as a race and as individuals." So bitter had Southern sentiment become that when Lincoln was assassinated there were some at least who welcomed it as a sort of retributive justice.[8] The South emerged from the war with a strengthened conviction of Northern wickedness and a sense of having been unduly persecuted by the vindictive malignity of the Federal power.

The sentiment hardened into unyielding prejudice. Defeat came, and to those who had staked all and lost all it meant that the bitter road of the conquered must be traveled. *Vae victis!* C. C. Clay spoke of it as a crucifixion in body and in soul. Many heard the cry, "The Yankees are coming," only to find that the words meant "the fall of loved ones, the burning of homes, the wasting of property, flight, poverty, subjugation, humiliation, a thousand evils, and a thousand sorrows."[9] The flag of the Union meant chastisement. Too often the emissary of the victorious power expected from the fallen atonement as though they had been in sin.[10] The South submitted but had

[8] J. S. Wise, "End of an Era" (Boston, 1899), 454; *Southern Review* (Baltimore), I (1867), 236–237.

[9] J. W. DeForest, "Chivalrous and Semi-Chivalrous Southrons," *Harper's Monthly Magazine*, XXXVIII (1869), 339.

[10] Mrs. R. A. Pryor, "My Day" (New York, 1909), 275.

no love for its master. July 4, 1865, the birthday of the American people, was silently ignored.[11] Not independence but a yoke heavier than their ancestors of 1776 had worn seemed the Southern lot.

Not glory but pathos encompassed the Southerner's first adjustment to the new regime. Lost were the dreams of greatness. Yet ruin, poverty, and defeat could not altogether destroy memory of the aspiration. The yearning for the vanished beauty of the past became a part of the Southern heart. Never was it more beautifully expressed than in the poem of Timrod, which itself became part of the tradition.

> Sleep sweetly in your humble graves,
>   Sleep, martyrs of a fallen cause;
> Though yet no marble column craves
>   The pilgrim here to pause.

Timrod dying from undernourishment himself personified the spirit that slept beneath the Southern ashes.

Memory, indeed, was the only solace in "these days of public shame, in this conquered land." [12] If in some it sealed the heart to reconciliation, to many it was the one thing that made life bearable. The dark shadow of mourning blackened the land. Productive of the greatest grief was the necessity of interring the Lost Cause. Father Ryan expressed the emotion of his people in the despairing yet acquiescing poem, "The Conquered Banner."

> Furl that Banner, softly, slowly!
> Treat it gently — it is holy —
>   For it droops above the dead.
> Touch it not — unfurl it never,
> Let it droop there, furled forever,
>   For its people's hopes are dead.

[11] Typical was Mrs. Preston's diary, "July 4, 1865. The Confederacy disowns forever as sacred the Fourth of July." E. P. Allan, "Life and Letters of Margaret Junkin Preston" (Boston, 1903), 208. Not until 1876 did the *Charleston News and Courier* urge renewed commemoration of the day.

[12] See the *Annual Report of the Home for the Mothers, Widows, and Daughters, of the Confederate Soldiers* (Charleston, 1871), 7.

The spirit of the South seemed dead in the dreary summer of 1865.[13] It was beyond the power of comprehension to realize that everything the South represented had suddenly become unfit for future life. The premises upon which past confidence had rested were now demolished. Had God willed the conflict? Had God made right to triumph over wrong? Had then the South been wrong? Such logic which would turn even the nobility of sacrifices into sin was impossible for an impoverished and bereaved people to accept. There must be an alternative. The South groped until it found an answer in admitting that Northern wealth and power had been invincible. Force, not reason and not right, had been the arbiter. It was easier to admit the strength of the North than to admit its righteousness. If the new equation proved more acceptable to Southern pride, it nevertheless carried a price tag of its own. The South must henceforth feel its own inferiority. And so to old, still sore, and cankering wounds was added a new factor which made for still greater emotional instability.

The admission of utter defeat was everywhere apparent in the South of 1865. From this followed the corollary of general acquiescence in the political consequences of the war. The apprehensive North little appreciated the completeness of its triumph, missed the extent to which the bankruptcy of Southern morale went, and so found it difficult to receive without some questioning the many assurances given by reporters of all shades of opinion that the South "accepted the situation." [14] The South, to be sure, showed no enthusiasm in this submission, and it is also probably true that none of its fundamental beliefs were immediately altered. The conviction of the Negro's inferiority remained, and while emancipation was accepted the need for discipline was still insisted upon. As for the political issues that had been so long in dispute the Southerner did not feel that they had been settled correctly, but he did know that

---

[13] "There was in the people themselves, especially in the women, an air of sadness which was as painful as it was natural. The ladies generally dressed in black or in dark colors, and there was not in King Street, at the busiest time, any of the chirping and chattering which are now so common." Dawson, "Talks by the Way," *Charleston Sunday News*, November 14, 1886.

[14] Truman, *Report*, 2; Andrews, "The South since the War," 9; Schurz, *Report*, 45–46.

they had been settled.[15] "The God of battles," wrote the Governor of Louisiana in language many could subscribe to, "has irrevocably decreed that we are one people. We must live together as brethren."[16]

"I am satisfied," wrote General Grant, "that the mass of thinking men of the South accept the present situation of affairs in good faith."[17] Much evidence substantiated Grant's opinion. Trowbridge, hardly a friendly observer, noted that most of the men who had "been lately fighting against us" wanted peace.[18] Truman wrote that "The soldiers of the late rebel army are, if possible, infinitely more wearied and disgusted with war and all its works than those of our army, and long for nothing so much as quiet."[19] Sidney Lanier in "Tiger Lilies" made an allegory of his war experience. Picturing the struggle as a "strange, enormous, terrible flower," he fervently hoped that it was forever destroyed. Lee urged all Southerners to "unite in honest efforts to obliterate the efforts of war and to restore the blessings of peace."[20] Roger A. Pryor, a Virginia fire-eater of the secession crisis, now advised his friends "to adjust their ideas to the altered state of affairs; to recognize and respect the rights of the colored race; to cultivate relations of confidence and good-will toward the people of the North; to abstain from the profitless agitation of political debate, and to employ their energies in the far more exigent and useful work of material reparation and development."[21]

The political leaders who were vocal in the period following the surrender were also in agreement as to the wisdom of a policy of acquiescence. The men who had been prominent in the affairs of the Confederacy were for the moment silenced. In their place a group of conservatives from the old union

[15] In a letter to Governor Letcher of Virginia, General Lee pointed out that while the issues had not been settled by reason they had been referred to the decision of war and decided unfavorably to the South. "It is the part of wisdom to acquiesce in the result and of candour to recognize the fact." Lee to Letcher, August 28, 1865, as quoted in H. A. White, "Robert E. Lee" (New York, 1897), 431.
[16] Governor D. S. Walker, *Appletons' Annual Cyclopedia* (1866), 326.
[17] *Report*, 106.
[18] Trowbridge, "The South," 188.
[19] Truman, *Report*, 3.
[20] White, "Robert E. Lee," 431.
[21] Mrs. Pryor, "My Day," 327.

party of the fifties acted as spokesmen for the South. These
men had for the most part opposed the policy of secession in
1860 and so seemed available to effect a renewal of contact
with the North. At the same time they had given support to
the Confederacy after the war had begun and so they commanded the respect of the South. Among them were individuals of substantial integrity and ability. Without exception
they urged the practical wisdom of concurring in the outcome
of the war.[22] The *Charleston News* in reviewing the events of
1865 summarized the matter by saying that the two great
issues, the permanence of the Union and the freedom of the
Negro, had been irrevocably decided. "Let us not unfit ourselves for the destiny which is marked out for us by cherishing any prejudices." [23]

It is a false impression, however, to assume that the South
of 1865 was much concerned with politics. The North itself
was so preoccupied with the issue of deciding a Reconstruction policy that everything Southern was distorted. Purveyors
of Southern news to the North were curious as to what the
South thought, especially about the Negro and the political situation. They pried into minds that would never otherwise have
expressed opinions and the opinions were relayed North to be
printed in newspapers, reports, and books. But while the dominant section was active in its interest, the South was mainly
passive. The people had had their fill of politics. Let the conqueror solve the problem of the nation's future. The South
had a more intimate task to meet, an immediate one that en-
grossed every energy. That task was the personal one of
salvaging from the general ruin the elements of livelihood
itself.

"I have no political aspirations of any kind," wrote one obscure Southerner whose attitude was typical of many. "I could
not indulge them if I had them." [24] "Our interest lies in eschew-
ing political excitement," advised a Governor. "Whilst others
rage and wrangle over ephemeral issues, let us be busy with the

[22] B. F. Perry of South Carolina and Jonathan Worth of North Carolina
were outstanding representatives of this group.
[23] *Charleston News*, Jan. 13, 15, 1866.
[24] "Bryan-Hayes Correspondence," *Southwestern Quarterly*, XXV, 231.

real, abiding concerns of life." [25] Political responsibility was a
luxury to men whose total strength was needed in the battle
with poverty.[26] The South sank to a dead level of unremitting
struggle for the necessities of life.

The newspapers of Savannah, one student has observed,
treated political news far less conspicuously than reports of
crops.[27] Charles Bruce found little politics in "the isolated life
of a Virginia farmer." "Simple routine and comparative seclusion" were for him a contrast to the prewar interest in politics he and his planter friends had known.[28] "People are thinking about their private business," reported another Virginian.
"They want to go to work to repair their losses." [29] Frances
Leigh, who had her own problem of rehabilitating a disor-
ganized plantation, saw men living "only in the daily present,
trying, in a listless sort of way, to repair their ruined fortunes.
They are like so many foreigners, whose only interest in the
country is their own individual business." Mrs. Leigh recalled
no discussion of politics in her entire experience. "Night after
night gentlemen met at one house or another, and talked and
discussed one and only one subject, and that was rice, rice,
rice." [30] This preoccupation with the worries of broken lives
made it all the more difficult to purge the heart of the resentment and prejudice engendered by the war. "I could be happier," wrote C. C. Clay, "almost anywhere than here, the scene
of so many departed joys never to return, of so many sorrows
never to be forgotten, of so many wrongs so hard to forgive.
That command of Christ, 'Love your enemies,' so like a good

[25] Governor Jenkins, Message to the Legislature, November 1, 1866, *Journal of the Georgia House of Representatives*, 1866, 31.
[26] The case of John and William Tison, of Beaufort, South Carolina, was
typical. They belonged to the planter class and had been educated at Harvard College, graduating in 1847. William became a state legislator before
the war. John was a colonel in the Confederate army. In the autumn of 1866
William wrote that he was living in two rooms, unprotected from the weather.
His family of wife and eight children lacked food and clothing. His gun was
his only dependence for meat. Corn and hominy were his chief articles of diet.
He had no horses, mules, or oxen, and no money to buy them. Manuscript in
Harvard College Library, *Harvard Class of 1847*, 429, 430, 441.
[27] C. M. Thompson, "Reconstruction in Georgia" (New York, 1915), 164.
[28] Manuscript in Harvard College Library, *Harvard Class of 1847*, 99.
[29] As quoted in Fleming, "Documentary History of Reconstruction," I, 10.
[30] F. B. Leigh, "Ten Years on a Georgia Plantation since the War" (London, 1883), 12-13, 152-153.

God, and so unlike a wicked man, is kept constantly in memory, to wound and reproach." [31] The war had given to many the most intense experience of their lives. For such people the dead past could not die. It clung tenaciously, making some permanently unreconcilable and giving to all an instability of emotion that could be directed into unfriendly channels in much the same manner as the Northern apprehension had been turned into vindictiveness. There were memories in the experience of all that could not be forgotten or remembered with pleasure. When new irritations such as undisciplined Negroes, contact with the military occupation, thoughtless slander by visiting Northerners, or the imprisonment of Jefferson Davis, were added to the dark social and economic outlook of 1865, the spirit of the South grew sullen and unfriendly. Yet it remains true that most of the hatred of the South found expression at a later date. During the summer of 1865 it was hushed.

It would be more accurate to say that the South in 1865 was unadjusted rather than unreconciled. The people had not yet found a basis in the shifting sands of the new conditions. The planting aristocracy had lost heavily in wealth and political influence. Many had to make new starts in life for which little in past experience had given preparation. The professional and middle classes, if they had less to lose, were nevertheless confronted with the equally grim necessity of fighting a long engagement with impoverishment. The poor were brought to the brink of actual starvation. The clergymen were rendered almost useless from the point of view of constructive influence. They had preached the righteousness of the Southern cause as fervently as their Northern brethren had invoked God to aid the Union. But their cause had failed and the adjustment to God's will was more than they could gracefully accomplish. It was in the churches that one found the utmost intolerance, bitterness, and unforgiveness during the sad months that followed Appomattox. [32]

The greatest problem of adjustment was that which faced the women of the South. Upon no class of the population did the

[31] Mayes, "Lamar," 122.
[32] The Reverend Doctor Girardeau of Charleston, South Carolina, might be offered as typical. See his address, *Confederate Memorial Day, Charleston, S. C.* (pamphlet), 17, 20.

war leave a more indelible impression. The enthusiasm aroused in them found no easy outlet in bearing arms as it had in the case of men. It festered as they sat silently, waiting and enduring. "The poverty which war brings to them," wrote one Confederate in his recollections, "wears no cheerful face, but sits down with them to empty tables and pinches them sorely in solitude." [33] The man who fought learned to understand that an attitude toward an opponent could be dissociated from the enmity directed against a cause. That the women were never given the opportunity to learn. To them the enemy was individually and collectively identical.

The Southern woman suffered a triple agony in the war. First was the physical suffering that came from deprivation and impoverishment. Hers was the responsibility of managing farms from which the men had gone into the armies and of feeding families left unprovided for. Secondly was the personal loss of fathers, husbands, sons, and brothers killed in battle or by disease. So large a percentage of the white male population of the South went into the army that nearly every family circle knew in time the cost of war. Finally, the Southern woman had an experience her Northern sister more fortunately escaped — the crucifixion of soul that came from sacrifices made in vain. And in the end it became their lot to face personal insult, humiliation, and, in cases, actual danger. [34]

So heart-rending and irremediable were the effects that thousands of Southern women seemed unable to appreciate that the cause for which they had given so much was actually destroyed. The peace had meant to them the ultimate in mortification. What abasement of the female spirit could be greater than the infliction placed on them of having little left with which to cheer the return of their beaten loved ones? The greater the humiliation the more imperative it seemed that the struggle must go on. And yet again there was no effective line of action. The only outlet was hate.

[33] G. C. Eggleston, "Rebel's Recollections" (New York, 1875), 58.
[34] The Northern women "were in no danger themselves. There was no Milroy, no Butler, no Hunter, no Sheridan, no Sherman, to taunt and upbraid them, to strip them of their most precious mementoes, to steal or scatter their scanty store of provisions and burn their homes over their heads." F. W. Dawson, "Our Women in the War," 3.

Possibly the most revealing expression of this emotion appeared in the poetry written by Southern women during the year and a half following the surrenders. It is a poetry of black-robed women:

> Weak their hearts from too much sorrow,
> Weak their frames from want and toil,
> Toiling where the earth is reeking
> With the blood that soaked its soil.

It is a poetry of the dead:

> We who live are living buried,
> Ye will ever live who died;
> For ye represent a struggle
> That your deaths have glorified.

It is a poetry in which the dead are considered happier than the survivor:

> He knew not the sorrow the conquered must feel,
> The grief of a fruitless endeavor.

It is a poetry of despairing courage:

> We do accept thee, heavenly Peace!
> .   .   .   .
> Upon our spirits, Fear — distrust —
> The hopeless present on us thrust —
> We'll meet them as we can, and must.

Fannie Downing in "Dixie" seemed to reflect the entire range.

> To die for Dixie! — Oh, how blest
> Are those who early went to rest,
> Nor knew the future's awful store,
> But deemed the cause they fought for sure
> As heaven itself, and so laid down
> The cross of earth for glory's crown.
>   And nobly died for Dixie.
> To live for Dixie — harder part!

More ambitious was the long narrative poem, "Beechen-brook," by Mrs. Margaret J. Preston. The poem was one of the most widely read of books of any sort in the prostrate South. It was dedicated to "every Southern woman who has been widowed by the war . . . as a faint memorial of suf-ferings, of which there can be no forgetfulness!" The poem is highly sentimental. Its tone is irreconcilable. The emphasis is on despair, grief, trouble, poverty, ruin. But the reader would be dull indeed if he failed to sense the depth of emotion that was put into "Beechenbrook." Here was pride in sacred memo-ries and the unshaken determination of a widowed lady that the "glorious *South must be Free!*" Such women would be hard to reconcile.

It seems necessary to emphasize that it was this legacy of hatred and shattered hopes, rather than an inadequate early training, that left the Southern women unadjusted to the new conditions of the postwar South. So far as formal education was concerned it may well be true that the Old South sought to develop grace and charm, but it can scarcely be maintained that the Southern women were much more superficially trained than the women of the North. The plantation women had their discipline and their responsibility, and it would be absurd to imagine the great mass of Southern women who lived on farms as free from care. Yet it remains true that the new order which followed the war was to revolutionize the outlook of the Southern woman. American women, North and South, had been sheltered from unfriendly exposure to the world. The South had gone further than the North in romanticizing the role of women in society. The grim necessities of the prostrate South precipitated the Southern woman on her painful road of adjustment in a way the Northern woman was never to experience.

To illustrate, one could cite young Bessie Allston, of Charles-ton, whose mother had been widowed in the war. The family's rice plantation was in ruins, and Mrs. Allston's immediate task was to make a livelihood. "August 25 [1865]," reads the daughter's diary. "A letter from Mamma today has upset me completely . . . she has determined to open a boarding and day school, and she expects me *to teach!* . . . I wrote

'Mamma, I cannot teach.'. . . Now that I have sent the letter
I am awfully ashamed. . . . Am I just a butterfly?" Mrs. Allston was inexorable, or rather the force of poverty dominated,
and so on October 20 the diary reads, "My irresponsible life
ends. . . . I have been able to enjoy being young and foolish.
I love dancing and I love admiration and I love to be gay." [35]
So also Frances Butler Leigh, taken to a Georgia plantation by
her father, learned how to be "very busy, very useful, and very
happy"; how to cook and how to doctor Negroes, and how in
time to manage the plantation on her own responsibility.[36]
A new discipline came to Southern women. "The iron," wrote
one, "entered my soul very early in this great battle we call
life. I looked about me with wide-open eyes, full of comprehension and a heart full of bitterness. . . . Silk dresses were
displaced by cotton ones, the parlor was deserted for the
kitchen, the piano for the sewing machine. The grind was on
us." [37] Only the future could reveal what relation the adjustment this womanhood made would have to sectional peace.

In summary, it can be noted that a gravitational pull was
causing the complex currents of Southern reaction to defeat to
flow down the lines of least resistance until they joined in a
common outlet. The experiences of 1865 made perhaps for a
greater unification of Southern emotion than had existed in any
earlier period of the section's life. It was not climate, or geography, or the agriculture of staple crops, which made the South
the entity that stood confronting the victorious North, and
gave to the American nationalist his problem of assimilation.
The South was a people who had had a history of separate aspiration and who still possessed the memory of a cause that
was lost. The South was a people united by a feeling of common helplessness before the overwhelming display of Northern might. And finally, the South was a people living in the
presence of the Negro who had been freed from the discipline
which had governed ante-bellum society. It was the common
experience of aspiration and defeat, of a sense of superiority

[35] "Patience Pennington," pseudonym for Mrs. Elizabeth W. Allston
Pringle, "Chronicles of Chicora Wood" (New York, 1913), 289–290, 296.
[36] F. B. Leigh, "Ten Years on a Georgia Plantation Since the War," 40–41.
[37] Belle Kearney, "A Slaveholder's Daughter" (New York, 1900), 22–23.

passing into loss of confidence, of a feeling of social security changing into the instability of race relationship, that knit the section together. While the North had been steeling its heart to play the victor's role, the South in turn had learned the implications of defeat. Between the two yawned a vast chasm.

CHAPTER III

THERE IS NO PEACE
1865–1880

DURING the summer of 1870 John Anderson made a visit to the South. He stopped with his friends in Tennessee, the family of Confederates who had nursed him back to health after finding him wounded and deserted on the battlefield. Upon his return to Ohio, Anderson was unable to decide whether he had enjoyed his trip or not. To no one in all his acquaintanceship did he feel so much gratitude as to this Southern family. He had been relieved to find that they had survived the war and the upheaval of reconstruction. He had been pleased with their unqualified welcome and the friendly glow of happiness his coming evoked upon their faces. But contact had not ripened into cordiality. Some restraint, some variation in background, present outlook, or future expectation, seemed always present to prevent the harmony each was seeking. It was as though they were traveling different roads which, having once crossed, would forever afterwards diverge. True friendship could not be built upon the memory of a single meeting when the present and the future seemed governed by an unyielding destiny of dissimilarity.

"They are not us," Anderson was forced to admit to himself with considerable disappointment and not complete understanding as to why it should be so. "They are not us and we are not them. My visit was a bridge across a chasm. It enabled me to shake their hands, to eat at their table, and to sleep in their bed. But it was only a bridge, and neither they nor I ever forgot the void between us. We could not even mention it. Had we done so we would have been pushed even farther from each other. The only friendship possible was based upon a tacit ignoring of what was deepest in our hearts. And what sort of friendship is that?"

What Anderson experienced, most Americans experienced in the years that followed the Civil War. Much was said about the need of healing the wounds of strife. Optimists pointed to episodes that seemed to suggest the approach of reconciliation. But actually the years from 1865 to 1880 were dreary years in which there was no peace. The war had ended only on the battlefield. In the minds of men it still persisted. Memories of the past and issues living in the present combined to perpetuate and perhaps enlarge the antagonism that victory and defeat had created.

One observer made the comment that "it was useless to preach forgiveness and good will to men still burning with the memory of their wrongs."[1] A wrong so remembered became an endless source of virulence. Each section had its burden of grievances suffered from the other to carry into the future.

Deeply engraven on the Northern heart was the conviction that the Confederacy had deliberately maltreated the prisoners of war captured by its armies. The Southern prisons, for reasons not here pertinent to explain, were at best what one Confederate surgeon described as a "gigantic mass of human misery." Stories of extreme suffering and bestial brutality emanated from them to fan the Northern rage into a frenzy. Newspapers paraded exaggerated accounts of prison atrocities before their readers. Escaped or exchanged prisoners published lurid tales of their experiences. The worse cases of emaciation and disease were photographed and the pictures reproduced in every Northern community. Fear gripped every Northerner who had a relative in the army. "Nothing in the Civil War was harder to get over," wrote one who had felt the dread. "If anything could justify sentiments of undying hatred toward all who participated in the slaveholders' rebellion, it was the treatment of our defenceless prisoners."[2]

A war-crazed public could not dissociate this suffering from deliberate intent of the enemy. Rather it fitted the purposes of

[1] Trowbridge, "My Own Story," 287.
[2] F. A. Walker, *Oration Delivered at the Soldiers' Monument Dedication in North Brookfield, Jan. 19, 1870* (Worcester, 1870), 12.

propaganda to attribute the basest motives to the Confederates. It was not merely the people who so reacted; they were abetted by the government. A committee of Congress made an official investigation and reported that "there was a fixed determination on the part of the rebels to kill the Union soldiers who fell into their hands." [3] The great non-governmental agencies of relief and propaganda contributed to the spread of similar impressions. After making an inspection of its own the United States Sanitary Commission declared, "The conclusion is unavoidable . . . that these privations and sufferings have been designedly inflicted by the military and other authorities of the rebel government and cannot have been due to causes which such authorities could not control." [4] The Loyal League publicized both reports.

Northern opinion was thus rigidly shaped in the belief that "tens of thousands of national soldiers . . . were deliberately shot to death, as at Fort Pillow, or frozen to death as at Belle Island, or starved to death as at Andersonville, or sickened to death by swamp malaria, as in South Carolina." [5] Horror passed into fury and fury into a demand for revenge. The *New York Times* insisted that "every rebel official who had been concerned, directly or indirectly, in the torturing and murdering of our prisoners" should be excluded from the terms of presidential pardon.[6] Secretary of War Stanton ordered the officers in command of the Union armies advancing into the South to arrest the men who had been most prominent in the management of the prisons. Such "inhuman monters" as "Dick" Turner of Libby, Captain R. B. Winder of Andersonville, and Major John H. Gee of Salisbury, were caught in the net. Considering the emotions of the time it is surprising that of the lot only two were punished. An obscure private was convicted of manslaughter and sentenced to a term in prison. And the arch-fiend of iniquity, for so the North regarded him, Major Henry Wirz, was hanged as a murderer.

[3] "Returned Prisoners," *38 Cong., 1 Sess., House Report No. 67.*
[4] United States Sanitary Commission, *Narrative of Privations and Sufferings of United States Officers and Soldiers while Prisoners of War in the Hands of the Rebel Authorities* (Philadelphia, 1864).
[5] *New York Times,* May 28, 1865.
[6] *Ibid.*

It is not necessary to consider Wirz a hero or a villain in recognizing that he was the scapegoat upon whom centered the full force of Northern wrath. Andersonville prison represented the utmost in horror, and it had been Wirz's misfortune to be in command of that prison in the months of greatest misery. He personified the evil and he was made to pay. He was not given an impartial trial. He stood already indicted in the North as a wholesale murderer from whom "some expiation must be exacted for the most infernal crime of the century." [7] A man who was believed to have boasted, "I am killing more Yankees than Lee at the front," found no mercy.

Wirz was executed in November 1865. Other trials all ending in acquittal continued into August 1866. But if the peak of frenzy passed, the issue continued to divide the sections. The public press made constant references to the prisons. Ministers preached sermons about them as examples of the barbarous influence of slavery. Politicians exploited the theme. At least forty-eight narratives of prison experiences were published in book form during the seven years from 1865 to 1871. [8] Veteran groups gave prominence in their reunions to suffering survivors of the prison camps. In 1869 the House of Representatives published a committee report on the *Treatment of Prisoners of War by the Rebel Authorities*. The testimony of three thousand witnesses was taken to establish an "enduring truthful record, stamped with national authority." "The opinion of the committee carefully and deliberately formed [is] that the neglect and refusal of the rebel authorities to provide sufficient and proper rations was the result of a premeditated system and scheme of the confederate authorities to reduce our ranks by starvation, and that they were not forced to these deprivations from accident or necessity." [9]

Meanwhile the South had no effective way of meeting these charges of brutality. The Confederate government was defunct and so no official statement of the Southern side could be made to offset the Report of 1869. It was not until 1876 that the publication of R. R. Stevenson's "The Southern Side,

---

[7] *New York Times,* July 26, 1865.

[8] The count was made by W. B. Hesseltine, "Civil War Prisons" (Columbus, 1930), 247–248.

[9] *40 Cong., 3 Sess., House Report No. 45,* 216.

or Andersonville Prison" and J. W. Jones's "The Confederate View of the Treatment of Prisoners" gave to such unbiased
minds as might wish to know an adequate exposition of the
Southern side. It is not difficult to find, however, material in
these years that indicates the South received the Northern
charge with sullen hatred. Typical is an article contributed to
the *Southern Review* in January 1867:

The impartial times to come will hardly understand how a
nation, which not only permitted but encouraged its government
to declare medicines and surgical instruments contraband of war,
and to destroy by fire and sword the habitations and food of non-
combatants, as well as the fruits of the earth and the implements
of tillage, should afterwards have clamored for the blood of
captive enemies, because they did not feed their prisoners out of
their own starvation and heal them in their succorless hospitals.
And when a final and accurate development shall have been made
of the facts connected with the exchange of prisoners between
the belligerents, and it shall have been demonstrated, as even
now it is perfectly understood, that all the nameless horrors
which are recorded of the prison-houses upon both sides, were
the result of a deliberate and inexorable policy of non-exchange
on the part of the United States, founded on an equally deliberate calculation of their ability to furnish a greater mass of humanity than the Confederacy could afford for starvation and the
shambles, men will wonder how it was that a people, passing for
civilized and Christian, should have consigned Jefferson Davis to
a cell, while they tolerated Edwin M. Stanton as a cabinet minister.

So the endless argument continued. The wounds remained
unhealed festering their poison of unforgiveness.

If the prisons constituted a Northern grievance the South
likewise had its hurtful memories. While Northerners blamed
the evil genius of slavery for the war, Southerners pointed the
finger of responsibility to "those men who preached the irrepressible conflict to the Northern people" and "helped to bring
on that unlawful and unholy invasion of the South."[10] The
South felt that it had been betrayed. "Assuredly the subjugated
portions of this imperial republic (so called), with the bitter

[10] Major T. G. Barker, *Address* (Charleston, 1870), 7.

experience they have of outraged honour, justice, and humanity, on the part of those once their associates and friends, can never again by any possibility trust that vast engine of tyranny, a consolidated popular Union, nor derive from it one ray of hope for their own welfare, or for the happiness of mankind."[11] It was to this "deep spirit of hate and oppression toward the Southern people," and not to the necessities of war, that the South attributed the vast destruction of its property.[12]

The ineradicable sense of injury felt by the South took concrete form in condemning the ravages committed by General Sherman's army in Georgia and South Carolina. "No tongue will ever tell, no pen can record the horrors of that march," wrote an intimate associate of General Joseph E. Johnston whose surrender to Sherman is sometimes pictured as a love feast. "Ten generations of women will transmit, in whispers to their daughters, traditions of unspeakable things."[13] The hurt inflicted was accentuated by Northern pride in the achievement. The South resented the arrogant and jeering tone of the song, "Marching through Georgia," and bridled when Northern orators described Sherman's army going through the conquered land "like the plow of God." Sherman personified all that the South had suffered.

The most contentious bone over which the wrangling occurred was the destruction of Columbia. As much bitterness was generated over the issue of "Who burnt Columbia?" as the question of Confederate responsibility for the suffering of Andersonville. Sherman's own defense was to blame General Wade Hampton, who ordered the Confederate retreat from the South Carolina capital. The charge was made deliberately in Sherman's official report. "I did it," he later wrote, "pointedly to shake the faith of his people in him, for he was, in my opinion, a braggart, and professed to be the special champion of South Carolina." Hampton immediately countered by accusing Sherman of premeditated destruction of the city. And so a question of intricate perplexity to the historian became one on which partisans of the time took definite stands. "Hur-

[11] *Southern Review*, II (1867), 5.
[12] See B. W. Jones, "Under the Stars and Bars" (Richmond, 1909), 14.
[13] B. J. Johnson, "A Memoir of the Life and Public Service of Joseph E. Johnston" (Baltimore, 1891), 157.

rah for Columbia!" exulted Phillips Brooks in the North. "Isn't Sherman a gem?" But the South had the ashes of a city and the experience of a terrible night of pillage to remember.

The debate persisted. Books and pamphlets were written. Testimony of eye-witnesses was collected in public mass meetings held as late as 1867 in South Carolina. Claims for damages for property destroyed in the fire were made and Congress created a commission to take evidence. The report, made in 1873, freed the United States from responsibility for damages, but North and South each read in the accumulated evidence vindication of its accusation against the other.[14]

The South was further irritated by the arrest and imprisonment of Jefferson Davis. It was not unnatural, considering the bitter partisanship that every civil war breeds, to find the victors determined to exact some vengeance from the leader of the defeated side. There was a widespread clamor for the execution of Davis. Northern opinion considered him the chief author of secession, the fountain head of treason. "It was his hand," it was declared and generally believed, "that shed the blood or caused the death of more than a quarter million of men and the waste and destruction of more than six thousand millions of property." [15] Troops had marched to war singing the refrain "We'll hang Jeff Davis on a sour apple tree." The whole North laughed at the jeering newspaper reports of Davis's capture "in women's clothes." Davis was personally held responsible for the worst conditions at Andersonville. When Lincoln was assassinated high government officials charged Davis with complicity in the crime. Secretary of War Stanton summed up the Northern case against Davis when, as late as January 4, 1866, he asserted that the Confederate Presi-

---

[14] The official reports of Sherman and Hampton are found in *Official Records of the Rebellion,* XLVII, pt. 1, p. 21, and pt. 2, p. 596. See also, W. T. Sherman, "Memoirs" (New York, 1875), II, 287; Allen, "Phillips Brooks," II, 526; W. G. Simms, *Letter on the Sack and Destruction of Columbia* (Charleston, 1865); D. H. Trezevant, "The Burning of Columbia" (Columbia, 1866); W. H. Peck, "The McDonalds, or Ashes of Southern Homes" (New York, 1867); *Report of the Committee to Collect Testimony in Relation to the Destruction of Columbia* (Columbia, 1893); and *Report of the Proceedings and Results of the Mixed Commission on American and British Claims, 43 Cong., 1 Sess., Foreign Relations,* III, 50. For a typical debate in Congress see *Congressional Globe,* May, 1, 1866.
[15] Senator Howard of Michigan, *Congressional Globe,* Feb. 1, 1866.

dent was guilty of treason, "of inciting the assassination of
Abraham Lincoln," and of "the murder of Union prisoners
of war by starvation and other barbarous and cruel treatment." [16]

Davis was imprisoned in Fortress Monroe on May 22, 1865.
At first he was forcibly placed in irons, but these were removed four days later. Until October he was confined in a
cell that was deleterious to his health. After October his treatment was good. Meanwhile the prosecution against him moved
slowly. It was not until May 13, 1867, that he was brought before a court of law. By that time the hysteria prevailing at
the time of his arrest had abated. Charles O'Connor, an able
New York attorney, was able to prove that much of the evidence connecting Davis with the assassination of Lincoln was
perjury. The charge that Davis had murdered Union prisoners,
much as it might be fixed in public opinion, was recognized to
be unprovable in law. A Northern physician, Colonel John J.
Craven, who had attended Davis in prison, published early in
1866 a book, "The Prison Life of Jefferson Davis," in which
he conveyed the idea that Davis had been harshly treated.
Further delay in prosecuting Davis seemed unjust. He was
brought before the United States Circuit Court for Virginia.
The Government's case was still not ready for prosecution.
The Court thereupon released the prisoner on bond. The trial
was never held. Davis was finally freed from all charges against
him under terms of the general pardon extended to all who had
participated in rebellion by President Johnson in his proclamation of December 25, 1868.

The South received Davis's "persecution" with consterna-
tion. "If there was guilt in any," wrote Sidney Lanier, "there
was guilt in nigh all of us. . . . Mr. Davis, if he be termed
the ringleader of the rebellion, was so not by virtue of any
instigating act of his, but purely by the unanimous will and appointment of the Southern people. . . . The hearts of the
Southern people bleed to see how their own act has resulted in
the chaining of Mr. Davis, who was as innocent as they, and
in the pardon of those who were as guilty as he!" [17] Davis in

[16] *Official Records of the Rebellion,* Series II, vol. VIII, 843.
[17] Lanier, "Tiger Lilies," 120.

forcibly resisting the placing of irons around his ankles sounded the note of the Southern protest. "I will not submit to indignities by which it is sought to degrade in my person the cause of which I was a representative." The response could not be made moderately. And so it was the irreconcilable *Southern Review* that in this crisis acted as spokesman for the entire section in condemnation of the "barbarous violence" in Fortress Monroe.

The ultimate release of Davis on May 13, 1867, and his complete pardon under the President's proclamation of December 25, 1868, constitute one of the most important of the early triumphs of reconciliation. Had he been executed an irretrievable step would have been taken which would have indelibly stamped into the Southern heart a feeling of ineradicable wrong. Even as it was, bitterness over Davis remained to separate the sections. The *Boston Advertiser* interpreted Southern rejoicing over the release of Davis as defiance. Horace Greeley was made to feel the unpopularity of his action in contributing to the fund for Davis's bail by seeing the sale of his recently published history, "The American Conflict," almost cease. The *Nation,* a journal of moderate opinion, as late as 1876 maintained that Davis was morally responsible for Andersonville.

An episode in the summer of 1875 indicated that seven years after the imprisonment the North still wanted no peace with Jefferson Davis. In May the manager of the county fair to be held at Rockford, Illinois, invited Davis to deliver an address in September that would contribute to the "promotion of sectional peace." [18] A similar invitation to address the county fair at Columbus, Indiana, which would also meet in September, was extended. All mercenary motives were disclaimed, although the hope was expressed that the large funds required to bring the Confederate President North might be recovered through the larger attendance his presence would attract. Davis accepted the invitations, professing the hope that

[18] The episode is best followed through the correspondence exchanged between Davis and the manager, printed in D. Rowland (ed.), "Jefferson Davis" (Jackson, 1923), VII, 422–435.

an opportunity to speak in the North might be a means of allaying sectional antipathies.

An olive branch in the hands of Jefferson Davis was too shocking a spectacle for the North to endure. Disdainfully the token was refused. The proposed exchange of honeyed phrases of fraternal greetings did not materialize. Instead insults were beaten back and forth to exacerbate the sores of sectional unneighborliness. The ridiculous exhibition embarrassed the moderate men who found it difficult to promote peace and Davis in combination. Again the extremists throve on controversy unhappily aroused. No sooner had the invitation been extended than the Rockford post of the Grand Army of the Republic met to condemn the insult of asking this "arch-traitor to address the relatives and surviving friends of thirteen thousand men murdered at Andersonville alone by his orders." [19] The *Chicago Tribune* pointed the finger of scorn at what it considered the mercenary motives of the managers of the fair who asked Davis "to seal the era of reconciliation for $400" while Davis held out for five hundred dollars. Indignation meetings assembled throughout the state, the press of the entire country joined in the debate, and the proposed visit was canceled. The managers took consolation in the belief that the "best men among us approved your coming," while Davis expressed the pious hope that eventually "some of the prejudices generated by partizan factions and nurtured by individual and sectional hate" might be removed. Meanwhile it possibly occurred to neither to reflect on the mischief the ill-advised effort had accomplished. The weakest beam had been selected to bridge the chasm. Its wreckage would prove an embarrassment in the future to those who sought a more intelligent construction.

If Davis embodied in Northern opinion the hateful memories of the Civil War, the South in much the same manner cherished a hateful image of the martyred Lincoln. Lincoln, the candidate of 1860, had been represented as the blackest Republican preaching the House Divided. He became the President who carried out in action his prophecy of war and de-

[19] *Nation,* Aug. 19, 1875.

struction. He and his cabinet, wrote the *Southern Review*, had a

> perfect comprehension of the passions, prejudices, susceptibilities, vices and virtues, knowledge and ignorance of the people upon whom they had to practice. They knew every quiver of the popular pulse, and what it signified. They could weigh out, to a grain, the small quantity of truth to which the public appetite was equal, and they perfectly understood and measured the supernatural extent to which the popular conception could assimilate falsehood. They were masters of every artifice that could mystify or mislead, and of every trick that could excite hope, or confidence, or rage. . . . Understanding their pit thus well, they played to it, with wonderful tact and effect. They filled their armies, established their financial system, controlled the press, and silenced opposition, by the same ingenious and bold imposture.[20]

Lincoln, the South believed, won by trickery and by force vindictively applied. Here was a further grievance that time alone could remedy.

As long as these hurtful memories persisted a true union of emotion necessary to nationalism was impossible. This was revealed in a number of minor incidents. The South sneered at a North which observed the Fourth of July and "at the same time denounced as damnable heresy the doctrines of the Declaration of Independence." When the North celebrated the completion of Field's transatlantic cable as an American achievement the South felt no similar thrill of pride. When Chicago was destroyed by fire in 1871 it was considered no national tragedy by at least the more radically tempered Southerner who deemed it a "demonstration of Divine vengeance," because it had been in Chicago that "the rowdy Lincoln, the prime official agent of all our woes, was nominated." When dirges in the North expressed the nation's sorrow for the loss of General Custer in the massacre of 1876, it was remembered in Virginia that the gallant martyr of the Little Big Horn was also the Custer who had executed seven captured Confederates

[20] *Southern Review*, I (1867), 236. See also Jubal A. Early, *Address before the South Carolina Survivors' Association, November 10, 1871*, 37.

of Mosby's command without treating them as prisoners of
war.

It was impossible for moderation to flourish in such an
atmosphere. The man of vindictive bias and recriminating
taste commanded more than normal influence. Typical of the
group in the South was A. T. Bledsoe, the founder and editor
of the most recalcitrant of the Southern journals of opinion.
For eleven years from its founding in 1867 to Bledsoe's death
in 1878, the *Southern Review* was a channel of vituperative
hatred directed against the North. In the North the most influential organ in the same period was possibly *Harper's Weekly*,
with its editorials by G. W. Curtis and its cartoons by Thomas
Nast. Its prevailing tone was the non-forgetting and the
non-forgiving of men "who had betrayed their trust," and
forced "Union soldiers to rot in Andersonville and Libby
prisons."

The unreconciled impressions were kept alive in the earliest
memoirs written by the leading actors in the conflict. No book
of this time received greater acclamation in the South than
Admiral Semmes's personal narratives, "The Cruise of the Alabama and the Sumter," and "Memoirs of Service Afloat."
Apart from the interest in the story of Confederate successes
on the high seas, the South was gratified to find that the books
embodied an argument justifying secession on constitutional
and political grounds. Sherman's "Memoirs," published in
1875, was equally popular in the North and gave pleasure in
much the same way. The General was unequivocal in condemnation of the South (far more so here than in his private
letters) and took an almost lustful pride in describing the
tremendous power his hand had wielded in spreading terror
and destruction. Read together the books are eloquent of the
division between the sections.

The desire to be moderate stumbled against the necessity
to maintain the right. This is well exemplified in the cases
of a prominent clergymen and a distinguished scholar. Henry
Ward Beecher was never a Radical in the Reconstruction era.
He found much to admire in the way the South had borne its
burden of defeat. He believed that forgiveness was both
Christian and statesmanlike. "But reconciliation," he asserted

as late as 1878, "would be a weakness if it glozes over the criminality" in the Southern past. "We dishonor our dead when we make no distinction between those who died for liberty and those who died for slavery. Reconciliation purchased by rubbing out the whole meaning of the war, the moral significance of its results, the grandeur to mankind of its influence, is not a compromise, but a surrender." [21]

Much the same psychology dominated John W. Draper, who in the years 1867 to 1870 published a three-volume "History of the American Civil War," the first detailed survey of the struggle by a trained scholar. According to his own confession he listened to "the voice of philosophy . . . calming our passions, suggesting new views of things about which we contended, whispering excuses for our antagonist, and persuading us that there is nothing we shall ever regret in fraternal forgiveness for the injuries we have received." Draper did try to shoulder "climate" with the responsibility of "making us a many diversified people" who "in the nature of things . . . must have our misunderstandings and our quarrels." But in the narrative Draper emphasizes the sin of slavery as the factor which brought the nation to the brink of destruction, he declares secession a conspiracy, and he speaks of the outcome of the war as a retribution to those who had started it. Finally there appears this bit of moralizing,

Shall he who writes the story of this hideous war hide from his readers its fearful lesson? . . . If in the future there should be any who undertakes to fire the heart of his people, and to set in mortal battle a community against the nation, let us leave him without the excuse which the war secessionist of our time may perhaps not unjustly plead, that he knew not what he did. Let us put our experience in the primer of every child; let us make it the staple of the novel of every school girl; let us tear from this bloody conflict its false grandeur and tinsel glories, and set it naked in the light of day — a spectacle to blanch the cheek of the bravest man, and make the heart of every mother flutter as she sits by her candle.

[21] Beecher, *Address to the Society of the Army of the Potomac,* Springfield, Mass., June 5, 1878.

This being sober history of the day, it is perhaps not surprising that Bledsoe, who was attempting to put a different experience into the primer of every Southern child, should condemn Draper's book as one "literally stuffed with the lying traditions, the cunningly devised fables, and the vile calumnies, with which a partizan press and a Puritanical pulpit have flooded the North." [22]

Unreconciled views entered into the textbooks used in the schools and were so transmitted to the youth of the country. Thus Worcester's "Elements of History, Ancient and Modern" (1866 edition) affirmed that "Confederate prisoners at the North were comfortably housed and fed; but the inhuman treatment and horrible suffering of Federal soldiers in Southern prisons form one of the most shocking chapters in the history of the Rebellion." The widely used Peter Parley "Pictorial History of the United States" (1867 edition) by S. G. Goodrich was surcharged with the spirit of Northern superiority quietly introduced in contrasts such as the statements that Virginia was settled by "vagabond gentlemen" while New England was settled by a "pious and excellent people." A different sort of bias appeared in Emma Willard's "History of the United States" (1869 edition). Her factual narrative is inoffensive to the extent of being dull, but much greater emphasis and space is given to New England's rôle in the nation's history than to the South's. Also temperate in tone was Quackenbos' "Illustrated School History of the United States." The prewar editions of this text had been characterized by evasiveness on all debatable issues. The editions of 1867, 1868, and 1871 seemed equally noncommittal. Nevertheless both Willard and Quackenbos were condemned in the South along with more extreme partisans. Perhaps their chief fault in Southern eyes was the moralizing tone which saw in Southern defeat retribution for the sins of slavery and secession.

As was to be expected, Southern textbooks were fewer in number and later in date. They were written from a bias which emphasized Southern achievement in the colonial and national periods, expounded the constitutional doctrines of state rights and secession, and told the story of the Civil War from the

[22] *Southern Review,* III (1868), 4-5.

Confederate point of view. J. S. Blackburn and W. N. McDonald's "New School History of the United States" (1870), was apparently the first in the series of Southern school histories. It was as moderate in its pro-Southern bias as Quackenbos or Willard were in their pro-Northern. More partisan was Alexander H. Stephens's "Compendium of the History of the United States" (1872), designed for purposes of a textbook. In general a perusal of these early textbooks reveals not so much intemperance in the authors themselves as in the public which received them. North and South, parents were more insistent than the textbook writers that only their special brands of "truth" be taught.

Organized religion offered another battleground of acrimonious controversy. At one time all the great protestant sects, with the exception of the Congregational churches, which existed only in New England or where New England influence extended, had been truly national in organization and membership. As national bodies it had been in the interests of unity to maintain a moderate and conciliatory attitude toward the bitter animosities which political rivalries engendered. Conservatives, interested in preserving their churches as "dwelling houses of Christian unity," had worked constantly for peace, hoping to avoid dissension through evasion, by insisting that it was not the rôle of religion to assume a position on political issues. But the clash of interests over slavery and disunion had sectionalized the churches and bred in churchmen the virulence of radicalism. Moderation of men seeking unity was replaced by the extremism of men justifying division. Faiths which had once been bonds of national communion had now become agencies of discord.

The unity of the Methodist Episcopal Church had been disrupted as early as 1844 when the Northern majority resolved that slavery was a moral sin and therefore came within the purview of the church, and that bishops of the church could not be slaveholders. The Southern delegates had denounced this action as interference with established civil institutions and declared that the establishment of a separate Southern church was necessary to enable them to perform their proper function of preaching the gospel to a slave-owning community.

Such a church, organized in 1846, justified its secession and independence on the tenet that the "peculiar mission of the Methodist Episcopal Church South is that it alone stands for the Christian principle of keeping out of politics." [23] While the split was in process of development churchmen were governed by intense passion. Charges of sinfulness, blasphemy, and heresy were freely made on either side and read into solemn resolutions where they remained to rankle in the future.

The Baptist church divided in 1845 on the same issue of the propriety of moral agitation of slavery. The more conservative Presbyterian church cohered until the Civil War had actually begun. Then in May 1861 the Assembly adopted the comparatively mild resolution that in its judgment "it is the duty of the ministry and churches under its care to do all in their power to promote and perpetuate the integrity of the United States, and to strengthen and encourage the Federal Government." [24] This was sufficient provocation to cause the secession of the Southern element and the establishment of a Southern Presbyterian church which, like the Southern Methodists, "planted itself upon the Word of God and utterly refused to make slaveholding a sin or non-slaveholding a term of communion." [25] In the same year the Protestant Episcopal Church separated as an incidence of the war, and, peculiar to itself, with the exchange of a minimum of contumely.[26]

Had division accomplished peace and good neighborship in two houses it would have been preferable to the internecine war that had existed around one hearthstone. But in this instance division meant merely the drawing off of extremists into opposite camps from which they could better direct their warfare against each other. The moderates were crushed between the accomplished fact of disunion which they had attempted to prevent and the swelling enthusiasm for the war. Each section of the church moved steadily to more extreme positions.

[23] *Southern Review*, X (1872), 338.
[24] L. G. Vander Velde, "The Presbyterian Churches and the Federal Union, 1861–1869" (Cambridge, 1932), 50.
[25] Address of the Southern General Assembly to all the Churches of Jesus Christ, printed in R. E. Thompson's "History of the Presbyterian Church in the United States" (New York, 1895), 388–406.
[26] M. Mohler, "The Episcopal Church and National Reconciliation," *Political Science Quarterly*, XLI (1926), 567–595.

North and South, patriotism was preached as a religious duty. The objectives of the combatants were translated into moral values. Northern pulpits assailed slavery and disunion as sins. Southern pulpits upheld them as sacred foundations of society and charged the North with sinful conduct in acting against them. It is no exaggeration to affirm that the churches in both sections became the chief recruiting agencies and the chief builders of morale.

In the heat of the war years the Southern churches descended from the high spiritual ground of aloofness from politics which they had taken to justify their secession from their Northern brethren. Thus the Southern Presbyterian Church, somewhat inconsistently with its action of 1861, passed in 1862 a resolution which read in part,

Deeply convinced that this struggle is not alone for civil rights and property and home, but also for religion, for the church, for the gospel, for existence itself, the churches in our connection have freely contributed to its prosecution of their substance, their prayers, and above all of their members, and the beloved youths of their congregations. . . . The Assembly desires to record, with its solemn approval, this fact of the unanimity of our people in supporting a contest in which religion as well as patriotism now summons the citizens of this country, and implore for them the blessing of God in the course they are pursuing.[27]

In 1864 the same body announced that "we hesitate not to affirm that it is the peculiar mission of the Southern Church to conserve the institution of slavery, and to make it a blessing both to master and slave."

Meanwhile the Presbyterian Church in the North was undergoing a similar transformation from conservatism to radicalism. The Assembly of 1862 resolved that "this whole treason, rebellion, anarchy, fraud, and violence" was "utterly contrary to the dictates of natural religion and morality, and plainly condemned by the revealed will of God." The Assembly of 1864 was even more plain spoken in extreme condemnation of the "wickedness and calamities of the rebellion," and "the

[27] T. C. Johnson, "History of the Southern Presbyterian Church" (New York, 1894), 427.

evil and guilt of slavery." As one conservative ruefully inquired, "Could the Church go further in its adulterous intercourse with the State?" [28]

The extreme commitment of organized Protestantism to the war objectives of their respective sections was the first great barrier to church reunion after the war had ended. The Southern Methodists and Baptists early affirmed that the abolition of slavery did not affect the basic principle, which the North had violated and was still violating, of the impropriety of mixing religion and politics.[29] Curiously blind to their own activity, the Southern Methodists never forgave the Northern Church for the active part it had assumed in the waging of the war. The Southern Presbyterians refused to accept fraternal greetings from the Northern church because they were unaccompanied by apologies and withdrawals of the earlier accusations of sinfulness and heresy.[30]

Added injuries were inflicted when Northern missionaries moved into the South with the advancing armies. Secretary of War Stanton in 1863 adopted the policy of seizing the property of Southern churches that came within the Union lines and turning it over for occupancy to the officials of the corresponding Northern sect. Here was an "unnatural crime" that deeply wounded the susceptibilities of the Southern religious bodies. The practice also produced a great number of acerbating lawsuits for the recovery or retention of churches thus allocated. Here was some bad history that was not soon forgotten. As a prominent Southern Methodist stated, it "has made reunion impossible for at least a generation. There cannot be the confidence and respect for the men engaged in this business which would make church fellowship with them profitable or even tolerable." [31]

While the Southern churches were sullenly determined to have no communion with the victors, the Northern churches assumed an attitude that was ill adapted to the delicacy of the situation. This attitude was based upon a confident assump-

[28] *Minutes of the General Assembly, 1862, 1864.* See also Vander Velde, "Presbyterian Churches," 127–130.
[29] *Appletons' Annual Cyclopædia* (1866), 553.
[30] *Ibid.* (1870), 621–622.
[31] *Southern Review,* X (1872), 417.

tion that the triumph of the Federal armies meant the end of separate churches in exactly the same sense it meant the end of Southern political independence. Just as the state had its problem of reconstruction, so also the Northern churches announced their policy to be the disintegration and absorption of the schismatical Southern bodies. Many believed that the "rebellious defiance of lawful authority which has racked the Nation to its foundations during the four years of war" was born in "the Church of God." [32] Prompt and decisive action seemed imperative if the "offspring of heresy, corruption, and all unrighteousness" were to be exterminated and "those who have gone out from us upon vain and wicked pretexts . . . may know the cost of setting at defiance the authority which Christ has given to his Church." [33]

The Presbyterian, Methodist, and Baptist churches adopted the policy of regarding the South as a missionary field. Among Presbyterians the prevailing sentiment was for making "enlarged and most vigorous efforts in all parts of . . . defunct Confederacy." Inasmuch as the secessionists had "knowingly sinned in slavery and in treason" conditions of repentance must be exacted. Thus ministers who had been active rebels "should never be permitted to return to our church as teachers or rulers." Others less sinful, "upon proper sense of their sins, and upon proper confessions and promises, might be restored." But in all cases "a scheme of readjustment or reconstruction" would have to be devised. The policy of the church was officially defined in the Assembly of 1865. The Board of Domestic Missions was directed to "take prompt and effectual measures to restore and build up the Presbyterian congregations in the Southern States of this Union by the appointment and support of prudent and devoted missionaries." Needless to say, no missionaries were to be appointed who could not give "satisfactory evidence of their loyalty to the national government." [34]

This action was obviously a declaration of war against the Southern Presbyterian Church, a war to be waged in the latter's field, for communicants whose past loyalties had been to

[32] Thesis of R. L. Stanton's "The Church and the Rebellion" (New York, 1864).
[33] Moderator's speech of acceptance, Presbyterian Assembly of 1866.
[34] Vander Velde, "The Presbyterian Churches," 197, 222–223, 500.

the Confederacy. It should have appeared obvious that such
people could have been won only by generous terms. But the
Northern missionaries came as conquerors. The Assembly
steeled them with rigid instructions contained in the following
resolves:

Whereas, During the existence of the great rebellion . . . a
large number of Presbyteries and Synods in the Southern States
. . . have organised an Assembly denominated "The General
Assembly of the Confederate States of America," in order to
render aid in the attempt to establish . . . a separate national
existence, and to "conserve and perpetuate the system of slavery,"
therefore

Resolved, 1. That this Assembly regards the perpetuation of
Negro slavery as a great crime, both against our National Government and against God, and the secession of those Presbyteries
and Synods from the Presbyterian Church, unwarranted, schismatical, and unconstitutional.

Resolved, 2. That this General Assembly does not intend to
abandon the territory in which these churches are found. . . .
On the contrary, this Assembly hereby declares that it will recognize such loyal persons as constituting the Churches, Presbyteries
and Synods, in all the bounds of the schism, and will use earnest
endeavours to restore and revive all such churches and church
courts.[35]

The Methodist Episcopal Church acted with equal vigor.
Conferences or mission conferences were established to include
all portions of the South. Theological schools were established
in New Orleans and Charleston and two weekly religious
journals were published from the same centers.[36] The Baptists
were also in the field. The General Assembly of 1865 expressed "a readiness to coöperate with their Southern brethren
in the fellowship of Christian labor," and then immediately
nullified the gesture by attaching to it the condition that the
Southerners must admit the sin of slavery and profess loyalty
to the Government.[37]

The answer to these threats of absorption was instantaneous.

[35] *Ibid.,* 198.
[36] *Appletons' Annual Cyclopædia* (1866), 488.
[37] *Ibid.* (1865), 106.

The South determined to "keep ourselves distinct in matters of faith and church government." "One thing is obvious at a glance," wrote a Methodist. "In case of reunion, the Northern Church would give its character to the whole organization." [38] No Southern church of the larger denominations believed that it could trust the direction of its destiny to the Northern majority.

The General Assembly of the Southern Presbyterian Church adopted resolutions in December 1865 to remain "a separate and distinct ecclesiastical body." The Southern Baptist associations that met during the year 1865 were unanimously in favor of a continuance of separation. They seemed especially intent on censuring the American Home Mission Society, an agency of the Northern Baptists, for obtaining from the Federal government authority to take possession of Southern church property. Likewise the Methodist bishops of the South issued a pastoral letter in which they asserted that "whatever banner had fallen or been furled, that of Southern Methodism was still unfurled; whatever cause had been lost, that of Southern Methodism survived." Grievances were mentioned which still made disunion imperative, notably the "political practices" of the Northern church and the intrusion into Southern pulpits of Northern missionaries. The General Conference of April 1866 officially declared for permanent independence and announced that if there "be any Church or Association wishing to unite with us, they shall be received on giving satisfactory evidence of belief in our articles of religion, and willing to conform to our discipline." The Episcopal Church alone of the larger churches was able to reunite.[39]

For the most part the policy of disintegration and absorption failed in its objective and resulted in perpetuating the fatal division among the churches. Its one achievement was the capture by the Northern churches of the great bulk of the Negroes. This was a further injury to the Southern churches. Thus the Methodist Episcopal Church South had 207,776 colored members in 1860 and only 48,742 in 1866. The Negro seemed as unwilling to take his religion as his politics from his former

[38] *Southern Review*, X (1872), 386.
[39] *Appletons' Annual Cyclopædia* (1865), 106, 553, 706; (1866), 490–491.

masters. The Southern churches were forced to relinquish much of their evangelical work among the freedmen, while the Northern missionaries, making no headway among the Southern whites, turned all their energies to the blacks. The American Baptist Home Missionary Society (North) was very active in organizing colored churches, sustaining ministers in the field, financing churches, and establishing schools. The Presbyterian Assembly (North) made special efforts to "instruct and evangelize and gather into churches" the colored population. The Methodists seemed to make greater progress than any of the other sects. African churches established in the North before the Civil War found in emancipation a golden opportunity to expand into the South. The American Methodist Episcopal Church Zion, the African Methodist Episcopal Church, and the Colored Baptists made tremendous strides. The Zion Church alone grew from 13,340 members in 1864 to 225,000 in 1876. The Southern churches attempted to hold their own by organizing separate colored churches under their jurisdiction. But it was a losing contest, and at best it converted the entire South into a tremendous battleground. The fight for Negro members was added to the memories of the original break, the disputes over property, and the threat of absorption, as an unmovable barrier to reunion.[40]

The hope of reconciliation within the Presbyterian Church was permanently defeated in 1866 when the rigid stand on reinstating Confederate sympathizers led to the dissolution of the "disloyal" Louisville Presbytery, further divisions in the border states, renewed recriminations, and additional suits at law over the possession of property.[41] Reunion was a topic for discussion among the bishops and in the assemblies of the Methodist Churches from 1869 to the end of the seventies. But in spite of delegations appointed to "convey fraternal greetings" from one group to the other and back again no headway was ever made beyond the fixed resolution of the Southern Church

[40] G. Alexander, "History of the Methodist Episcopal Church South" (New York, 1894), 86, 91–92; W. C. Whitaker, "History of the Protestant Episcopal Church in Alabama" (Birmingham, 1898), 197–198; *Appletons' Annual Cyclopædia* (1866), 468, (1867), 87; Johnson, "The Southern Presbyterian Church," 381.
[41] *Appletons' Annual Cyclopædia* (1866), 621.

that "it is the judgment of this Conference that the true interests of the Church of Christ require and demand the maintenance of our separate distinct organizations." [42] The most
that the Baptists could achieve was a resolution "not to propose any organic connection, but to cultivate fraternal affection." [43] Such resolutions of good will and the pious expressions
of fraternity usually came to naught in face of the vexatious
problems which arose out of the rival policies of the churches.
The suggestions to reconcile did little more than advertise the
fact that churchmen of the country's three largest denominations were still standing on the record of their Civil War divergences.

The net result was that the churches remained sectional
bodies, an antagonistic element in the integration of national
life. Not only did the work of religion and social improvement
suffer from the lack of harmony, the future was also to reveal
the sorry spectacle of clergymen standing as the most radical
of sectionalists. The *Nation* described the situation in the North
when it wrote, "Churches are doing their full share in causing
permanent division. Undoubtedly four fifths of Protestant
churches are Republican. In the Methodist Episcopal Church
fully nine tenths are. A part of their creed seems to be that
Southern people are sinners, and that it is the duty of good
Christians so to vote as to teach them that fact. They support
such men as Chandler, Morton, Logan, and Grant." [44] In the
South the presence of unreconcilable clergymen was also common. Such a figure was Robert Lewis Dabney, one of the most
eminent theologians in the Presbyterian Church. His aversion
to all things Northern made for a rock-ribbed conservatism
that opposed such doctrines as evolution and public schools,
partly because they prevailed in Yankeedom. Bitter and irreconcilable till his death in 1898, he led the Southern churchmen in resistance to reunion, in fighting the liberalism of Dr.
Woodrow, and in attacking the programs for wider educa-

---

[42] *Appletons' Annual Cyclopædia* (1870), 491.
[43] *Minutes of the Southern Baptist Convention* (1868), 27.
[44] *Nation*, June 12, 1879. The failure of the Presbyterians to reunite in the
1880's led to widespread editorializing in the press. See *Public Opinion*, III
(1887), 184–185, and *Appletons' Annual Cyclopædia* (1882), 702–703; (1883),
653; (1884), 667; (1887), 691–693; (1888), 698–700; (1889), 713–715.

tional advantages. Toward the North his attitude never changed from what it had been when in 1870 he declared, "I do not forgive. I try not to forgive. What! forgive those people, who have invaded our country, burned our cities, destroyed our homes, slain our young men, and spread desolation and ruin over our land! No, I do not forgive them." [45]

Moral agitation over the Negro in slavery, which had done so much to disrupt the unity of the churches, had also been a vital factor in sectionalizing the nation. "Our provincialism," wrote a Southern bishop, "is . . . explained by one fact and one word — slavery." [46] When emancipation came as a consequence of the war many professed to see in it the end of sectionalism. Thus a Georgian asserted that the South "will heartily embrace the political creed of the Union" now that the Southern "nationalizing tendency has been destroyed by the removal of slavery." [47] Beecher likewise wrote, "Slavery being removed, the cause of collision is removed. . . . Of all guarantees of future harmony of the North and South, the best is the effectual extermination of slavery." [48] Yet Beecher was wrong. The history of the fifteen years after 1865 was to demonstrate that the freedman was to be a source of sectional strife almost as baneful as the slave. The Negro remained a rock separating the current of national life in angry currents.

Emancipation dictated that the Negro was to have a new status without defining what that status was to be. The determination of the Negro's future thereupon became the issue. A bitter competitive struggle was precipitated in which the true interests of the Negro disappeared. The South maintained that the problem was a domestic one in which it alone should participate. The North in reply pointed to the responsibility it had assumed when it suddenly bestowed freedom upon the Negro. The South believed that its social stability required a discipline over the inferior race and expressed its program of

[45] T. C. Johnson, *"Life and Letters of Robert Lewis Dabney"* (Richmond, 1903), 352.
[46] A. G. Haygood, *The New South* (Sermon preached at Oxford, Georgia, Nov. 25, 1880), 14.
[47] J. C. Reed, *The Old and New South* (pamphlet, New York, 1876), 15.
[48] Beecher, "Conditions of a Restored Union, Oct. 29, 1865," in "Patriotic Addresses," 718.

what should be done in the "Black Codes" of 1865 and 1866. The North interpreted this action to mean that the South was attempting to perpetuate as much of slavery as conditions permitted, and read its conception of the civil rights needed by the Negro into the practices of the Freedmen's Bureau. The result was rivalry in the field of race relations. The South was horror-stricken with the idea of enfranchising a mass of illiterate and unpropertied people. The North could see no way in which a downtrodden class could defend itself unless it were granted the suffrage. The South could conceive of no society that did not recognize the validity of racial segregation. The North in time seemed ready to force upon the South an equality that extended through all the walks of life. The South in accepting freedom for the blacks believed that it had made all the surrender entailed by the war. The North under Radical direction held that anything less than "absolute equality of every man before the law" would "be a practical surrender of the North to the South."

The Negro and all that pertained to him accordingly formed a continuance of hostilities between the victors and the vanquished. Folly and passion characterized the approach to a problem that would yield only to the most considerate coöperation. The North was inclined to be impatient, to insist upon an immediate solution. The South in face of the constant pressure and menace of power from outside throughout the Reconstruction period failed to admit that there was any problem except to reassert control by the white man. Meanwhile the Negro, "drunk with freedom" and the football of Reconstruction politics, was largely unfitted for progress by the noise made over him.

Many Northerners went into the South with good intentions of bringing to the Negro religion, education, and a better life. There were zealots among them who had been swept into a frenzy of idealism by the wartime clamor of "making all men free." Some were unquestioned self-seekers. But most of the newcomers were good people volunteering for a service of uplifting the lowly and degraded. They had the urge to serve but not the knowledge either of the field in which they were to work or of the freedmen with whom they were to work.

The only possible hope for success was a combination of tact on their part, a welcome reception from the Southern whites, and sobriety among the Negroes. Not one of these elements was present. The Northern humanitarians arrogantly ignored the importance of the contribution that might have been made by the Southern whites. The latter ostracized the humanitarians, shutting them off as bad and dangerous influences. The Negro fell the prey first to the Carpetbagger who seduced him with the suffrage and then to Ku Kluxism of an aroused white population which beat him back into discipline. Mistakes, misjudgments, heartburnings, alienation of races, and division of North and South, were the consequences of this first essay in race relations under freedom.

The issue of whether the Negro should be the ward of the South or the ward of the Nation, took on a more sinister expression when the Republican party asserted a proprietary interest in the freedman. It is a truism of Reconstruction history that the Radicals enfranchised the Negro in order to build a Republican party in the South. This leads to a study of politics as the most important of all the divisive forces separating the sections and preventing the realization of harmony. To a subject so significant a special chapter must be devoted, and before turning to it one additional hurt inflicted upon the South can be disposed of.

The divisions over the Negro and politics in the Reconstruction era went so far as to create a situation of almost permanent sentimental disaffection on the part of Southerners. The injuries then experienced became a tradition. "The whites cannot forget that dismal period," wrote James Bryce in 1891, "and their recollection of it makes them vehemently resolute that power shall never again pass into hands which so misused it. It is not revenge, it is not hatred, it is the instinct of self-preservation which governs them." [49] The South had in fact suffered so much that from that day on a mark of a Southern man was his distrust of all who were not born below the Mason-Dixon Line.

The South later professed forgiveness to the men who

[49] James Bryce, "Thoughts on the Negro Problem," *North American Rev.*, CXLIII (1891), 549.

fought in the fair fight of war. But to those who came victorious and "heaped indignities upon a fallen foe" it exhibited
a "bitterness of heart that lasts as long as life endures." [50] The
South, as one of its spokesmen said, came to believe "that
what was desired and intended by the party in power was not
a restored Union of equal States, but a subjected South, a
dominant North, and a radical faction ruling all. The painful
and exasperating belief gained ground daily that nothing
which the Southern people could say or do . . . would avail
anything to change the course of their destiny. . . . The
whole history of the struggles between the North and South
had generated in the minds of the Southern people a profound
skepticism. . . . Distrust of the Northern people, such as the
fortunes of war and all the bitterness of surrender had failed
to arouse, began to stir in the South; and her people began to
look upon their brethren of the North as possessed of a cruel
hatred which rejoiced to believe evil, and by a malignancy
which would not stop at wrong or oppression." [51]

"Whether right or wrong," said General Gordon before a
Congressional Committee in 1871, "it is the impression of the
Southern mind — it is the conviction of my own mind, in
which I am perfectly sincere and honest — that we have not
been met in the proper spirit." [52] There is not a page written in
the vast literature of war and Reconstruction literature which
does not corroborate Gordon's judgment. Joel Chandler Harris poured out the emotional content of the Southern heart
when he wrote, "It was a policy of lawlessness under the forms
of law, of disfranchisement, robbery, oppression and fraud.
It was a deliberate attempt to humiliate the people who had
lost everything by the war, and it aroused passion on both
sides that were unknown when the war was in actual progress." [53]

The yawning chasm thus remained unclosed. Southerners

[50] J. W. Burgess, "Reconstruction and the Constitution" (New York,
1902), 297. See also R. Taylor, "Destruction and Reconstruction" (New
York, 1879), 236–238.
[51] Mayes, "Lamar," 154–155.
[52] Testimony taken by the Joint Select Committee to Inquire into the
Condition of Affairs in the Late Insurrectionary States (Washington, 1872),
VI, 316.
[53] Atlanta Constitution, Jan. 20, 1882.

still looked upon their connection with the Union as something forced and inevitable rather than as something desirable. The North was forced to realize that, although the Civil War had retired into history, the South remained a problem to embarrass the even flow of national life. Nothing revealed this tragedy more strikingly than the enmities which flourished in the world of politics.

CHAPTER IV

POLITICS AS A SECTIONAL DIVISOR

1865–1880

THE practice of American politics in the years that followed the Civil War seemed based upon a theory that the two great parties were hostile armies in camps irreconcilably divided. Democrats were to Republicans, and Republicans were to Democrats, not opponents to be persuaded, but enemies to be remorselessly pursued and destroyed. "He is a stupid visionary" stated Benjamin H. Hill, "who supposes he can ever make peace between the politicians." [1] The condition primarily responsible for this hostility was the unhappy fact that party divisions coincided with the sectional dualism whose corrosive influence ate into the vitals of every phase of national life.

The Republican party was born in strife on issues that won support only in the North. The tactics of the party had always been to appeal on strictly sectional lines to the numerically stronger portion of the Union, realizing that there were electoral and Congressional votes enough in a united North to control the national government. It was a party of sectional-consciousness. As such it operated to split asunder the fabric of national life.

The Democratic party claimed a more national composition. Even in the election of 1860 when the party was split into Northern and Southern groups, each with a sectional platform and a sectional candidate, Douglas the Northern candidate was able to poll a considerable vote in the South, and Breckenridge the Southern rights candidate was given more votes in New England than Lincoln gained in all the South

[1] B. H. Hill, Jr., "Senator Benjamin H. Hill, His Life, Speeches, and Writings" (Atlanta, 1893), 435.

including the border states. After the war the party continued to be in the North a strong minority group with more than an even chance to win such important states as New York, Indiana, and New Jersey. Control of these states in the North plus the solid support of the Southern states would carry a presidential election. Consequently the Southern vote became a prime consideration for the Democratic party. Its tactics aimed as much to placate the South as did Republican policy to excite the self-interest of the North. Thus the tragedy of postwar politics appears. The parties were rooted on opposite banks of the chasm.

The Republican party took glory in the war. It had been a Republican president, Lincoln, Republican cabinet members, Republican congressmen, and Republican governors who had been the chief components of the Union coalition which had waged the war. The Democratic party as an organization had maintained a critical opposition to the administration. When the war was won on the lines the Lincoln government pursued the Republicans were in a position to claim the credit and to them accrued the prestige of having saved the Union and freed the slaves. Meanwhile the Democrats could learn the bitter wisdom contained in Schurz's apothegm that "There is no heavier burden for a political party to bear, than to have appeared unpatriotic in war."

Thus it became the interest of the Democratic party to "forget" the war and to patch up quickly a truce which would re-admit their Southern allies to the political contest. But it was equally important to Republicans that the past be not forgotten and that a reunion which would increase the strength of their opponents should be postponed. The process of reconciliation was fatefully involved in this counterpurpose of party aims. When one party recommended peace it seemed as though it was prostituting a nation's interests for selfish ends. When the other party clung to the memory of past feuds hatred and suspicion lingered longer than conditions warranted.

In spite of the handicap of having opposed a war that succeeded, the Democratic party remained a dangerous foe. In the election of 1868, with a strong presidential candidate but with weaknesses in the platform and the vice-presidential

nominee, and running against the greatest living Northern
hero of the war, the Democrats polled two million seven hundred votes to the Republican three million. Had it not been
for the Reconstruction policy which deprived three Southern
states of the right to vote, the extensive disfranchisement of
Southern whites and the enfranchisement of seven hundred
thousand Negroes which gave the Republicans the vote of six
of the Confederate states, a Democrat, Seymour, would have
beaten the Republican, Grant, some three years after the latter
had stood under the famous apple tree at Appomattox. It was
an alarming situation for Republicans. Seymour carried New
York and New Jersey. A solid South would have given him
success, and the white South was turning solidly against Republican rule.

This was the sword which hung over a Republican party
already sorely beset by other worries. Its hold upon the North
was precarious and depended largely upon keeping "patriotism"
keyed to an emotional fervor of wartime pitch. The party was
in constant danger of factional disruption. In many respects
it was a coalition of tempers ranging from extreme moderation toward the South to extreme radicalism. There were
rivalries within the party based upon diverging economic interests. At any time Northeast and Northwest might divide on
tariff or finance and in doing so precipitate the party out of
power. Nascent rivalries of personal ambition were developing
from the conflicting leaderships of Blaine and Conkling, with
reformers growing more critically aloof. To offset these evils
the party had one blessing, its war record, and to that it clung
instinctively for protection against the enemy outside and the
weakness within.

The refusal to let the past fade into history, the exploitation
of war issues that were settled, the inherent selfishness of the
practice, all received censure from those outside the party. A
phrase of opprobrium was coined, "waving the bloody shirt,"
and applied to this feature of Republican politics. But the
"bloody shirt" was possibly the greatest weapon any American
party ever possessed and the Republican party would have
been an unusual assemblage of politicians indeed if it had not
exploited this instrument which was both a sword of offense

and a shield of defense. It served effectively five great needs. First it confounded the enemy, striking the Democrats where they were most vulnerable. Secondly it aroused the ire of the North against the South, as desirable a result to a sectional party as it was undesirable to the nation. Thirdly it provided an issue upon which all the factions within the party could unite and so, in the crises of elections at least, the dangers of division could be minimized. Fourthly, the appeal to patriotism was an easy evasion of the responsibility of accounting for mistakes and corruption in office. Finally, when new allies were necessary to save the Republican program in the South from the growing hostility of the whites, it served as a justification for the dubious statesmanship of Negro enfranchisement.

An analysis of the "bloody shirt" reveals, first of all, that it emphasized the continued disloyalty of the Southern whites. All evidence to the contrary was disregarded in the fixed creed of Republican belief that the rebels never changed. A cartoon in *Harper's Weekly* for July 1, 1871, portrays a 'possum labeled "Rebellion" which lies sprawled on the ground playing dead while a man pokes inquiringly into its ribs. In the background Jefferson Davis stands whispering to a friend, "Don't you be afraid; that animal ain't dead. Just wait and see." Worsted in battle the South, so it was claimed, had surrendered none of its objectives. Men "trained to hate the Union as their oppressor, and to despise the Yankees, or Northerners, as the meanest of mankind," had merely changed their tactics. "The solid South," asserted the influential *Cincinnati Commercial,* "is the Southern Confederacy seeking domination of the United States through the machinery of the Democratic party and by peaceable means." Consequently, "The North and South of the fiery quarrel and of the war are the living, acting North and South of today."[2]

Outrages against the Negro, intimidation of white Republicans in the South, displays of sectional temper, were repetitiously paraded as "little Providences" which "come along to save the forgiving North from losing itself in a mush of sentiment in regard to the South."[3] When a Southern newspaper, the *Mobile Register,* criticized President Grant as "the Jacobin tyrant who sits enthroned at Washington to the terror of all patriots, and the peril of free government," the Republican welcomes the opportunity of contrasting the record of "the modest and honest soldier" with that of the rebels whose plans he had frustrated.[4] When the South elected to Congress men who had been active in Confederate service it was interpreted to mean continued rebellion against the Union.

Republicans insisted that Southerners had learned nothing by the war. "I have seen no signs at the South of a desire for reconciliation in the party of the old slave power," wrote a New England member of the party. "They have a strong desire to regain power, and by a united South and a Democratic North to again govern the country."[5] So often was this hammered home that the "bare idea of the rebel States casting their votes for election . . . and giving us again a democratic and rebel government"[6] became intolerable to many Northerners who voted Republican to forestall the fancied evil.

The second step in the tactics of "bloody shirt" politics was to "charge the Democratic party with being the same in character and spirit as when it sympathized with treason."[7] There was much truth in John Sherman's observation that "the people will not trust the party or men who during the war sided with the rebels."[8] Republicans played upon this theme. The Democratic record was reviewed as one of friendship with slavery and subserviency to Southern economic interests before the war, treachery to the Union during the war, and non-acceptance of the fruits of victory since the war. The desired conclusion was that such an opponent so jeopardized the national welfare that it could not be trusted in power.

Even to moderates the Democratic organization seemed uninviting. First was the stigma of opposition in the war. "We all agree" wrote the *Nation* in 1872 when the editorial policy

---

[4] *Ibid.,* May 20, 1871.

[5] J. M. Forbes to Charles Sumner, Aug. 10, 1872, S. F. Hughes (ed.), "Letters and Recollections of John Murray Forbes" (Boston, 1899), II, 180.

[6] John Jay to S. P. Chase, Jan. 5, 1866, "Diary and Correspondence of Samuel P. Chase," *American Historical Association, Annual Report, 1902,* II, 519.

[7] Republican Platform of 1876.

[8] "Sherman Letters," 259.

of the weekly was distinctly critical of the Grant administration, "that the Democratic party has no high aims, no patriotic intentions; its purpose seems to be simply to get back into power. . . . If we remember, with any gratitude the 500,000 soldiers who perished in the struggle, we can never consent that the party which was sneering, dabbling, and hindering while they were fighting shall in its old form and character again come to the front." [9] Then there was the notoriety which came from membership in the party of Copperheads like Vallandigham, an honorable man but certainly not popular in the North, and political bosses like Tweed whose corruption was always a consolation to Republicans who had their own burdens of Credit Mobilier, Sanborn contracts, Belknap scandals, and whisky frauds to carry. Senator Hoar boasted without too great danger of being contradicted that most of the substantial men of the North in professions, business, and farming were in the Republican party, while the Democrats were "controlled by the foreign population and the criminal classes of our great cities, by Tammany Hall, and by the leaders of the solid South." [10] It was not mere prejudice that pictured to the normal middle-class, church-going Northerner a Democratic party that sought power by an alliance of rebel sentiment in the South, corrupt Tweed Ring politics in New York with Tammany and Irish support, and Copperheadism in the West. There was just enough truth in the fact that Democratic success depended upon an electoral vote built upon the solid South, New York where the party was largely foreign born and corrupt, and Indiana where Civil War Copperheadism had been strongest, to give Republicans excellent material for exploitation by the usual tricks of exaggeration and misrepresentation.

The country was not permitted to forget that the Democratic party was "an organization containing the opponents of the union, . . . men believing in state sovereignty, . . . men contemptuous of equal rights, . . . rebels, . . . repudiators of the war amendments, . . . tools of slavery and secession." [11]

[9] *Nation,* April 11, 1872.
[10] G. F. Hoar, "Autobiography" (New York, 1903), I, 200.
[11] *Harper's Weekly,* July 30, Aug. 20, Sept. 3, 1870.

When Thomas Nast in a cartoon of May 6, 1871 essayed to portray Democratic principles, he drew a motley assembly of wolves, demagogues, Ku Kluxers, and Jefferson Davis, tearing up the graves of settled issues, reviving the old causes, and preaching the Constitution as it was in 1860, with rebellion and slavery revived. When Vallandigham died in 1871 it was recalled that the "stigma of his treachery" was imbedded in the core of the party to which he belonged.[12] When a Democratic Senator from Kentucky, in a mistaken notion of what could be done in the name of reconciliation, proposed the removal of seventeen thousand buried Union soldiers from their graves in Arlington cemetery so that the estate could be returned to the widow of General Lee, Republicans were not unhappy. It was a beautiful opportunity to exploit "the grossest insult to the patriotism and good sense of the country" as a further revelation of "the real spirit of the Democratic party." [13]

After building the premises of a disloyal South and an untrustworthy Democracy in the North, the Republicans were ready to point the moral by luridly portraying the dangers such a combination threatened. "If the Northern majority weakens and the nation's representatives let themselves be persuaded in the interests of conciliation . . . to let the Southerners reënter Congress easily," wrote Clemenceau in 1867, "there will be no more internal peace for a quarter of a century." [14] Nine years later Garfield as a spokesman of his party was harping on the same theme. North and South to the Ohioan still represented irreconcilable conceptions of freedom and slavery, loyalty and treason. "Often," he confessed, "the blunders and faults of the Republican party have been condoned by the people [because the alternative was] the violent, reactionary and disloyal spirit of the Democratic party." [15] "Neither the jeers at the bloody shirt," wrote another oracle of Republicanism in the same year, "nor the natural and just desire of reconciliation, nor the extravagances and offenses

[12] Ibid., July 1, 1871.
[13] Ibid., Dec. 31, 1870.
[14] Clemenceau, "Reconstruction," 84.
[15] B. A. Hinsdale (ed.), "The Works of James Abram Garfield" (Boston, 1883), 356, 360, 381.

of the colored voters in the Southern States, nor the bland and smooth oratory of Southern Democratic politicians, nor the crafty declarations of Northern Democratic politicians . . . should cause any man to forget that the Democratic party is now what it has been for many years — the political organization of those who aimed to destroy the national Union." [16]

The Republicans thus stood frankly on the sectional issue boldly asserting that it was vain to deplore sectionalism when the sectional division of politics was so evident that it could not be winked out of sight. The North had only one decision to make. Would its future be safer entrusted to the party of Lincoln and Grant or to the Democracy which had compromised with treason, resisted emancipation, and still cherished the Confederate South?

From the day that Thaddeus Stevens asserted that "just so much as the Democratic party shall again gain the ascendancy just so much will that same spirit of despotism run riot which has disgraced this nation for a century," Republicans maintained that a return of Democrats to power would mean the debasement of the Negro. Whether the Negro needed the Republicans more than Republicans needed the Negro is a matter for speculation, but that there was an affinity between the two is unquestioned. Thus Senator Wilson in a moment of statistical-mindedness estimated that his party could count on six hundred and seventy-two thousand colored voters in the South to offset in part the nine hundred and twenty-three thousand Southern white voters, and give to the party control of South Carolina, Mississippi and probably Louisiana, Alabama, and North Carolina.[17] Even Sumner, the most ardent champion of Negro rights, thought his argument for enfranchisement would sound more plausible to his fellow partisans if he showed that the colored vote was necessary to "secure the new allies which are essential to the national cause." [18] But after the Fourteenth and Fifteenth Amendments were passed the party found it more dignified to assume the role of unselfish defender of the black man against the party of his natural

[16] *Harper's Weekly*, Jan. 29, 1876.
[17] *Congressional Globe*, March 15, 1867.
[18] E. L. Pierce, "Memoir and Letters of Charles Sumner" (Boston, 1893), IV, 319–320.

enemies. The Democrats, appreciating that few Negroes would enroll under their banners, were probably as selfishly motivated in resisting measures for Negro advancement.

The Republicans did not hesitate to point out that for a generation the Democratic party had devoted all its power to the inhumane oppression of the Negro. Evidence was found in the disorders in the South to convince the North that the Democrats were still a "nigger hating" party. Typical was Thomas Nast's portrayal of a Negro kneeling over the murdered bodies of his family, with a background of burning homes, schools, workshops, and churches of colored folk, inquiring, "Is *this* protecting life, liberty, property? Is this the equal protection of the laws?" [19] While Southern Ku Kluxers acted, so the Republicans declared, the Northern Democrats sympathized with this barbarism directed against the Negro. When the Democratic party regained control of the New York legislature it made the futile gesture of repealing the state's earlier ratification of the Fifteenth Amendment. This was used naturally enough as an indication of Northern Democratic hostility to the Negro. "The Democratic party," charged *Harper's Weekly,* "went out of power in this State trying to make the Negro a slave. It returns to power trying to prevent his becoming an equal citizen. Arrayed against justice, humanity, reason, and the American principle, the doom of the party is sure." [20]

To reach those who still wavered, the "bloody shirt" had other arguments. Time and time again it was asserted that a Democratic administration would lower the tariffs, partially repudiate the debt, and shower economic benefits upon the South. Not all Northerners, not even all Republicans, would have been disturbed to see tariff reduction and monetary inflation. But the appeal could be and was made selectively in areas where it would count and silenced where it would have no effect. Especially was it used to appeal to classes whose investments were in government bonds or whose livings were made in protected manufactures. Secretary of Treasury McCulloch, feeling that there was no justification in arousing

[19] *Harper's Weekly,* Sept. 2, 1876.
[20] *Ibid.,* Jan. 22, 1870.

fear on this issue, felt constrained to protest in a letter to Senator Sumner against the practice. "I have been greatly alarmed," he wrote, "at the disposition that seems to exist among our radical friends to induce the holders of our securities to take ground against the President's [Johnson's] policy by the argument that under it there is danger of a coalition between the recent Rebels of the South and the Democracy of the North for the repudiation of the obligations which have been created in the prosecution of the war. It will not do to make the faith of the nation dependent upon any such issue; and I entreat you as a leader and a creator of public sentiment not to encourage the idea." Sumner, however, was not only deaf to the entreaty, but acted immediately to encourage the fears of New England bond holders by making it the theme of his speech before the Republican Convention of Massachusetts.[21]

The "bloody shirt" led to the natural conclusion that the good of the Nation required the rule of the party of patriotism. "Reconciliation," the Republicans agreed, "will not result from taking the control of the government from New England, the Middle States, and the Northwest, and giving it to the Southern and border States. The power must remain where it is, because there the principles of the New Union are a living faith."[22] Or to put it differently, not until the Democratic party was utterly defeated and dissolved could a perfect accord be accomplished. The Republicans thus manœuvred, at least to their own satisfaction, the Democratic party with its millions of Americans into the category of enemies to the American state.

Time and time again representatives of the "Grand Old Party" asserted that it contained the "best elements in our national life . . . the survivors and children of the men who put down the Rebellion and abolished slavery, saved the Union, and paid the debt and kept the faith, and achieved the manufacturing independence of the country, and passed the homestead laws."[23] It was a record of proud achievement which

[21] J. F. Rhodes, *History of the United States* (New York, 1893–1906), V, 549–550.
[22] *Harper's Weekly*, July 20, 1872.
[23] Hoar, "Autobiography," 200.

drew to the party ranks "the more intelligent and moral part of the population," and one which served as a refuge in the evil days of corruption under Grant. "Corruption," the party could always argue, "is, unhappily, to be found in both parties, but he would be more daring than well informed who should allege that the Democratic party is more honest than its opponent." [24] To the one question which carried its own answer, Republicans always returned, — "Shall the men who saved the Republic continue to rule it, or shall it be handed over to the rebels and their allies?"

The political division, then, made for the survival of the ancient antagonisms between North and South, and the old issues were not permitted to die. "As in 1860," spoke the Republican candidate for the Vice-Presidency in 1876, "we are once more . . . face to face with a united South, with the Democratic party in the North its subservient and pliant ally. . . . Let your ballots protect the work so effectually done by your bayonets at Gettysburg and on so many a field of strife." [25]

Handicapped by its war record, embarrassed by the forcefulness of the "bloody shirt" attack, the Democratic party was for more than a decade compelled to remain on the defensive. During these years it made painful and for the most part unsuccessful efforts to find an issue substantial enough to carry the party back into the confidence of the Nation.

The first tactics assumed by the party chieftains was resistance to the Republican program of Reconstruction. Even before the war had ended Democrats assailed Radicalism as "impolitic and vindictive at this time when the minds of all good men are searching diligently for ways of reconciliation and peace." Feeling certain that majority sentiment favored moderation and that therefore they had the winning side, the Democrats were not unhappy in seeing Radicalism definitely develop into the official policy of the Republican party.

True to the tactics of non-acceptance of Reconstruction the Democrats pictured themselves before the public throughout

[24] *Harper's Weekly*, May 21, 1870.
[25] W. A. Wheeler, "Speech at St. Albans, Vt.," *Republican Campaign Pamphlets* (1876).

the elections of 1866 and 1868 as men of peace and reunion fighting hatred and vengeance. "The time I hope will come," a party spokesman piously wished, "when the foundations of our Government will again rest, as of old, in the affections and confidence of the whole people." [26] Democracy, a lady if the cartoonists are correct, drew back her skirts in shocked propriety when Republicans were so boorish as to recall her past. She posed as the advocate of a wiser and more philosophical statesmanship. "Why make enemies of eight millions of people who are giving every pledge that men of honor can give of their sincere desire to be your friends?" queried James Beck of Kentucky. "All experience teaches that magnanimity and generosity to a fallen foe will make him a friend, while cruelty and oppression will but intensify his hate." [27]

The party thus committed took official stand against the "revolution" the Republicans were directing. The entire range of Reconstruction legislation was first contested in Congress and then before the people as "usurpatious, and unconstitutional, revolutionary, and void," and of course unwise. The party also resisted the enactment and ratification of the Fourteenth Amendment which garnered what the Republicans defined before the Nation as fruits of victory, — equal civil rights of the Negro, definition of federal citizenship, disfranchisement of prominent Confederates, guarantees of the validity of the national debt, and prohibitions upon Congress ever assuming in any way any obligation of Confederate origin. Finally the Democratic party fought the Negro enfranchisement which was ultimately embodied in the Constitution by the Fifteenth Amendment. There is little doubt that party zeal led the Democrats to extremes that later proved a handicap. Their early acceptance of reconciliation seemed too hastily arrived at for a proper appraisal of the conditions necessary to safeguard the fruits of victory. When Republicans did give the safeguards, in too radical a form, it grated harshly upon many Northerners to hear the constant assertions made by Democrats that the North was persecuting the South.

Nevertheless Republican excesses gave to Democrats many

[26] *Congressional Globe*, March 13, 1867.
[27] *Ibid.*, March 11, 1868.

targets at which to shoot their darts of criticism. The intemperance of the politics of the times is again evident when one notes the "crimes" catalogued by Democrats against their opponents, — military despotism, Negro supremacy, violations of individual rights to jury trial and habeas corpus, arrogant abuse of Congressional power in encroachments against the executive and the judiciary, corruption, extravagance, encroachment upon the prerogatives of States, and in general the subversion of the established form of government and its replacement by a centralized and consolidated form. These were not issues for normal times. Nor did the Democratic party face them with the self-restraint their demand for moderate Reconstruction would seem to indicate. Most historians today agree that in a large measure their criticism of the Radical program was good. But the Democratic argument of sweet reasonableness lost much of its grace when advocated in a manner that was far from being sweetly reasonable.

There was also a selfish side to the Democratic espousal of moderation which cast suspicion on the party's motives. It appeared to be a conscious bid to wean from Republican ranks the large number of lenients who seemed restless in a party growing daily more radical. The Democrats needed very few recruits in the North to make them, as they had been before the Civil War, the dominant element in politics. Moderation seemed the way to the desired end. Furthermore it would bring back into the national balance the important Southern Democratic strength. In other words, while each had its idealistic aspects, "the patriotism of peace" was inherently as selfish as "the patriotism of the bloody shirt." Between the two true progress of reconciliation came dangerously near destruction in the wrangle of partisan ambitions.

Bright as seemed its prospects the tactics of non-acceptance proved an unwise step. The Democratic party had too many vulnerable weaknesses to pose successfully as the vehicle of patriotism. Who are the Democrats, these men who promise peace, forgiveness, and union? asked the vigorous Morton in the election of 1866. Every unregenerate rebel, was his answer, every bounty jumper, every deserter, draft dodger, murderer of Union prisoners, dishonest contractor, and corrupt pay-

master, were Democrats. "In short," concluded the Republican
whose own record as war governor of Indiana insured the integrity of his patriotism, "the Democratic party may be described as a common sewer and loathsome receptacle." [28] What
would Democratic success mean, asked Roscoe Conkling? The
Confederates, he answered, would be brought back to power to
appropriate Government money in payment for slaves and
Southern property damaged by Federal armies in the war.[29]

Even the plea for constitutionality proved a boomerang.
"Who pleads the Constitution?" queried Stevens. "It is the
advocate of rebels." [30] To many the phrases so common on
Democratic lips, "the Constitution as it is," "prerogatives of the
States," and "encroachments of the Federal Government,"
seemed painfully reminiscent of the old debates when Southerners had hurled against the North the epithets Democrats
now were using. After all, the war had settled something,
and all the talk Democrats were making about restoring fraternal relations seemed to boil down into suspicion that Democrats were unaware of this fact. Cartoonists pictured the
Democratic party as a wolf masquerading in the skin of a
sheep. Moderates took what appeared to them the lesser evil
of joining with Radicals whose loyalty they respected rather
than with peacemakers who were suspected of prostituting a
noble aspiration for a selfish end.

The futility of Democratic efforts at conciliation through
politics was demonstrated in the fiasco of the Philadelphia
Convention during the Congressional elections of 1866. The
meeting was planned to be a great love feast of sectional peace.
Moderate Southerners journeyed North to meet Democrats
and Johnsonian Republicans. Arm in arm men from Massachusetts and South Carolina, New York and Georgia, and
so on through the States (like the animals entering Noah's ark,
jeered Blaine), paraded into the convention hall as a token
of harmony between the erstwhile foes. Resolutions were
passed giving assurances that the South was loyal, and much

[28] W. D. Foulke, "Life of Oliver P. Morton" (Indianapolis, 1899), I, 475.
[29] A. R. Conkling, "The Life and Letters of Roscoe Conkling" (New
York, 1889), 370.
[30] E. B. Callender, "Thaddeus Stevens" (Boston, 1882), 111.

was made of the fact that Southerners stood on chairs cheering the assertion that slavery was dead.

The show did not impress dominant opinion in the North. Thomas Nast destroyed such good as it might have accomplished by a few strokes of his pencil. His cartoon showed the presiding officer of the convention busily placing padlocks on the lips of the delegates to prevent them from giving utterance to any unpatriotic sentiments.[31] The Convention smacked of artificiality, especially since the managers straining after the effect of peace had excluded the Copperhead Vallandigham who sought admission and who as a prominent Democrat belonged where other Democrats assembled. As one Southerner who was present later wrote, the effort at fraternity was "of as little avail as the waving of a lady's fan against a typhoon. . . . [We] were again taught the lesson that is ever forgotten, namely, that it is an easy task to inflame the passions of the multitude, an impossible one to arrest them." [32]

The unsubstantial basis upon which the Democrats were erecting their edifice of reconciliation was again demonstrated in the same campaign in relation to the Soldiers and Sailors convention that met in Cleveland on September 17. This meeting of Union veterans was intended to demonstrate a loyal element supporting Johnsonian policies. Unfortunately for the effect on the public, however, a group of Southern veterans meeting in Memphis at the same time and harmoniously inclined felicitated the Northern body by sending a telegram of sympathy. The name of N. B. Forrest was among those appended to the telegram.[33] Forrest was the man Northerners held responsible for the massacre of Fort Pillow, one of the unforgettable and unforgivable tragedies of the war.

The Democratic assault upon the Reconstruction program of the Radical Republicans also failed to win recruits from the moderate Republicans. Pressure from outside solidified the Republican party, and, during elections at least, moderates coöperated with Radicals. When Democrats made gains in the fall elections of 1867 in the States, John Sherman expressed

[31] Harper's Weekly, Sept. 29, 1866.
[32] Taylor, "Destruction and Reconstruction," 253.
[33] Appletons' Annual Cyclopædia (1866), 759.

the apprehension common to all Republicans when he wrote that the "danger now is that the mistakes of the Republican party may drift the Democratic party into power." [34] When the failure to remove Johnson upon the impeachment charges threatened momentarily to divide the party, a Radical outside Congress wrote to Fessenden, who had voted against conviction, that "it is sheer madness to add . . . the risk of splitting up the Republican party, now the only bulwark of freedom. We owe it to the living and the dead to keep together until we have absolutely secured the fruits of our dearly bought victory." [35] Here indeed was the cement to unite all factions in the party.

A consolidated Republican party was the result. The Reconstruction program originated by Radicals became the test of party loyalty with hatred of the white South and distrust of Democrats as fixed tenets of the creed. An additional party reason for support of Reconstruction was the knowledge that the election of 1868 could not be won without Southern votes in the electoral college. The only way of securing those votes was by maintaining carpetbag governments built upon Negro suffrage. So party interest again dominated the situation to the detriment of reconciliation. While Democrats courted the Southern whites, Republicans courted Southern blacks, and, since neither party could hope successfully to invade the premises of the other, strife, passion, and even bloodshed became the weapons of this political struggle.

Gradually such idealism as had earlier existed in the quest for Negro enfranchisement dropped into the background. A grimmer and more permanent phase began. The Negro became a shuttlecock in the rivalry for party mastery. Necessity drove one party to give the Negro more rights than he possibly could exercise with profit to his advancement. Necessity drove the other to a brutal position of robbing the Negro of that little he might with justice claim. Between the two the true friends of the race were left in confused indecision. From the disorder that arose as the inevitable corollary of the struggle each party sought that interpretation which served its purpose.

[34] "Sherman Letters," 299.
[35] Hughes, "Forbes," II, 165.

Democrats charged Republican Radicalism as the breeder of race dissension. Republicans charged Democratic hatred of the Negro as the source of the black man's woes.

With this change also came a change in the direction of the "bloody shirt." An excuse might possibly be made for the originators of the practice. Men like Stevens, Sumner, Fessenden, Trumbull, Grimes, and Julian were idealistically or at least unselfishly motivated. But these men who had been the leaders in the early period, one by one, died, retired, or were rendered powerless. Their places were taken by chieftains whose use of the war issues was motivated by little more than party or personal ambition. Blaine, Conkling, Morton, Logan, Cameron, Sherman, and Butler professionalized the issue and robbed it of the small justification it might once have claimed.

This more professional use of the "bloody shirt" was common to all Radical Republican politicians. But it may best be illustrated in the cases of two prominent Ohioans neither one of whom had other than party reasons for expressing hatred of the South. The indictment of John Sherman can be given through a private letter written by his fellow Republican James A. Garfield.

I have never been more disgusted with Sherman than during this short session. He is very conservative for five years and then fiercely radical for one. This is his radical year which always comes before the Senatorial election. No man in the Senate has talked with so much fierceness as Sherman. . . . You will see an attempt made by his partisan friends in Ohio to show that he is more zealous than the rest of us. His conduct deceives nobody here but it may at home.[36]

But Garfield also had elections to carry, and on such occasions he too had his moments for blowing hot. Especially was this true of him when the Credit Mobilier scandal threatened to end his promising career. He then found it a convenient thing to talk of patriotism when Democrats talked of reform.

In the election of 1868 both the Democrats and the Republicans posed as reconcilers, but with a difference. The Demo-

[36] T. C. Smith, "The Life and Letters of James Abram Garfield" (New Haven, 1925), I, 471.

crats stood upon a platform of non-acceptance, insisting that
not until the wrongs of Reconstruction inflicted by Republicans
upon the South were undone could harmony be accomplished.
The Republicans asserted that this stand of their opponents
threatened to "unsettle the settlement" and would lead only
to a recrudescence of sectional strife. The South must be
"pacified" to the extent of accepting the results of the war.
The strong hand of the Hero of Appomattox as President
would convince the South that it must yield. Then, the Republicans declared, the road to true reconciliation upon right
principles would be opened. With this definition Grant's "Let
us have peace" became the party's slogan. By a curious irony
the Democrats saw their plea for reconciliation twisted into
an augury of strife. They fought the campaign squarely on
the evils of Reconstruction, and lost. The country decided to
follow the Republican signpost to peace and the Democrats
had no other alternative than to scrap the "non-acceptance"
program and go searching for a substitute.

If, as one of their own members had said, the "most effective battery against the Democratic party today [1868] is,
that they are willing to abandon to you [the South] some or
all of these trophies [fruits of victory]," it was obvious that
a change of tactics was imperative and that the party must
move to better fighting ground.[37] The Republicans were assured of four more years in power. It did not seem possible
to undo in 1872 what could not be undone in 1868. Consequently "reconciliation by acceptance" became the future basis
of action. In the political parlance of the day this change
of front was styled the "New Departure" of the Democratic
party.

It was a shrewd manœuvre which promised to win accretions to the party ranks. By emphasizing acceptance of the war
amendments and the acts of Reconstruction as accomplished
facts, it answered the Republican charge that Democrats were
attempting to reopen settled issues and perpetuate the sectional
division for party ends. By insistence that bygones were bygones and emphasis on present problems, it freed the party
from the vulnerable tactical and defensive position of explain-

[37] John Quincy Adams, II, *Massachusetts and South Carolina* (pamphlet).

ing its record, and carried the fight aggressively into the weaknesses of Republican corruption in Washington and misgovernment in the South. The Republican party could ill afford to surrender the offensive. Consequently while the Democrats shouted "New Departure," Republicans clung to "bloody shirt." The question was whether the North would accept the Democratic shift as a true reformation of party objectives, or whether they would believe the Republicans who said that it was merely the old ruse of the wooden horse in which unregenerate partisans were seeking to capture the citadel of power.

For the next four years the Democrats advocated the politics of the "New Departure." In the same period the evils they attacked, corruption of the Grant regime and carpetbag excesses in the South, threatened seriously to disrupt the unity of their opponents. The Liberal Republican movement started as a factional fight for the control of the party machine in Missouri in 1870. It rapidly developed into a nation-wide movement that seemed to promise the necessary accretions the Democrats were seeking to gain majority control.

The relation of the Liberal Republican revolt to sectionalism in politics is best shown in relating the transformation it effected in Carl Schurz, the original genius of the movement. Schurz had been a Radical close to Sumner. In the election of 1868 he spoke the language of normal Republicanism, attacking Democrats as rebels, and advocating Grant's election as "the only road to peace." In 1869 when the Missouri legislature elected him United States Senator, he declared that "only such acts of grace to our late enemies are in order as will be consistent with the safety of our loyal people. . . . I will not consent to arm the late rebels with power in a manner which would enable them to deprive loyal men of their rights." In the Senate as late as May 19, 1870, he attacked the Democratic views on constitutionality, asserting that they were false and that the American people "will never consent to placing power in the hands of men who still speak of overthrowing the great Constitutional amendments."

But in becoming a Liberal Republican Schurz faced the necessity of justifying his bolt from the party of Union and freedom. The only possible arguments available to him were those which softened the asperities between himself and the Democrats. Thus in an address to the people of Missouri, September 10, 1870, he made for him the new discovery that the "Civil War is over. . . . The exigencies of a great public danger have ceased to exist. . . . New measures are necessary. . . . If the Democrats support us we have abandoned no principle to gain such support." But Schurz had abandoned the "bloody shirt." From advocating the removal of political disabilities of ex-Confederates, to an attack on Republican corruption, to a speech on "Grant's usurpations," to exposure of "the insane Ku Klux legislation," he moved steadily to the grounds where Democrats were fighting. Finally at Nashville, September 20, 1871, he became a reconciler, "happy to stretch out my hand to all men who, having stood against us in the Civil War, are now ready to work for the restoration" of peace and harmony. To be sure Schurz never became a Democrat. "We liberal Republicans," he was careful to make clear, "are honest enough to speak out frankly what displeases us in the Republican party, but the same honesty compels us to say that there is still more in the Democratic party that displeases us." [38] Nevertheless Democrats could not be other than pleased to see their enemies divide on issues that brought one faction so near the line of Democratic attack.

So far as reconciliation is concerned this is the chief significance of the Liberal Republican movement. It was the first great event in the political narrative which made an appreciable number of Republicans soften the harshness of their attitude toward Democrats and the South. Few men had been more bitter in the past than Horace Greeley. Yet divergence from Grant brought him into the road of sectional accord. During the summer of 1871 he visited the South from which he wrote letters published in the *Tribune* critical of carpetbag government, urging amnesty, and suggesting ways toward the economic union of the sections. So also the veteran abolitionist, Julian, who once had wished to hang Jefferson Davis "in the name of God," withdrew from the party he had helped to

[38] Schurz's changing attitude can be traced in his "Writings," I, 472, 476, 484–509, 510–518; II, 2–254, 257–306.

build, and sought other agencies through which to effect a reformation of government.

Equally arresting was the sight of Sumner reprimanding Blaine for waving the "bloody shirt." Sumner, who had quarreled with Grant, supported Greeley and advised his many Negro friends to vote the Democratic ticket. Blaine thereupon charged Sumner with treason to his party and to his principles, and, giving the "bloody shirt" a wave, asserted that it was singular to see Sumner in alliance with the party of Preston S. Brooks. Sumner's answer is eloquent of the change a shift in party position can effect. "What has Preston Brooks to do with the Presidential election? . . . I will not unite with you in dragging him from his grave where he sleeps, to aggravate the passions of a political conflict, and arrest the longing for concord." [39]

Not merely did men like Schurz, Greeley, Julian, Sumner, David Davis, Charles Francis Adams, Jacob D. Cox, and Lyman Trumbull, politicians whose loyalty and integrity were unassailable in the North, henceforth speak the language of harmony. The Liberal Republican movement also brought into the same position the most powerful journals and the ablest editors in the North. Greeley's *New York Tribune,* White's *Chicago Tribune,* Bowles' *Springfield Republican,* and Halstead's *Cincinnati Commercial* were foremost among Republican journals. To have this group secede from the party and join a reform movement that stressed moderation toward the South seemed a progressive step toward reconciliation.

The Greeley campaign of 1872, when Liberal Republicans and Democrats united on a common candidate and a common platform, was important to reconciliation for much the same reason. This first effort of reformers to use the Democratic party as a vehicle ended in failure at the polls. But reconciliation won a partial victory in that certain obstacles to ultimate success were definitely removed.

In this respect it was important that the South conceded as much as it did in accepting not only the Reconstruction acts as accomplished facts but Horace Greeley as well. To many it was indeed a bitter pill. "The New Departure" wrote one

[39] M. Storey, "Charles Sumner" (Boston, 1900), 416–417.

irreconcilable, "is so low a descent from principle as to reach the extreme depths of political profligacy. It is simply a shameful . . . acknowledgement that the animating and actuating motive of its contrivers is the lust of office." [40] More typical, however, especially among Southern politicians, was the shrewd and practical view espoused by Benjamin H. Hill. It was futile, Hill urged, to waste energy in efforts to undo the measures of the past. The South would gain all she could ever hope for if she recaptured control of her own State governments. Greeley was a means to that end, and the end seemed so attractive as to make palatable the means.[41]

In the campaign proper Greeley not only promised deliverance from radical misgovernment in the South. He made reconciliation an issue of the campaign. "They [my opponents] talk about rebels and traitors," he said at Pittsburgh in September. "Fellow citizens, are we never to be done with this? . . . You cannot afford to teach a part of your country to hate you, to feel that your success, your greatness is identical with their humiliation. . . . I ask you to take the hand held out to you by your Southern brethren in their adoption of the Cincinnati platform . . . and say . . . 'The war is ended, let us again be fellow countrymen, and forget that we have been enemies.' " [42] At Portland, Maine, after stating that the two great issues of the campaign were reconciliation and purification, he defined the three steps in reconciliation to be the driving out of carpetbaggers, universal amnesty, and restoring to Southerners all the rights of citizenship. This actually was a narrow political approach, but it permitted Greeley a basis from which to make a strong emotional plea for peace.

Historians have often said that the nomination of Greeley ruined the chances of the Liberal Republican movement for success, that the reformers would have followed Adams or Trumbull but not the New Yorker. It is true, as Schurz wrote in a letter of May 11, 1872, that the battleground was neither in the South nor among Democrats, — those votes

[40] A. D. Mann to Jefferson Davis, Dec. 5, 1871, Rowland, "Davis," VII, 299–300.
[41] Hill, "Life and Speeches," 350–366.
[42] *New York Tribune*, Sept. 20, 1872.

were assured any candidate, — but in the North among elements which might be won away from Grant. It was in this respect that Greeley was weak and brought defeat. But while other candidates might have garnered a greater harvest of votes, the historian of reconciliation has still this to say, that no other candidate could have put a greater warmth, a purer sincerity, or a more unselfish devotion in his plea for peace than Horace Greeley did in his memorable speaking tour of the late summer and fall of 1872.

The Republican party fought the "New Departure," the Liberal Republican movement, and the Greeley campaign by the familiar methods of the "bloody shirt." Why does the South support Horace Greeley? inquired *Harper's Weekly*. "It is not fraternity, nor reconciliation, nor unity which the representative Southern leaders desire. They wish power; and their way to power is the success of the Democratic party." Greeley, so it was charged, was pledged to "undo as much of reconstruction as possible," to pension Confederate veterans, and to let Southerners "take care of the niggers." [43]

Nast's pencil was busy. One of his most effective cartoons was devoted to the "New Departure." At the North a Democrat plays "the New Organ" to the tune of the "lost cause lost," while Tammany in the background says, "Let him play those Tunes and we will see if they will take." At the South Jeff Davis (Davis was rarely absent from Nast's cartoons) plays a hand organ — "Bonnie Blue Flag" — to the tune of "the lost cause not lost" while "K K K" listens with approval and a group of men exclaim, "That's the Talk! That's the real Democratic Dixie." [44]

So savage did Nast's cartoons against Greeley become that G. W. Curtis, the editor, whose language as the reader of these pages can appreciate was not mild, protested, but Fletcher Harper, the owner, let Nast have his way. In fact the campaign can be told in terms of Nast cartoons. On August 3 appeared a striking one, "Baltimore 1861–1872, Let Us Clasp Hands over the Bloody Chasm," in which Greeley (the 1872 Democratic Convention met in Baltimore) reaches for the

[43] *Harper's Weekly*, July 20, Sept. 14, 1872.
[44] *Ibid.*, July 1, 1871.

dripping hands of a Southern bully who, revolver in hand, stands on the American flag and the bodies of soldiers of the Sixth Massachusetts regiment (fired upon in 1861 when marching through Baltimore). September 14, "the Wolf in Sheep's Clothing" idea was used again. A week later Greeley, Boss Tweed, and Brown represent "Lost Cause," "Repudiation," "White Supremacy," "K K K," "The Constitution of 1860," and so on, in an attack against a virtuous Uncle Sam defended by the Republican party. The same issue also carried a "Bloody Chasm" cartoon, with Andersonville prison feeding the chasm with blood, and Greeley fawningly reaching across to shake the hands of the perpetrators of the horrors. Possibly the limits of decency were reached when Greeley was depicted as a vulture resting on the ruins of colored orphan asylums and school houses. But Mark Twain, for one, thought that this greatest of American cartoonists now in his prime was, in this campaign, working for "civilization and progress."

The Republican campaign probably was successful in making reconciliation seem the cheap staple of Democratic ambition and lust for power. The North was cautioned that "letting the South have its way" would not bring peace but struggle.[45] Henry Adams and James Russell Lowell wrote that if Greeley were elected "we should again witness that hideous uprising of exulting disloyalty and violence which greeted the reactionary course of President Johnson."[46] "The Greeley orators," wrote Curtis, "represent the Southern States as full of prostrate and ruined brothers sighing for fraternal reconciliation and the Northern States as haughty and tyrannical, insolently insisting upon holding their hapless associates under an iron heel."[47] This approach was an effective prelude in manœuvring the Democrats on to fatal ground. The Republicans could argue that peace on Greeley's lips was surrender, while peace from Grant meant that reconciliation would wait upon the right settlement of basic issues.

The argument seemed convincing. Such moderates as Godkin

[45] *Harper's Weekly,* Oct. 26, 1872.
[46] *North American Rev.,* CXV (1872), 421–422.
[47] *Harper's Weekly,* Nov. 2, 1872.

and Winthrop chose the lesser evil, Grant, primarily because they were not yet ready to believe that Southerners and Democrats were honest in their "New Departure." The mouthpiece of Republicanism was quite correct in saying that the results indicated that "the vast majority of the American people know very well what they have won at such tremendous cost, and that they intend to maintain it to the last and the utmost." [48] It was the suspicion that the restoration of the Democratic party to power notwithstanding its assurances of acquiescence would imperil Northern interests and disturb the war settlement that explained Grant's second victory.

Possibly it weakened the cause of reconciliation thus to have made it an issue. Certainly it did little good to have again the friendly gestures of Southerners spurned. "People weary," as one lamented, "of continued self-control, self-abnegation and self-sacrifice, if all their efforts are turned back upon them as evidences of cunning, hypocrisy and deceit." [49] But still the impression remains that Greeley's work was not all in vain. Emotion is an elusive thing, often impossible to analyze. Greeley's defeat was a personal tragedy made complete by his death shortly after the election. A universal sense of pity stilled for a moment the indecent abuse that had made the preceding six months a turmoil of strife. It may well have been that Greeley as President could have done no more than cause a continuance of party warfare of the sections. In such a death as his, however, he gave the country its first experience of a common heart throb since before the ancient divisions had begun.

Four more years of Grant demonstrated the futility of expecting peace through the Republican policy of pacification. Evils of carpetbag misrule in the South grew worse and the administration bogged in a morass of confusion that made more convincing the Democratic argument that solution could be realized only after "home rule" was restored to the South. Four more years of Grant also demonstrated the futility of expecting reform from within the ranks of the administra-

[48] *Ibid.*, Nov. 23, 1872.
[49] Guy M. Bryan to Hayes, Aug. 29, 1871, "The Bryan-Hayes Correspondence," *Southwestern Historical Quarterly*, XXVI (1922), 61.

tion and raised again the possibility of using the Democratic party as a broom to sweep clean the filth of office. As a consequence the Democrats gained strength in the years from 1873 to 1876. In reverse, the Republicans were pressed to use more than ever the defensive weapon of the "bloody shirt."

The most effective criticism directed against the pacification policy was made by Godkin in the columns of the *Nation.* Godkin began his attack well before the Greeley campaign, but it grew in volume as events in the South confirmed the accuracy of his trenchant observations and dire predictions. Through years of emphasis Godkin built up a complete dogma of the folly of Republican rule in the South and applied it to every episode that raised the Southern issue. His central conception was that the evils in Southern social and political conditions were not curable by legislation applied from outside. They were evils which could disappear only under the influence of a general improvement of Southern society. Meanwhile Radical interference, which Godkin asserted was selfishly motivated, acted only as an irritant. The proper men to solve Southern problems were Southern men in whom the South had confidence.

The growth of this critical attitude towards Reconstruction robbed the Republican party of some of its strength. Dana, editor of the *New York Sun,* originally a Radical, became a Democrat and made "No force bill! No Negro domination!" the constant cry of his newspaper throughout Grant's second administration. Pulitzer was another Republican who by 1876 had become a Democrat. Winthrop, who had been unable to support Greeley in 1872, by 1876 had come around to the support of Tilden. At last he could say that "I have no fear that such a change will endanger the great issues of the late war." [50]

On the other hand many men were still unready to trust the Democratic party. William Cullen Bryant, editor of the *New York Evening Post,* thought Tilden to be the best qualified man in politics for the Presidency. Yet he could not support a Democrat and so cast his vote for Hayes. Carl Schurz acted likewise. James Russell Lowell, at last cured of his

[50] Winthrop, "Memoir," 298.

Radicalism by the "shameful condition of things at the South,"
was "ready for a movement now to emancipate the whites."
But he still thought "that the intelligence of the country is
decidedly on the Republican side" and so preferred to work
from within the party.[51] So also the *Nation,* in spite of its
exposure of Reconstruction frauds, thought that the war had
taught some "tremendous lessons" which would better be
expounded by Republican teachers than by Democratic. From
the point of view of reconciliation it was not unfortunate that
these men remained Republican. Within the party they constituted a "better element," certainly an unselfish one, which
worked against the use of the "bloody shirt." As Democrats,
even they would not have escaped the suspicion that vexed
that party's every proposal of reconciliation.

Tilden, the party's nominee in 1876, felt some embarrassment in this respect. On every issue of the campaign, except
the North-South rivalry, he seemed a stronger choice than the
Republican Hayes. As Governor of New York his first inclination was to keep silent on national issues. But urged by no
less a person than Whitelaw Reid, a Republican, who had
been made wise by what had happened to Greeley, Tilden
finally made "a ringing declaration" accepting the results of
the war. Again in his letter accepting the Democratic nomination he had preferred to stress reform as the major issue and
remain silent on the matter of his patriotism, which he felt
could stand on its record. But before the campaign had proceeded far he was influenced to speak specifically to the effect
that the repose of the country need fear no unsettlement from
his election.[52]

Throughout the years that criticism of Republican policy
was developing, Republicans clung to the practice of inter-
preting Southern news so as to maintain the fierce war spirit
of the North. "Nowhere," wrote the editor of *Harper's
Weekly* concerning outrages in the South, "except in the States
where Republicans rule is there any safety for life and freedom. It seems a fixed purpose of the Democratic politicians

[51] Lowell to Thomas Hughes, July 12, 1876, "Letters," II, 174–175.
[52] R. Cortissoz, "The Life of Whitelaw Reid" (New York, 1921), 247, 292,
297–298; J. Bigelow (ed.), "Tilden's Public Writings and Speeches" (New
York, 1895), II, 359–373, 381–382.

to prevent the restoration of peace at the South, and in this policy they are unhappily encouraged by the Democratic and Liberal Republican leaders at the North. Both hope to keep up their party organization by inciting insurrection in Louisiana, and by charging upon the Administration those scenes of fatal discord which have sprung up from their evil promptings." [53] In 1876 the party met the reform issue by going outside the administration circle and nominating a "pure" candidate, Rutherford B. Hayes, of Ohio. But to meet what Charles Francis Adams, Jr., in 1875 had described as a vast majority of Northern sentiment against Southern abuses, the party had only the "bloody shirt" for defense.

Whether the Democratic eagerness to embarrass their opponents, or the Republican desire to evade responsibility caused the phenomenon, or whether it was inherent in the situation, the sectional division rapidly became the major talking point of the election of 1876. From the day in January when James G. Blaine tore "from the throat of treason the tongue of slander [and] snatched the mask of Democracy from the hideous face of the rebellion" (as Robert Ingersoll described it), by deliberately charging Jefferson Davis with responsibility for the old tragedies of Andersonville, until the votes were cast in November, the country was again deluged in a flood of sectional abuse. It was a great contest of recrimination in which selfish partisan ends triumphed over every other consideration of national good. The feeble efforts of moderates like Schurz, Reid, Tilden, Lowell and Godkin to keep the issue on reform failed miserably. Democrats used language as vindictive as the Republicans. Most men went one road or the other to extremes, as did Thomas Wentworth Higginson who, having first sought compromise, later let himself be aroused by the stories of Negro persecution.

The hopes of moderates that Hayes would keep a balance were also dissipated. A year before his nomination he had expressed disgust with Radical tactics. Reformers like Schurz were intimately in touch with him, giving advice to stand on reform and "honest money" and to avoid the sectional issue. For years Hayes had been in correspondence with a close

[53] *Harper's Weekly*, May 3, 1873.

Southern friend, Guy Bryan, who urged him to be the statesman of good feeling. But the transformation of Hayes
began in his letter of acceptance, July 8, when he agreed to
the Republican definition of peace as meaning the "permanent
pacification of the South." By August he was convinced that
a "vast majority of the plain people think of this as the main
question in the canvass, — *A Democratic victory will bring
the Rebellion into power.*" Hence it was not difficult for him
to see the utility of appealing to the sentiment. By September
he had convinced himself that the danger of a "united South
victory and Tilden's [war] record were the two major issues
of the canvass." By election day he was the prey of his own
fears and fully believed that if he were not elected the "poor
colored men of the South will be in a more deplorable condition than when they were in slavery." [54]

The election ended a deadlock in which it was impossible to
decide whether the people wanted Hayes or Tilden. The comment of Governor Seymour, in retirement, made in April 1876,
that the "Republicans have lost the confidence of the country and the Democrats have not gained it," seemed evident in
the result. [55] Or as Godkin expressed it, the real issue had been
how to get rid of Republican rascals without handing over the
government to that portion of the country lately in rebellion. [56]
The solution came as a compromise effected between November 1876 and March 1877, but only after the nation again
faced the grim prospect of civil war brought on by the reckless
indulgence of party enmity.

The Compromise of 1877 pleased those Northerners who
still dreaded the prospect of a national Democratic administration, by placing Hayes in the White House to purify the
Republican party. Hayes was tacitly committed to the restoration of white rule in the South, and Southerners seemed
perfectly satisfied with their share of the spoils. [57] Only the
Northern Democrats got nothing for their efforts. But even

[54] On Hayes see, C. R. Williams, "The Life of Rutherford Birchard
Hayes" (Boston, 1914), I, 383, 461–462, 493–494; "Bryan-Hayes Correspondence," *Southwestern Historical Quarterly*, XXVI, 292–293; Schurz,
"Writings," III, 161, 215, 240, 248, 252, 258, 284, 285, 338.
[55] As quoted in *Harper's Weekly*, April 22, 1876.
[56] *Nation*, Sept. 28, 1876.
[57] *Charleston News and Courier*, Feb. 19, March 3, 1877.

they could take consolation in knowledge of the fact that Reconstruction now come to an end had given them a solid Southern vote as a source of strength in future elections.

The removal of Federal troops from the South by a Republican President and the restoration of home rule to Southern whites had important consequences in shaping the future course of the sectional issue in politics. The editors of the *Nation* and *Harper's Weekly* were over optimistic in expecting that the end of Reconstruction would mean the end of the Solid South. But it is true that the last of the three great political factors that had rent the nation asunder (the debate over slavery, the struggle for Southern independence, and the trials of Reconstruction) no longer existed. The hurt was in the past, and, while the South remained a problem often vexatious, the proportions of that problem were never again to reach the degree where they would overwhelm the good sense of the country.

The Compromise of 1877 implied a surrender to those who had insisted upon a thorough establishment of strong nationalism and complete equality as the results of the war. It was the first great compromise in which the Republican party, originated largely as an enemy of compromise, had participated. It seemed almost as though the parties were returning to the politics of sectional adjustment by trial and error, give and take, that had characterized the era before 1850. Had this "surrender" been made under Democratic auspices it would have been exploited by Republicans as material for the "bloody shirt." But accomplished by a Republican administration as the concession to the privilege of peacefully retaining power, the burden of defense rested upon the party which prided itself upon its adherence to the strictest standards of loyalty. Hayes, not Tilden, had the burden of proving that he had not sold for party advantage the nation's well-being and the Negro's future.

As President, Hayes completely committed himself to a policy of leniency. The Federal troops were removed from the South. Carpetbag governments toppled. White men governed from Virginia to Texas, a vast Democratic area, anti-Republican in politics, in which the Negro became again what he had been in 1860, the ward of the dominant race. An ex-Confederate, Keys of Tennessee, was given a cabinet position — the first evidence that Republican officialdom admitted the self-professed reformation of a rebel. Hayes's first message to Congress, justifying his Southern policy, is eloquent of the change that had taken place.

To complete and make permanent the pacification of the country continues to be, and until it is fully accomplished must remain, the most important of all our national interests. . . . There was [1876] a widespread apprehension that the momentous results in our progress as a nation marked by the recent amendments to the Constitution were in imminent jeopardy; that the good understanding which prompted their adoption, in the interest of a loyal devotion to the general welfare, might prove a barren truce, and that the two sections of the country, once engaged in civil strife, might be again almost as widely severed and disunited as they were when arrayed in arms against each other. [To end this situation Hayes withdrew the troops, a policy] which pointed to the time . . . when a genuine love of our whole country . . . shall supplant the destructive forces of mutual animosity of races and of sectional hostility. . . . The discontinuance of the use of the Army for the purpose of upholding local governments . . . was no less a constitutional duty and requirement . . . than it was a much needed measure for the restoration of local self-government and the promotion of national harmony.

Here indeed was a curious medley of old phrases and new necessities in imperfect adjustment. On one hand the passage of the amendments was associated with national progress and was said to have been prompted in the interests of the general welfare. On the other the enforcement of the amendments by federal power was destroying the Union. Actually force of circumstances dictated the course Hayes pursued. His discomfort arose primarily from the fact that the only possible justification he could find was the familiar Democratic arguments of unconstitutionality and reconciliation.

The country also had the novel spectacle of seeing a Republican President attempting to ingratiate himself with the South. On Memorial Day Hayes participated in ceremonies in Tennessee where flowers were strewn upon the graves of both

Federal and Confederate dead, while his ex-Confederate Post-master General took part in a similar ceremony in Ohio. In the fall Hayes made a good-will tour of the South. At Louisville prominent Southerners sat on the same platform with the President, and earnest and patriotic pleas for a fraternal union of good will were exchanged. Most prominent among the Southerners with whom Hayes associated in the deeper South was Wade Hampton, the storm center of the South Carolina election of 1876. It was a gratifying picture, the *Nation* observed, to see the President who had been elected by the "bloody shirt," within one short year, "traveling triumphantly through the South, pleading before joyous multitudes for union and conciliation." [58] No less significant, perhaps, was the spectacle of Hampton, who had won his governorship on what might be termed the Southern model of the "bloody shirt," also advocating peace and harmony.

The Compromise of 1877 also affected reconciliation in that it committed the Republicans favorably disposed to Hayes to the necessity of preaching before the country the finality of the truce. The disputed election had taught the nation concretely to what extremes sectional partisanship might lead. In the sober afterthought most Northerners welcomed as salutary a change which would emphasize concord rather than discord. This change in psychology was reflected even in such rigid abolitionists as Whittier, who expressed the opinion that the Negro would be better off without the protection of Federal troops and Republican support in the South than with them, really a remarkable change in opinion impossible to explain except in terms of how grave the crisis before the Compromise had appeared.

The change in tone was most strikingly if not brazenly shown by certain of the "bloody shirt" spellbinders. Most notably was this true of Robert Ingersoll whose heart-rending speech on Andersonville had been given throughout the North and had been a chief reliance of the Republicans. During March 1877 Ingersoll delivered a series of lectures in leading Northern cities in which he not merely recommended the policy of conciliation but also admitted that his different line of

[58] *Nation*, Sept. 27, 1877.

talk had been deliberately directed to arouse Northern hostility against the South so as to elect a Republican President.

Curious also was the complete revolution in the editorial policy of *Harper's Weekly*. This important Republican journal saw a new light when Hayes lifted from its back the burden of defending corruption and carpetbaggery. Almost with unseemly haste the "bloody shirt" came down and the flag of reconciliation took its place. *Harper's Weekly* essayed the task of defending the President's policy and did as complete a job for leniency as it earlier had done for Radicalism.

Striking while the moment was opportune, prominent Southern Democrats embarked upon a conscious program of impressing the North with their loyalty. A good beginning had been made in February 1877 when Southern Congressmen stood by the bargain which permitted Hayes to reach the presidency and cautiously refrained from joining in the wild assertions of some of the Northern Democrats. So moderate was their stand as to evoke from *Harper's Weekly* the comment "if this is Southern Democracy, it is wonderfully like the best Northern Republicanism." [59] Hill, Lamar, and Gordon, especially strove to make a good impression. Senator Hill not only spoke frequently and at length about the Southern desire to cement a true union between the sections, but also took decisive steps to kill any action within Democratic ranks toward recognizing Southern war claims.

The conservative East was also gratified to find Hill and Lamar giving effective aid to "sound money" in the silver crisis of 1878. Hill spoke convincingly for the absolute recognition of the obligation of all contracts in terms of gold. Lamar, although instructed by his State to vote for silver, also stood on the conservative side. It was commented that two former Confederates were "earnestly and eloquently insisting upon keeping faith and redeeming in their full spirit and intention the promise of the government, [while] . . . devoted supporters of the Union during the war now were insisting the government shall partially repudiate its obligations." [60] Hill seemed especially deserving of applause in the

[59] *Harper's Weekly*, May 5, 1877.
[60] *Ibid.*, Feb. 16, 1878.

eyes of Eastern conservatives when he said, "I tried my best [during the war] to make the bondholder who purchased at sixty cents lose the sixty cents he gave, but now I am for giving him the dollar he was promised." [61] Apart from the economic merits of the case, it is significant that on the money question the conservative East and the liberal West were again seeking, as of old, political support in the South. Here was promise of a future division on grounds other than the war issues.

The South also began in this period the practice of sending some of her most persuasive orators into the North to play upon the emotions of the people. Senator Gordon, of Georgia, with a romantic background of Confederate service, beloved of ladies, handsome and ingratiating, was among the first of these emissaries. "I care not what mere politicians may say," said the mere politician Gordon in an address before the Commercial Club of Boston, in the spring of 1878, "the true sentiment and intuitive perceptions of the people of the country will refuse to believe and refuse to base the future legislation of the country on the unceasing assertion that any portion of the people are the enemies of the country. In his heart of hearts the politician himself does not believe it. You men of Massachusetts, you Republicans or Democrats, do not believe it. . . . The causes that divided us are gone, and gone forever. The interests which now unite us will unite forever." [62] If it be said that the business men who thus mixed food with oratory were thinking of profits in the South, and that Gordon was interested in developing in the North an opinion favorable to the advancement of Southern ends, it can be answered that that is just what makes the episode significant. Another thread of interest was being woven into the rent fabric of national life to offer some resistance to the separating pull of "bloody shirt" politics.

A year earlier, in June 1877, Wade Hampton, the stormy petrel of so many sectional issues, visited Auburn, New York. He was introduced by a Northern Republican, who developed the theme that the "war is ended. . . . The record is made up

[61] Mayes, "Lamar," 333.
[62] As quoted in *Harper's Weekly*, May 18, 1878.

and the issues can now be retired." Hampton began by crying "Amen" to this sentiment, and then explained that the
contest in South Carolina had not been against the North, or
primarily for party success, but for good government and
civilization. He also made assurances of future protection to
the Negro. "I come," he concluded, "to do honor to my distinguished friend General Shields. He wore the blue and I
wore the gray, but we can let the curtain drop over these years,
and go back to the time when that flag borne by him waved
alike over the men of the South and the men of the North,
and we can look beyond to the future, when through all time
that flag shall float over a free and prosperous and reunited
country." [63]

Typical also was the speech of a North Carolina Congressman, Wadell, in New York, in May 1878. As a Confederate
veteran, he made a glowing tribute to the "boys in blue,"
promised to support every bill in Congress that the Northern
veterans needed, and asked for nothing for the South except
the privilege of local self-government. His conclusion struck
a note that would ring time and time again in the later years of
the century — "whenever in the future it [the Stars and
Stripes] shall be unfurled in war, the Confederate soldier
will be found beneath it, ready to give his life in its defense." [64]
When finally Alexander H. Stephens, former Vice-President
of the Confederacy, now in Congress, participated in the
ceremonies honoring Lincoln's memory on February 12, 1878,
old Jubal A. Early, having seen with rising indignation Hill
fraternizing with Blaine, Lamar seeking "to instill into the
hearts of Mississippians principles of morality and honesty
gathered from the 'land of steady habits,' " broke out wrath-
fully in a letter to Davis, "Are our Southern representatives,
and bitterest revilers of the North, about to resolve themselves into a mutual admiration society, leaving such 'irreconcilables' as you and myself out in the cold?" [65] To those,
however, who were looking for the rainbow this Southern
policy of ingratiation seemed a hopeful sign.

[63] *Harper's Weekly*, July 7, 1877.
[64] *Ibid.*, May 25, 1878.
[65] Early to Davis, Feb. 16, 1878, Rowland, "Davis," VIII, 82.

Not all, however, felt inclined to soften the issues between the sections. In fact the major portions of both parties sought to keep alive old issues and rekindle the fire of the people. The Northern Democrats had not been pleased with the compromise and were not prone to sit back quietly permitting "His Fraudulency," as Hayes was dubbed, to enjoy his administration. The Democratic majority in the House of Representatives reopened the quarrel in the session of 1877–1878 by investigating the election of 1876 in the hope of discovering Republican fraud. This was the signal for the professionals in the Republican party to come back to life and wave with renewed vigor their beloved garment. "I can't go this new policy" of Hayes, wrote Blaine, who was nearer the center of gravity in the Republican party than was the President. "Every instinct of my nature rebels against it, and I feel an intuition amounting to an inspiration that the North in adopting it is but laying up wrath against the day of wrath. In any event its success means the triumph of the Democratic party, against which I wage eternal war! *Carthago delenda est.*" [66]

The first element responsible for the persistence of the "bloody shirt" was a large, if somewhat nebulously defined, group which had developed, in the long years of dispute, fixed beliefs in regard to sectional issues. Thomas Nast was of this type. While the editorial policy of *Harper's Weekly* changed, Nast continued with unabated fury to draw his cartoons of hatred and suspicion. Deep into Northern homes had penetrated the idea that disloyal Southerners were still conspiring to destroy the Union and reënslave the Negro. In such circles the Democratic party was viewed as the treacherous ally of the enemy. Such ideas died slowly, and while they lasted the "bloody shirt" orator had reason to believe an appeal to sectional distrust might win votes.

A second element was composed of honest zealots who had "labored so long for the emancipation of the slaves that the Negro has undergone a sort of transfiguration in their minds and appears to be right in any conflict with his old master." [67]

[66] Blaine to Reid, April 12, 1877, Cortissoz, "Reid," I, 377.
[67] *Nation,* April 12, 1877.

Wendell Phillips in an article in the *North American Review*
revealed the mental content of this group.

> The cement of the [Republican] party was a principle. . . .
> The men who created the Republican party were men of con-
> viction. They sought, more or less directly, but in dead earnest,
> to limit and kill slavery. . . . Lacking its old cement — a great
> purpose — the party is falling to pieces, like boulders from a
> wall without mortar. Its managers have been so dull and timid
> in using the great victory, they have so wasted their opportunity,
> that they have suffered the Southern question — their whole cap-
> ital — to fall prematurely into abeyance. On their own theory
> they stand today with no *raison d'être*, no excuse for their exist-
> ence. Their strength lay in a public opinion well informed as to
> the Southern purpose and the nature of Southern civilization, and
> watchful of the possible reaction from its sore defeat.

Phillips was adamant in his disbelief that "such a conspiracy
as that of the South [ever] surrenders the hope of success,"
that "it was the Republicans' duty to keep alive at white heat
the lesson and vigilance of the war," that Hayes' policy was
a betrayal, and that Lamar and Gordon in their "pretty
speeches" were hypocrites.[68]

The third and most important element consisted of partisans like Blaine, Conkling, Logan, and Garfield, about whom
it may be said that they cared less about patriotism and the
Negro than that they regarded them as trophies of the war
to use for party purposes. To this group the Democratic
party was still an enemy to be destroyed, Southern whites
were irreconcilable, and any hostility or prejudice against the
Negro was a sign of a "new rebellion." This group which
had been dominant under Grant accepted Hayes only with
great distaste and were soon in open hostility to his policy of
leniency toward the South.

Not only were the old aspects of the "bloody shirt" re-
tained; new patches were added. Thus Agnus Cameron, of
Wisconsin, bemoaned that the "divine compassion" of the
Republican party in its treatment of rebels had been rewarded

[68] Wendell Phillips, "The Outlook," *North American Rev.*, CXXVII
(1878), 97, 98, 100, 101.

by establishment of a Solid South directed against the Union. "Without the Solid South the Democratic party would be a feeble fiction — a moral night-scavenger's cart, laden with the offscourings of Tipperary civilization, instead of a war-chariot armed with disciplined and exultant soldiers, confident of an early victory over their benefactors." [69] The Republicans now had a grievance to talk about — the Solid South built upon fraud. "As the matter now stands, all violence in the South inures to the benefit of one political party," wrote Blaine in 1879. "And that party is counting upon its accession to power and its rule over the country for a series of years by reason of the great number of electoral votes which it wrongfully gains. Financial credit, commercial enterprises, manufacturing industries, may all possibly pass under the control of the Democratic party by reason of its unlawful seizure of political power." [70]

To these men "the cure for all the evils we endure — all of them spawned by rebellion — is not to be found in conciliation . . . but in sustaining the party that restored the Union of the fathers, clad now in the white robes of freedom, unsullied and irreproachable." [71] Soon the cry was raised that a Solid North must be effected to oppose a Solid South. [72]

A fourth element, partly an outgrowth of the third, was made up of those who found distasteful the policies of the Democratic party in control of the House of Representatives since 1875. Every step was carefully scrutinized by Republicans who hoped to find mistakes that could be made the occasion for a new development of the "bloody shirt." Typical was General Sherman, who seemingly grew more Radical with age. He was especially disturbed by Democratic efforts to cut down the size and expense of the military establishment. In his irritation he immediately jumped to the conclusion that the Democratic majority in the House was unpatriotic. "They are resolved to cut down the Army, so as afterwards to increase it by new regiments commanded by the Southern officers

[69] Agnus Cameron, "The Irrepressible Conflict Undecided," *North American Rev.*, CXXVI (1878), 488.
[70] Blaine, *North American Rev.*, CXXVIII (1879), 282–283.
[71] Cameron, *op. cit.*, 490.
[72] *Nation*, Aug. 15, 1878.

who deserted in 1861," he wrote privately on November 12, 1877.[73] The next spring he asserted in a public address that the Confederates had been welcomed back into the family group so early and so completely as to impair the position "of the remainder of the family who stood faithful all the time." [74] Throughout the Hayes administration General Sherman talked and wrote of treasonable Democrats and unrepentant rebels. The man who in 1866 had spoken contemptuously of Radicals, twelve years later could write, "I do fear that unless the Union men of the North are careful, the Southern Democracy will govern the party, consequently Jeff Davis and his men will become the patriots whilst Mr. Lincoln and those of us who fought will be regarded and treated as traitors. This is no chimera, but is a struggle now in progress, and may lead to further strife and blood." [75]

By 1878 it was apparent that the Congressional elections of that year were to be fought on lines of the ancient antagonisms and not under the new dispensation of peace and harmony. The tug of war within the Republican party was decided. In 1877 the State conventions had varied in sentiment, Ohio and Massachusetts speaking in favor of Hayes, New York and Pennsylvania lukewarm and somewhat noncommittal, with Iowa and Maine distinctly inclined to extremism. On the other hand every Democratic convention held in 1877 had congratulated "the country upon the acceptance by the present Administration of the Constitutional and pacific policy of local self-government in the States of the South, so long advocated by the Democratic party, and which has brought peace and harmony to that section." But in 1878 the Republican State Conventions were distinctly bellicose in tone. Hayes was subordinated. Chief emphasis was given the Solid South "built upon a fraudulent base," its threat to national security, rebel claims, persecution of the Negro, and the "treasonable" attacks of the Democrats upon the military establishment.[76] In this year the apparent material from which all

---

[73] W. T. Sherman, "Home Letters," 386–387.
[74] Memorial Day Address, May 30, 1878 (pamphlet).
[75] Sherman, "Home Letters," 387–388.
[76] E. McPherson, "Handbook of Politics for 1878" (Washington, 1878), 152–168.

Republican platforms were built was, to quote the *Nation,* a conception "that a state of war exists in this country, and that there is a body of public enemies encamped on our soil now seeking to seize the Government." [77]

Harper's Weekly admitted the party was divided on the wisdom of using the "bloody shirt," insisting however that the rank and file were favorable to Hayes.[78] The curiously inconsistent Garfield opined after the election that the "man who attempts to get up a political excitement in this country on the old sectional issues will find himself without a party and without support." [79] Yet Garfield and the party chieftains had done exactly that, and made of the campaign of 1878 the same weary story of sectional distrust.

The conduct of the elections in the South deprived the moderates, who had banked so much upon Hampton's assurances of fair play for the Negro, of their main argument that if let alone the South would accept party divisions and permit the Negro equal enjoyment of his constitutional privileges. But the South remained solid, and built its unanimity upon a general disfranchisement of the Negro that in places, notably Hampton's South Carolina, descended to sheer brutality. This was of course rare political capital for the Republican leaders, who exploited it with increasing fervor from November 1878, through 1879, until they made it a prime issue in the presidential canvass of 1880. Even the friendly *Nation* and the new convert to moderation, *Harper's Weekly,* were affected, concluding that the Southern whites had betrayed a trust, and that somehow a remedy must be found through the Republican party. "If the South is to be solid for foul play," wrote *Harper's Weekly,* falling back into its old habit of distrust, "the North will be equally solid against it." [80]

So another projected bridging of the chasm collapsed in ruin. The North and South had so many dissension-making differences, so few harmony-making communities of interest, that the engineers of peace seemed working on a hopeless task.

The "bloody shirt" now proceeded on the argument that the

[77] *Nation,* July 4, 1878.
[78] *Harper's Weekly,* March 2, 1878.
[79] *Congressional Record,* Dec. 10, 1878.
[80] *Harper's Weekly,* Nov. 2, 1878.

"systematic terror of Southern Democrats," and not "Republican misdeeds," had reopened the sectional issue.[81] Hayes took this stand in his second annual message to Congress in December 1878, and from that time on there seemed to be a complete surrender to those elements in the party who had never sought peace with the Democrats. When to this was added in the Congressional session of 1878-1879 a Democratic attack upon the Federal election laws, enacted by Republicans in the Grant Administration for safeguarding a "loyal" vote in the South, the Republican leaders thought they had an invincible case for the application of "bloody shirt" tactics. Garfield, upon whom the mantle of party leadership was about to fall, was especially active in attacking Democratic "nullification" in Congress and the "revival of State Sovereignty ideas."[82]

The campaign of 1880 began, as one commentator observed, with "looseness of opinion on all questions except the condition of the South."[83] On this issue the Republicans sought purposely to foster strife, while the Democrats made no honest effort at any solid solution, contenting themselves with continued repeal of Republican safeguards for the Negro. Between these two positions there was little comfort for the moderate who again saw the extremes triumph over the middle. Again the nation participated in the old, prolonged debate as to whether the people of one half the country were or were not to be trusted in their fidelity and patriotism.

Thus the unanswered question was raised as the issue of the campaign — Shall "the people who rebelled against the United States government . . . gain full possession of that government?" "The war has now been over more than fifteen years," wrote the veteran Julian in ironic criticism of the Republican methods, "and yet the Rebels have so fair a prospect of capturing the government that the effort to save it cannot be balked in the slightest degree by any inquiries into the management of public affairs since the close of the conflict."[84]

[81] *Harper's Weekly,* Nov. 30, 1878.
[82] Garfield, "Works," II, 679-722.
[83] *Nation,* March 6, 1879.
[84] Julian, "Later Speeches," 195.

The Republican Campaign Text Book for 1880 devoted more than half its space to "bloody shirt" themes. *Harper's Weekly* resumed its old cudgels. Garfield, who at first indicated a desire to stand on the financial issue, soon retreated into the shelter of the war record issue.

> Treason may make its boast, my boys,
>   And seek to rule again;
> Our Jim shall meet its hosts, my boys,
>   And strike with might and main!
> Once more he'll crush the foe, my boys,
>   With arm and bosom bare;
> And this shall be his field, my boys, —
>   The Presidential Chair!

Before election day, Republicans were declaring the South to be the major issue of the campaign.

The "bloody shirt" was probably not so important in causing Garfield's election in 1880 as were Hancock's inability to force a more positive discussion on economic issues and the purity of Hayes's administration, which quieted the reform issue. Nevertheless this chapter ends with politics exercising the same divisive influence upon national life that it had exercised in 1865. To be sure there was much evidence that many people were wearying of the prolongation of the old quarrel between North and South in politics. As Lamar observed, "it required no courage [to wave the bloody shirt]; it required no magnanimity to do it; it required no courtesy. It only required hate, bitter, malignant sectional feeling." [85] It was also perfectly understood that partisan extremity North bred partisan extremity South. Yet each recurring election saw the nation slip back again into a practice apparently become habitual.

It could not be otherwise so long as the chasm between North and South remained unclosed. The day might come when the lurid red of the "bloody shirt" would fade into an inoffensive pink, and the garment through constant usage be worn into rags so disreputable that few would care to don it. But when that day came the chasm would first have been

[85] Mayes, "Lamar," 365.

closed. So far as the reconciliation of North and South was concerned politics were ever a negative force. It is time that we turn to the positive influences that even in the turbulent fifteen years after 1865 were raising the promise of ultimate peace.

CHAPTER V

LET US HAVE PEACE
1865–1880

THROUGH the long years of controversy that bred in North and South an unyielding sense of difference, there could also be found a persistent desire for peace. It was in the daily experience of all Americans to observe, with the editor of the *New York Tribune,* that "the bulk of the people of this country North and South do not hate each other, and it is a wretched piece of dishonesty on the part of the politicians whose trade is loyalty to make them believe they do." [1] "There is but one sentiment among the thinking men of the South," wrote a Texan, "and it is, Give us peace. Give us confidence, hope, and a foundation on which we can rebuild." [2] Grant's "Let us have peace," while prostituted to party ends, nevertheless demonstrated that the North too sought surcease from strife.

The excitement through which the country had passed and was passing, the suffering and the sorrow, the inflammatory appeals and constant agitation, and the never-relenting bitterness, filled the hearts, as Governor Vance of North Carolina said, "with indescribable yearnings for national peace, for a complete moral as well as physical restoration of the Union." [3] Those who looked to the future of the country which war had reunited appreciated the desirability of softening the animosities between the sections. "We are Americans," an orator before the New England Society of New York declared in 1876. "Sons of the Pilgrims, you are not to war with savage men and savage beasts, you are not to tame a continent nor

[1] *New York Tribune,* April 29, 1874.
[2] "Bryan-Hayes Correspondence," *Southwestern Historical Quarterly,* XXV, 296.
[3] C. Dowd, "Life of Zebulon B. Vance" (Charlotte, 1897), 238–239.

even found a State. Our task is nobler, is diviner. Our task, sir, is to reconcile a nation." [4]

Confronted by the prejudices and passions of the war and postwar periods, this sentiment often seemed hopeless. But good will is a slow distillation of many inchoate promptings. Its workings are rarely so dramatic or so capable of such neat analysis as dissension. Often it is taken for granted as though it needed no explanation. It came to a yearning people with no sudden realization, but quietly permeated the humblest folkways of the nation. Thus it was that the desire for peace found its first outlet in reconciling those who mourned at the graves of their dead soldiers.

The origin of Memorial Day, like everything that grows from common clay, is a development from obscure beginnings. During the war women of the South found relief for their saddened hearts by strewing flowers upon the fresh graves of husbands, sons, and brothers. The tragedy of defeat made dearer and perhaps more necessary this practice, which soon became customary. Northern troops of occupation moving South in late April and early May 1865 observed that communities everywhere were decorating their Confederate graves. The practice commended itself to the conquering invader. Especially did it seem fitting that the lonely graves of Federal soldiers buried in the South should be remembered. Small groups of Unionists, sometimes an individual alone, performed the rite in communities scattered throughout the South. Frequently Negroes joined in bringing flowers to the graves of their deliverers. One such occasion transcended others in importance and, attracting nation-wide attention, introduced the idea of Memorial Day to the North. In Charleston, South Carolina, on May 30, 1865, James Redpath led a throng of Negro school children to the bleak spot near the city where rested the remains of several hundred Union soldiers in four long trenches. Quietly the ugly mounds were covered with flowers strewn by black hands which knew only that the dead they were honoring had raised them from a condition of servitude.

[4] G. W. Curtis, Address before the New England Society of New York, C. E. Norton (ed.), "Orations and Addresses of George William Curtis" (New York, 1894), I, 129.

The movement spread to the North. The spring of 1866 and that of 1867 witnessed a growing number of ceremonies. The thought occurred to several men prominent in the newly organized Grand Army of the Republic that the practice might well be sponsored by their society. Consequently on May 5, 1868, a general order was issued by the Commander in chief, John A. Logan, designating the thirtieth day of May as a national Memorial Day "for the purpose of strewing with flowers the graves of comrades who died in defense of their country during the late war of the rebellion, and whose bodies lie in almost every city, village, and hamlet church-yard in the land." Soon it was made obligatory for every post to observe the day and for every comrade to attend unless illness prevented. In 1868, the first national Memorial Day, one hundred and three such services were recorded. In 1869 the number grew to three hundred and thirty-six. It was to increase many fold in later years as the Grand Army of the Republic perfected its organization, reaching into every community in the land. In 1873 the legislature of New York designated the thirtieth of May as a legal holiday. Rhode Island did likewise in 1874. Vermont and New Hampshire followed in 1876 and 1877, Wisconsin in 1879, and Massachusetts and Ohio in 1881. Within a decade thereafter every State in the North observed the day as a legal holiday. In the South a Confederate Memorial Day was legalized, but the date of its observance varied.[5]

The holiday thus initiated had an original significance it no longer possesses. The Civil War had saddened virtually

[5] Two fat volumes, "National Memorial Day" (Washington, 1868, 1869), describe the ceremonies held under the auspices of the Grand Army of the Republic on the first and second generally observed Memorial Days. E. Marble, "Origin of Memorial Day," *New England Magazine*, XXXII (1905), 467–470, is typical of the accounts written from memory of personal experiences. Redpath's part is narrated in C. F. Horner, "The Life of James Redpath" (New York, 1926), 111–119. H. L. Matthews and E. E. Rule, *Memorial Day Selections* (Lynn, 1893), is a sample of the many books and pamphlets prepared for school use. The newspapers, especially the *New York Tribune*, annually noted the day in editorials and news stories. Typical of the many magazine sketches is B. Matthews, "A Decoration Day Revery," *Century*, XL (1890), 102–105. Stories like C. F. Woolson, "Rodman the Keeper" (New York, 1880), and S. O. Jewett, "Decoration Day," in "A Native of Winby and Other Tales" (Boston, 1894), show insight into what the day meant to ordinary people. A mass of pamphlet material exists, composed of speeches, programs of ceremonies, poems, and records of the activities of veteran organizations.

every homestead in the land. Few were the persons who could not number among near relatives one who had given his life in the war. It should also be remembered that holidays were not in the seventies so numerous as they have become. A visit to the graves of the dead was not merely a sad rite of remembrance but also a diversion. The excitement of speech-making, the mingling with crowds, the appeal of marching men, the pageantry of school children bearing flowers, and the playing of martial music made Memorial Day a recreational feature in the lives of our mothers and fathers.

It was feared at first that the annual event would prove a permanent reminder of sectional enmity. Could men honor the memory of the fallen, cherish the cause for which the sacrifice had been made, and exhort the living to remember without perpetuating passions that perhaps should be set aside? Indeed no cordiality of sentiment toward erstwhile foes was possible in the early years after Appomattox. Rather there was a tendency to assume that only Federal soldiers deserved remembrance while those who had fought on the losing side should remain unhonored. Occasionally a note of reconciliation was ventured, but it rang hollow and unconvincing. Especially did this appear true at Arlington Cemetery in 1869 where the orator pleaded for a brotherly union between the sections while Union veterans stood guard over the graves of Confederates to prevent flowers being spread over the remains of rebels.

The same contrasting tendencies were revealed in 1867 when Francis Miles Finch published his poem, "The Blue and the Gray." [6] Finch, reading that some women in Mississippi had placed flowers impartially over the graves of Confederate and Union soldiers, was inspired to write what later became the great folk poem of Memorial Day.

> From the silence of sorrowful hours
>   The desolate mourners go,
> Lovingly laden with flowers
>   Alike for the friend and the foe; —
>   Under the sod and the dew,
>   Waiting the judgment day; —
>   Under the roses, the Blue;

[6] First published in *Atlantic Monthly*, XX (1867), 369–370.

Under the lilies, the Gray.
Sadly, but not with upbraiding,
The generous deed was done;
In the storm of the years that are fading,
No braver battle was won: —
Under the sod . . .

No more shall the war-cry sever,
Or the winding rivers be red;
They banish our anger forever
When they laurel the graves of our dead!
Under the sod and the dew,
Waiting the judgment day;
Love and tears for the Blue,
Tears and love for the Gray.

The abrupt appearance of this poem just two years after the war had closed startled a public not yet attuned to its sentiment of mellowed and forgiving sadness.

Yet the fears remained unrealized. Memorial Day was transformed into an agency of reconciliation and school children throughout the land memorized "The Blue and the Gray." From the start vindictiveness and contention played but a minor rôle in the remembrance ceremonies. The inherent pathos of the situation was obvious. Its softening influence was appreciated by the orators called upon to express the public's tribute to the dead. When one such speaker, as early as 1869, stood in a Union cemetery which overlooked a plot in which Confederates were buried, he spoke inevitably of the peaceful repose that had come to the slain soldiers on both sides. As they were now united in death, why, he inquired, "cannot we who survive catch the inspiration which swells the chorus of these who, once estranged, are now forever glorified." [7] Others were ready to dwell upon the similarity of the sacrifice, North and South, that had led to the silent mounds they were now decorating.[8] What could these memorials signify

[7] Mayor Pillsbury, Charleston, S. C., *Magnolia Cemetery* (pamphlet), 6.
[8] A Southern example, Major Thomas G. Jones, *Address at Montgomery, Alabama, 1874* (pamphlet). A Northern example, J. P. Thompson, *Address in New York, 1870*, reported in the *New York Tribune*, May 31, 1870.

except that war had bound together all in a common destiny that must be sealed in friendship?

While expressions of fraternity might in time have grown commonplace, it was a strong desire to escape the partisan excesses of Reconstruction that first produced a popular enthusiasm for Memorial Day as a means of reconciliation. In 1874 and 1875 the public showed an ever-growing interest in the new phenomenon of Northern and Southern soldiers cordially coöperating in honoring the dead of either side. "Only a little while ago," noted the *Tribune* in 1874, "many people of the North regarded it dangerous and criminal" for the South to decorate its graves. Now officers and men of the United States army stationed in the South were taking part in the ceremonies for the Southern dead, while Southern women did not refrain from scattering their flowers on Union graves.[9]

In 1875 the editor of the *Boston Daily Advertiser* felicitated himself with the observation that "all now esteem themselves Union men." Looking over the country he found that in Cincinnati the committee on arrangements for Memorial Day had sent a formal invitation to an association of officers of the Southern army to participate in honoring the dead of both sides. The invitation had been accepted, and the speeches delivered on the occasion were characterized by a "fraternal and charitable spirit that is a satisfaction to contemplate." At Sandusky, Ohio, the graves of both Union and Confederate soldiers on Johnson's Island were decorated by Union veterans, while in Louisville, Secretary B. H. Bristow delivered an address that caused comment for its eloquent tribute to the Southern soldiery. In Memphis the Confederate generals, Forrest and Pillow, participated in the Union ceremonies. But the scene that evokes a passing smile for its conscious effort to convince a doubting world occurred in Little Rock, Arkansas. A holiday having been declared, all places of business were closed and a large portion of the population, white and black, moved out to the cemetery to witness a joint service commemorating both Confederates and Unionists. The speakers' platform had been erected to overlap portions of both the ad-

[9] *New York Tribune*, April 29, 1874. The editorial is entitled "Peace in the Graveyard."

joining cemeteries. A Northerner therefore could speak from Confederate ground, while a Southerner could stand over soil consecrated to the Union veterans. The climax was reached when an ex-Confederate buried a hatchet in the Union cemetery, while a Union veteran did likewise in the Confederate cemetery.[10]

In seeking a reason for the "significant fact" that the incident of the Memorial Day exercises most commented on by the public was the fraternizing of former foes, the *Tribune* found it in the strong desire of the people to be friends again. "Politicians may have their own ends to serve in probing the still gaping wounds, but the great mass of intelligent Christian people in both the South and North are heartily glad of any occasion which brings them together . . . or gives them a chance to show kindly feelings."[11] Wearied of the partisan excesses into which they had been led by the difficulties of Reconstruction, not yet knowing the solution, yet conscious that the implied hostility and hatred were not of their seeking, the people of the mid-seventies found in Memorial Day an escape through which they could express their yearning for sectional peace. The holiday thus took on a significance it never fully lost.

The essence of Memorial Day in relation to reconciliation was its appeal to sympathy. North and South the sacrifice of war had led to a common meeting place, the cemetery, where strife and bitterness were hushed in death. On the Confederate monument in Columbia, South Carolina, an inscription may be found which reads, "Let their virtues plead for the just judgment of the cause in which they perished." It was the silent pleading of the dead that softened the asperities in living hearts. A leaven of forgiveness was introduced which in time permeated the entire national life.

In another respect the sections were nearer together than surface trends seemed to indicate. This was in regard to am-

[10] *Boston Daily Advertiser*, June 2, 1875. See also *New York Times*, May 31, 1875, for Bristow's address, *New York Tribune*, May 31, 1875, for Forrest's remarks.
[11] *New York Tribune*, May 30, 1876. Sample addresses are C. A. Bartol in Boston, 1874 (pamphlet), R. A. Pryor in Brooklyn, 1877, and Henry Watterson in Nashville, 1877 (*New York Tribune*, May 31, 1877).

nesty. The Confederate was susceptible to a variety of penalties. In addition to the general liability to a charge of treason for taking up arms against the Federal Government, the Confiscation Act of 1862 annexed penalties of property losses. The President, however, was granted power to amnesty offenders by proclamation and both Lincoln and Johnson liberally exercised ·the pardoning power. Johnson brought an end to all liability under this head by granting a full and complete pardon to all Confederates for the "crime" of waging war against the United States. Henceforth no Southerner was in jeopardy in person or in property. Even Davis, as has been seen, was released under this proclamation.

The Fourteenth Amendment, on the other hand, placed the former Confederate in a condition of political disability. The third section read as follows:

No person shall be a Senator or Representative in Congress, or elector of President and Vice-President, or hold any office, civil or military, under the United States, or under any State, who having previously taken an oath, as a member of Congress, or as an officer of the United States or as a member of any State legislature, or as an executive or judicial officer of any State, to support the Constitution of the United States, shall have engaged in insurrection or rebellion against the same, or given aid or comfort to the enemies thereof.

Probably less than one hundred thousand Southerners were placed under disabilities by this Amendment.[12] Inasmuch as Congress was empowered by a vote of two thirds of each House to remove disabilities the question of amnesty after 1868 became a matter for Congressional debate.

That the bark of the North was worse than its bite was

[12] Any such estimate is at best a guess because of the impossibility of ascertaining how many State officials had taken an oath supporting the Federal Constitution. Curiously enough the only estimate made in Congress was very vague. Senator Ferry, Republican, of Connecticut, made an estimate of fifty thousand at the lowest to three hundred thousand at the highest. A Washington correspondent of the *New York Tribune,* May 23, 1872, estimated that the Amnesty Act of 1872 relieved 150,000 Confederates, leaving from three hundred to five hundred still under disability. Rhodes somewhat uncritically accepts this figure as a basis for saying that between 150,000 and 160,000 individuals were excluded from holding office by the Fourteenth Amendment. Rhodes, "History of the United States," VI, 329.

quickly indicated by the large number of special amnesty bills passed by Congress. That the Southern pride was not so haughty as represented was suggested by the large number of prominent Confederates who petitioned and were granted amnesty.

The first acts of amnesty were passed during the second session of the Fortieth Congress even before the Amendment was proclaimed in force on July 28, 1868.[18] Thus an act of June 25 pardoned a group of more than one thousand individuals, an act of July 20, approximately three hundred, and an act of July 27, twenty. It is certainly true that the bulk of these early petitioners were "scalawags" needed for purposes of building up the Republican party in the South. Among the more important persons who were relieved of their disabilities by the Fortieth Congress were General James Longstreet, Joseph C. Brown, of Georgia, J. L. Alcorn, Reconstruction Governor of Mississippi, R. F. Bullock, Reconstruction Governor of Georgia, W. W. Holden, Reconstruction Governor of North Carolina, and F. J. Moses, the later notorious Radical of South Carolina.

The partisan spirit in which the Fortieth Congress acted on amnesty seemed to promise little good for sectional peace. Time and time again the Republican majority, which was more than the two thirds required by the Constitution, insisted that the only test was the petitioner's complete accord with the Reconstruction program of the Radicals. Even Senator Trumbull agreed to this, saying on February 16, 1869, that "I shall not be prepared to vote for any bill that will remove disabilities from that class of persons [non-Republicans] within any period that I can contemplate." On the other hand the Democrats bitterly assailed the selfishness of this attitude, and clamored for an act of general amnesty that would qualify members of their party as well as those of their opponents.

The Forty-first Congress, which sat in three sessions during the period from March 4, 1869, to March 4, 1871, relieved more than three thousand individuals and made distinct progress toward achieving a more liberal policy. For the first time

[18] My account of amnesty is based on the debates reported in the *Congressional Globe*, Fortieth, Forty-first, and Forty-second Congresses.

resolutions were introduced seeking general amnesty and received powerful support from prominent Republicans, notably
Senators Ferry of Connecticut and Seward of Nevada and
Representative Farnsworth of Illinois. These men pointed to
the waste of time involved as well as the inability of Congress
carefully to scrutinize the many bills presented for individual
amnesty. They also argued that the disqualification from holding office was incorporated in the Fourteenth Amendment not
as punishment but as a guarantee of public safety. In this respect they felt it had gone too far. Public safety did not require
the exclusion of more than a few leaders. Meanwhile a wider
disqualification was operating as an irritant which drove the
South into blind resistance of all Reconstruction measures. It
was also probably true that opinion in the North was definitely
in favor of sweeping away the disability except in very few
cases.

A new and unsuspected demand for general amnesty appeared in this same Congress from Southern Republicans, who
wanted all disabilities removed in order to deprive their opponents in the South of what was proving a powerful political
weapon. The threads of Southern politics in Reconstruction
years were much too complicated to permit of many easy
generalizations. But it seems true that the Republican Congressmen from Alabama, Arkansas, Louisiana, Tennessee, and
North Carolina, during 1869 and 1870 were actively seeking
a bill of general amnesty and that Southern Republicans were
the most liberal members of their party on this issue.

A combination of influences — pressure of public opinion,
increased strength of the Democratic minority as a result of
the Congressional elections of 1870, the rise of the Liberal
Republican movement, and a growing feeling among Republicans that the extensive disqualification of Southerners had
been a tactical error — made possible the passage of a general
amnesty bill through the House of Representatives during the
first session of the Forty-second Congress, which sat from
March 4 to May 27, 1871. Beck, Democrat, of Kentucky,
on March 9 introduced a bill for the removal of legal and
political disabilities from all persons affected by the Fourteenth Amendment. The impossibility of securing a two thirds

majority for so liberal a measure, however, influenced him
to accept an amendment by Poland, Republican, of Vermont,
which excepted from amnesty members of Congress and Army
and Navy officers who withdrew from their offices to support
the Confederacy, and also the men who had voted for ordinances of secession. The measure was debated on March 14
with Poland speaking vigorously for its passage. The vote on
the measure revealed 120 in favor, 82 opposed and 21 not voting. Inasmuch as a two thirds majority was wanting the bill
failed. The Republican division was 32 for, 82 against, and
16 not voting, while the Democrats stood 88 for, none against,
and 5 not voting.

Shortly after the defeat of the Beck bill, Hale, Republican,
of Maine, introduced a second bill of general amnesty, with
exactly the same exceptions contained as in the Beck bill but
with an additional requirement that the beneficiary of amnesty
should take an oath supporting the Constitution of the United
States. The bill was passed without debate by more than the
required two thirds majority on April 10, one hundred and
thirty-four voting in favor while forty-six opposed and forty-
seven did not vote. The bill was sent to the Senate, however,
too late for action during the short session.

When Congress reconvened for a second time in December
it was met by a message from President Grant urging the
enactment of a measure providing general amnesty. The
Senate immediately began discussing the Hale bill. It seemed
certain that Senators would bow to the now prevailing sentiment for leniency. "We are now in circumstances which render it necessary to render relief," confessed one Radical who
would have preferred to see no bars let down, "a necessity
forced upon us by the overflowing and superabundant sympathy of generous conquerors for misguided public enemies."

The smooth momentum of the bill towards passage, however,
was utterly destroyed when Charles Sumner endeavored to at-
tach to amnesty a Supplementary Civil Rights bill which provided equal civil (actually social) rights to Negroes in railroad cars, theaters, inns, cemeteries and churches. Staunch
Republicans like Conkling and Edmunds, who had never been
in sympathy with amnesty, came to the support of Sumner's

measure, realizing that if the Civil Rights bill were tacked
to the Hale bill Democrats would never accept it and it would
therefore be defeated. As Trumbull who favored the Hale bill
said, every person in heart opposed to amnesty voted for the
Sumner amendment while friends of amnesty voted against it.
The vote on the amendment was an even division with Vice-
President Colfax casting the decisive vote in its favor. The
vote on the combined amnesty–civil-rights bill was thirty-three
in favor, nineteen opposed — two less than the required two
thirds majority.

A storm of protest met the Senate's action. The Hale bill
was passed again by the House and sent to the Senate for
consideration. Once more Sumner, this time supported by
Sherman, succeeded in tacking on his amendment and again the
combined measure failed.

The Grant party leaders, unwilling to face the coming Presidential campaign without an amnesty bill enacted, now took
command of the situation. Benjamin Butler, determined to take
the amnesty issue out of politics, presented a final bill in the
House where it passed easily on May 13, 1872, "the best and
most liberal bill on this subject that has ever been passed by
this House." The Senate this time rejected Sumner's plea, and
passed on May 22 the Butler bill without amendment by a vote
of thirty-eight in favor to two opposed.

The General Amnesty Act of 1872 reduced the number of
Southerners disqualified from holding office to less than five
hundred men and probably the number was not far in excess
of two hundred and fifty.[14] Almost immediately special acts
began to be passed removing disabilities from individuals still
excluded. Zebulon B. Vance, for example, was granted amnesty

[14] Fifteen former Senators were excluded, among them being, Davis, Clay
of Alabama, Mallory, Toombs, Benjamin, and Hunter of Virginia. Twenty-
five former Representatives were excluded, among them, Curry, Lamar,
Vance, Reagan, Pryor. One Supreme Court Justice remained excluded,
John A. Campbell. Among prominent military officers still excluded were
Generals J. E. Johnston, Beauregard, Bragg, Pemberton, Hood, D. H. Hill,
Ewell, Early, Fitzhugh Lee, and Hardee. Among former Confederates who
after 1872 were to occupy important Federal offices whose disabilities were
removed by the Act of 1872 were A. H. Stephens, Wade Hampton, B. H. Hill,
and A. H. Garland. Prominent among those whose disabilities were removed
by special act after 1872 were Lamar, Curry, Vance and Reagan. See *New
York Tribune*, May 23, 1872.

by this same Congress by act of June 10, 1872. Within the next eight years Congress removed disqualifications from more than one hundred Southerners excluded by the Act of 1872. It became a truism that any man the South elected to office could, if he needed it, receive amnesty from Congress, Jefferson Davis alone excepted.

Thus pressure of public sentiment won an important concession and one hurt of Reconstruction was early remedied. But in a more positive manner amnesty also proved wise statesmanship. It permitted the return to national life of the respected and natural leaders of the South. Excluded from office their careers were narrow, crabbed and unreconciled. Brought back to participate in national affairs a broader and more constructive view of politics and Southern future became characteristic of their attitude.

The first fruits of amnesty in this sense appeared in the career of L. Q. C. Lamar, of Mississippi. During the early years of Reconstruction the proscribed Lamar was bitterly unreconciled, clinging to prejudice, and passionately resistant to Northern influences.[15] But in November 1872, although still excluded by the Act of 1872, he was elected to Congress as a Democrat. Immediately new horizons opened. Lamar's ambition was quickened. Without hesitation he asked the Republicans of Mississippi to favor a bill before Congress granting him relief from disabilities. "You may be assured of one thing," he wrote, "I am a patriot — that is, my heart beats with more fidelity to the interest and happiness of the American people, and to the principles of public and individual freedom, than it does to my own tranquillity." [16] The change in Lamar was not hypocrisy, but the difference between enforced banishment and the privilege of participating in a world he understood.

But another barrier still remained. In Washington Lamar found distrust of Southerners a hampering influence. "Is this not an appalling spectacle?" he wrote privately to a friend. "On

[15] *Cf.* Lamar's speech before the Agricultural Association of Carroll and Choctaw Counties, Mississippi, 1870, and his Letter on the death of Lee, 1870, both quoted in Mayes, "Lamar," 129–131, 658. An excellent recent biography of Lamar is W. A. Cate's "Lucius Q. C. Lamar" (Chapel Hill, 1935).
[16] Mayes, "Lamar," 175.

the one hand a brave, impulsive, but too sensitive people full of potent life and patriotic fire, ready — aye, eager — to abide with knightly honor the award of the bloody arbitrament to which they appealed; and yet, as if dumb, unable to speak intelligibly their thought and purpose. On the other hand a great and powerful section, . . . flushed with victory and success, but full of generous and maganimous feeling toward their vanquished brethren; and they too, as if under some malign spell, speaking only words of bitterness, hate, and threatenings. He indeed would be a patriot and benefactor who could awake them from their profound egotism and say with effectual command: 'My countrymen, know one another.' For then nature herself with her mighty voice would exclaim: 'Love one another.' " [17] To play this rôle of patriot benefactor became so strong a desire in Lamar's ambition as almost to be an obsession.

For months Lamar labored with the idea of making a great speech that would bring the estranged North and South together. Quietly he perfected the phraseology, seeking especially words that would not cause offense. Reflection, for example, suggested that the description of the North "as if under some malign spell, speaking only words of bitterness, hate, and threatenings," might arouse the ire of those he sought to pacify. So out it went and in its place was substituted, "as if mastered by some mysterious spell, silencing her better impulses, her words and acts are the words and acts of suspicion and distrust." Word for word, idea by idea, the project was carefully deliberated. So perfect was the preparation that when the opportunity for the great gesture came it had the final mark of supreme artistry. It seemed the spontaneous outpouring of a generous heart.

Such a speech required a dramatic setting. The opportunity for which Lamar was patiently preparing came in March 1874 when Sumner died and the Senate invited the Mississippian to deliver a memorial address in honor of the Massachusetts statesman. The eulogy which Lamar delivered had all the essentials of a great oration. If words could reconcile, it would have made the sections one. Praise for Sumner, the great

[17] *Ibid.*, 182. The letter was written July 15, 1872.

protagonist of the Union and of Negro equality, and emphasis
on the nobility of his efforts, were joined with a picture of the
South, noble also in its aspirations, defeated and knowing suffering, yet loyal to the restored Union.

I see on both sides only the seeming of a constraint, which each
apparently hestitates to dismiss. The South — prostrated, exhausted, drained of her lifeblood, as well as of her material resources, yet still honorable and true — accepts the bitter award
of the bloody arbitrament without reservation, resolutely determined to abide the result with chivalrous fidelity; yet as if struck
dumb by the magnitude of her reverses, she suffers on in silence.
The North, exultant in her triumph, and elated by success, still
cherishes, as we are assured, a heart full of magnanimous emotions for her disarmed and discomfited antagonist; and yet, as
if mastered by some mysterious spell, silencing her better impulses, her words and acts are the words and acts of suspicion
and distrust.
Would that the spirit of the illustrious dead whom we lament
today could speak from the grave to both parties to this deplorable discord in tones which should reach each and every heart
throughout this broad territory: "My countrymen! know one
another, and you will love one another." [18]

There is no gainsaying the personal triumph Lamar achieved,
with Blaine weeping in the Speaker's chair, and "bloody shirt"
newspapers throughout the North raising a chorus of praise.
But Lamar did not, as his biographer seemed inclined to believe, close the chasm between the sections. The real significance
of the eulogy was that it gave Lamar national status as a
reconciler. For the remainder of his life he devoted his chief
energies to the removal of misunderstanding between North
and South.[19]
If this was true of Lamar it was also true of the great number of former Confederates whom a liberal policy of amnesty
made possible to return to Congress. Republicans attempted to
make political capital of the "Confederate Brigadiers" in politics. But a careful examination of their conduct in Congress

---

[18] Mayes, "Lamar," 186.
[19] For typical speeches see *ibid.*, 218–223, 294–297, 673, 686.

and of their addresses before the public invariably reveals this group to be one of the most reconciled elements in the country.[20]

But it is doubtful whether any man in public life could inspire confidence enough in the unselfishness of his objectives to make headway in the removal of distrust between the sections. Misunderstanding rested upon deep and basic convictions. In some way it was these which had to be reached and changed. It is important, therefore, to note that one of the most constructive forces making for peace in this period was the beginning of better reporting of the South.

Newspapers, magazines, and publishing houses poured out a steady flood of articles and books descriptive of all phases of Southern life and problems. Most notable of the reports made in the 1870's were Robert Somers' "The Southern States Since the War," published in 1871, Edward King's "The Southern States," published serially in *Scribner's Monthly Magazine* during 1873 and 1874 and in book form in 1875, J. S. Pike's "The Prostrate South," published in 1874, and Charles Nordhoff's "The Cotton States in the Spring and Summer of 1875," published first as a series of letters in the *New York Herald* during 1875 and then in book form in 1876.

Somers' book lost some influence in the North because it was known that he was an Englishman who sympathized with the South during the war. Yet the "Southern States Since the War" was impartial and intelligent in tone and was based upon diligent and accurate observation. Somers' attitude was marked by modesty and restraint both in criticism and in praise. He pointed out the ignorance of the blacks, their need for education, and their incapacity for participation in government. But while he never hesitated to place stricture on carpetbag politics his chief message was optimism concerning what he pictured as the bright economic future of the South.

More elaborate was the "Great South Series" prepared by

[20] Notably true of B. H. Hill, A. H. Garland, W. Hampton, H. A. Herbert, J. H. Reagan, A. H. Stephens, Z. B. Vance, G. C. Vest, E. Walthall, and J. Wheeler. In the Congress of 1876, nine senators and forty-three representatives had seen service in the Confederate armies. The late seventies and early eighties witnessed the greatest number of "Confederate Brigadiers" in Congress. Typical delegations of this period were Alabama's eight Confederate veterans in eight Congressional seats in 1878, Georgia's seven in eight in 1878, and Arkansas' five in five in 1883.

Edward King for *Scribner's Monthly Magazine. Scribner's,* under the editorship of Dr. J. G. Holland, was the most energetic of the monthly periodicals of the seventies. King, who had served under Bowles on the *Springfield Republican* and had "covered" the Franco-Prussian war and the Commune disorders in Paris as a war correspondent, was one of the ablest of the younger American journalists. Accompanied by an illustrator, J. Wells Champney of the *Scribner's* staff, King spent all of 1873 and most of 1874 on an extensive tour of the South. The result was a series of profusely illustrated articles which filled an average of forty pages of each issue of *Scribner's* for two years. The book published from these articles was a volume of eight hundred large pages.

The preparation of this series was an enterprise of unprecedented size by an American periodical. King and Champney were instructed by Holland to "exhibit, by pen and pencil, a vast region almost as little known to the Northern States of the Union as it is to England." And they were to make their observations "sympathetically" so that the reader would be informed of the social, economic, and geographic features of the South.

The central theme of King's reporting was that if the South were treated fairly by the North prosperity would speedily return to a region of vast material resources. "Of course I encountered many bitter people," he wrote, "but these were certainly the exceptions. The citizens [of the South], . . . as a class are as loyal to the idea of the Union today as are the citizens of New York." Chapter by chapter the series piled up an overwhelming mass of evidence pointing to the evil results of Reconstruction. King also had his eyes open to the economic possibilities of the South, discussing such opportunities as the marl deposits of South Carolina, the iron deposits of Alabama, and the development of Southern health resorts. Once the "dreary transition period" was over he predicted the area would enjoy great opulence. Adding greatly to the popular effectiveness of the work were the more than four hundred sketches of Southern character and scenery drawn by Champney. Commenting editorially upon the conclusion of the "Great South Series," Holland justly took "no ordinary pride and satisfaction" in the completion "of a task undertaken with the desire to enlighten our country concerning itself, and to spread before the nation the wonderful natural resources, the social condition, and the political complications of a region which needs but just, wise and generous legislation, with responding good-will and industry, to make it a garden of happiness and prosperity."

J. S. Pike during the fifties had been the very capable Washington correspondent of the *New York Tribune,* and from 1861 to 1866 he had served the United States as minister resident at The Hague. His background was Republican and abolitionist. During the months of February and March he visited South Carolina and observed the State legislature in session. From this experience he wrote an effective little book conveying his first hand impressions to the public. "The Prostrate State: South Carolina under Negro Government," caught a vivid picture of radical Reconstruction at the moment and in the place of its grotesque flood tide of corruption. The book in no sense developed a theory of Reconstruction or gave a balanced view. But it did present a selection of facts freshly witnessed so colorfully as to fix permanently its picture as the one most remembered of all that have emerged from Reconstruction literature. The "Africanization of South Carolina" as the acme of misgovernment, corruption, and injustice became a tradition, carrying with it the conclusion Pike suggested,—"Is it not time to bring to an end the punishment of the innocent many for the crimes of the guilty few?"

While King reached best the popular level, and Pike played most effectively with the emotions, Charles Nordhoff gave the ablest analysis of Southern conditions. One of the most scholarly newspaper men the United States has known, Nordhoff during the war years had been the managing editor of the *New York Evening Post,* a strong Unionist, and an advocate of Negro betterment. From 1874 to 1890 he served, with freedom to develop his own projects, as Washington editor of the *New York Herald.* During the 1870's he performed two notable assignments of high journalistic merit. His "Communistic Societies in the United States" was published in 1875, and in 1876 appeared "The Cotton States in the Spring and Summer of 1875."

Nordhoff wrote without passion or excitement. He probed beneath the frothy surface of Reconstruction into a calmer analysis of the deeper and truer currents of Southern life. His "forty-two conclusions" were a complete negation of the "bloody shirt" attack. He forecast an optimistic social and economic future for the South.

These four studies of the South were the most influential of the period. They commanded the widest reading public and they were treated with greatest respect by reviewers. There was in none of their pages the expression of any sentiment which did not tend to soften the Northern attitude toward the South and thus make for better understanding. What was true of them was generally true of the great mass of material which found its way into print. *Harper's, Lippincott's, Appletons',* and the *Atlantic* vied with *Scribner's* in reporting Southern scenes.[21] The net result of this activity was to convey a new impression of the South to the North. In general it was maintained that Southerners were amicably disposed to the Union and that sectional bitterness was declining rather than increasing. A note of pathos, some pity, and understanding of what burden the white South was carrying, also entered for the first time in the Northern outlook. And finally the emphasis upon the economic potentialities of the South was offered as an indication of the way in which the two sections might be brought together.

When one looks back to the journalism of 1865 and 1866 it can be appreciated that something of a revolution had been accomplished in this reporting of the South. The earlier reporters had considered it "news" to describe a South that was disgruntled, rebellious, and unregenerate. The Negro had been the hero and the Southern white the villain. But while Republican orators still played upon these themes, the editors of newspapers and magazines apparently sensed among Northern readers a demand for narratives which sympathetically por-

[21] Most significant of the articles on the South prepared for these magazines were those written by Sidney Lanier, George Fitzhugh, E. A. Pollard, J. W. De Forest, E. De Leon, C. D. Deshler, G. C. Eggleston, T. W. Higginson, and N. S. Shaler.

trayed the Southern white society in its efforts to achieve a richer participation in the national life.

The emotional yearning for peace reached a climax in the series of centennial celebrations recalling the progress of the Revolution which began in 1875 and continued until 1881. The major event in the cycle was the great exposition held in Philadelphia during the summer of 1876 to commemorate the centenary of independence. But even closer to the life of the ordinary citizen and remarkable for the sustained interest shown in them were the innumerable observances of lesser centennials.

The observances were intended to be more than fitting memorials of the nation's birth. They were to harmonize a country estranged by Civil War. "Let us see to it, North and South," asserted an editor of *Scribner's,* "that the Centennial heals all the old wounds, reconciles all the old differences, and furnishes the occasion for such a reunion of the great American nationality as shall make our celebration an expression of fraternal good will among all sections and all states." [22] The *New York Tribune* undertook to warn "all fools, bigots, and scheming politicians" that there would be no room for sectional hate and bitterness while both sections were commemorating their common origin.[23] Many hoped that a national sentiment would be aroused in the South. Others suggested that the North too had concessions to make before the desired results could be attained. It was generally expected that the decade of historical reminiscence upon which the United States was about to venture would intensify the national spirit and create a consciousness of sectional interdependence and community of interest.

A handsome gesture on the part of Charleston, South Carolina, Confederate veterans before the Lexington celebration struck a note of good feeling at the start. In the assault on Fort Wagner the Fifty-fourth Massachusetts regiment of Negro soldiers led by Robert Gould Shaw had lost its battle flag. The South had bitterly resented the use of Negro troops,

[22] *Scribner's Monthly,* XX (1875), 510. See also *Harper's Weekly,* July 3, 1875; and *Nation,* June 3, 1875.
[23] *New York Tribune,* Jan. 1, July 3, 1876.

while Massachusetts had placed Shaw, killed in combat, high
on its list of heroes. Consequently when the Charlestonians
now voluntarily returned the lost flag the deed was warmly
applauded in Boston. "I deem it decorous," wrote the Southern
officer who tendered the trophy, "if not a positive duty, to
promote the oblivion of the animosities which led to and were
engendered by the war." [24]

The note of reconciliation dominated the observances at Lexington and Concord in the spring of 1875. Governor Chamberlain of South Carolina appeared to remind the people of
Massachusetts of the friendship and coöperation that existed
between the two States during the Revolutionary period. The
Governor of Massachusetts in reply assured all that the hearts
of the two States beat again in unison. Skeptics, however,
might entertain doubt as to the sincerity of these assertions,
since one came from a carpetbagger unloved in the South and
the other from a Democrat. But when the toast, "The North
and the South," was offered a soldier responded against whom
no charge of insincerity could be made. General Francis Bartlett, the youthful possessor of an heroic record in the Union
army, assailed the "selfish and excessive partisanship" which
divided the country and for which all who had fought in the
war had unmixed contempt. "As an American," he continued,
"I am as proud of the men who charged so bravely with Pickett's
division on our lines at Gettysburg, as I am of the men who so
bravely met and repulsed them there." He concluded by suggesting to the sons of men who fought for conscience against
their government in 1775 that they should be the first to forgive men who also fought for conscience in 1863. The bold
novelty of these opinions just ten years after the Civil War
had ended found a ready response in the sentiment of the
moment and made Bartlett the outstanding figure of the celebration.

Two months later Boston observed the anniversary of Bunker Hill with excitement keyed to an even greater pitch. The

[24] *Boston Daily Advertiser*, April 5, 1875. My account of the celebrations
at Boston, Lexington, Concord, and Bunker Hill is based upon the *Advertiser*,
April 5, 20, June 17, 18, 1875; *Nation*, June 24, 1875; *Harper's Weekly*,
June 12 ,1875; and F. W. Palfrey, "Memoir of William Francis Bartlett"
(Boston, 1878), 260.

focus of attention was the presence of military companies, composed largely of former Confederates, from Virginia and South Carolina. On the evening before the celebration a "peace and good will" meeting was held in which courtesies were cordially exchanged between representatives of North and South. All spoke of a common country and a common heritage. The redoubtable Fitzhugh Lee was presented "amid the wildest enthusiasm. A perfect babel of applause rose from the vast audience. The men threw their hats into the air and yelled themselves hoarse, while the ladies in the galleries waved their handkerchiefs and clapped their hands in patriotic fervor and sisterly affection."

The next morning the Confederates joined the procession of fifty thousand marching men that paraded through the streets of Boston to Charlestown and the Bunker Hill monument. It was soberly reported that an eminent physician who once had refused the sale of his respirators in the South, unwilling to stop the progress of tubercles in pro-slavery lungs, now, under stress of excitement, eagerly came forward to shake the hands of erstwhile rebels. When the Southerners paid a visit to Harvard University, President Eliot reminded them of the many names from their section honorably engraved upon the college records. Prompt was the answer he received: Might the college "hereafter promote, as in the past, not the greatness only, but the unity of the nation."

The reader may draw his own inferences as to the significance of remarks thus made under the contagious influence of mass excitement. It may, however, be noted that Charles Eliot Norton, not unduly affected by passing fancy, observed privately that in his opinion the peace making was genuine, the actors sincere, and the effect throughout the country instant and great.[25] Beneath the hyperbole of stimulated imagination the desire to reconcile showed deep and strong. "Mere politicians," as Norton was quick to observe, might be surprised at the strange behavior of their constituents. It seemed to others that the prophecy of Lincoln — "The mystic chords of memory, stretching from every battlefield and patriotic grave to every

[25] S. Norton and M. A. DeW. Howe (eds.), "Letters of Charles Eliot Norton" (Boston, 1913), II, 55.

living heart and hearthstone all over this broad land, will yet swell the chorus of the Union when again touched, as surely they will be, by the better angels of our nature" — was coming true.

It was shortly thereafter that James Russell Lowell, who had fought so long and so sturdily from the days of Hosea Biglow through the Civil War and postwar decade, made public his conversion to the gospel of peace and forgiveness. On July 3 Cambridge, Massachusetts, observed the event of Washington's taking command of the Continental army. Lowell was chosen to write the ode commemorating the event. With a consciousness of purpose almost naïve, he "took advantage of the occasion to hold out a hand of kindly reconciliation to Virginia." Closing his mind to the strife of his own times, he returned to the "Age of the Fathers," and the common hero Washington. The burden of the poem is revealed in its concluding lines.

> Virginia gave us this imperial man,
>
> .   .   .   .
>
> What shall we give her back, but love and praise
> As in the dear old unestrangéd days
> Before the inevitable wrong began?
> Mother of States and undiminished men,
> Thou gavest us a country, giving him,
> And we owe alway what we owed thee then.
>
> .   .   .   .
>
> Across more recent graves,
>
> .   .   .   .
>
> We from this consecrated plain stretch out
> Our hands. . . .
> Through battle we have better learned thy worth,
> The long-breathed valor and undaunted will,
> Which, like his own, the day's disaster done,
> Could, safe in manhood, suffer and be still.
> Both thine and ours the victory hardly won;
> If ever with distempered voice or pen
> We have misdeemed thee, here we take it back.
> Be to us evermore as thou wast then.

While the people of the North were thus participating enthusiastically the situation in the South was somewhat different. In the year of the centennial John C. Reed, a Georgian, published a pamphlet which aptly portrayed the Southern attitude toward the nation's birthday. He contrasted the "vast and happy population" of the North, her "great material prosperity and the fresh fame of a world renowned success," with the South suffering the "pangs of a sudden impoverishment and the incalculable discomfort of complete economic unsettlement." It was proper, he observed, for the North to exult, but the South should not be expected to rejoice greatly over a nation preserved at the cost of her recent defeat. Preoccupied with the work of "doing painfully the slow task of repairing lost fortunes; . . . striving to make homes pleasant again and to give . . . children a fair hope in the land," the South had little energy or interest in celebration. And yet "these intent workers, who are most of them scarred Confederate veterans — even if they will not say it loudly — have come to hold in steadfast faith that it is far better the Blue Cross fell, and the American Union stands forever unchallengeable hereafter." [26]

Much as it was hoped that the nation might be brought together at Philadelphia "to meet and embrace as brothers," [27] not many Southerners attended the Centennial Exhibition during the summer of 1876, and the industry of that section was meagerly represented. Impoverishment and preoccupation with the lingering evils of Reconstruction might suffice to explain the absence of Southerners. But more fundamental was the nonexistence in the South of the spirit which gave to the international exposition its significance in the North. During and after the war the North had been making tremendous strides along the road of economic revolution. The war itself had been an indication of her greatly increased power; the exposition was to be an appreciation of the fact. Northerners might take pride in the hundred years' development from feeble colonies to a powerful nation that was still moving on to an even greater future. But Southern social and economic life was not yet integrated to that development, and the South could share none of the optimism it created. Rather it seemed to her that the North in fact was becoming the nation, and she an appanage. The centennial came in due season for the North to

[26] John C. Reed, "The Old South and the New" (New York, 1876).
[27] *Scribner's Monthly*, XI (1876), 433.

rejoice, but for the South it was still premature. Yet wistfully the South looked on, and when Sidney Lanier, one of her dearest sons, was chosen to write the Cantata sung on that glorious Fourth of July celebration of 1876 her heart responded to his earnest faith in a beneficent American nationality.[28]

But it was something that the spirit of the centennial was one of reconciliation and pride in a common Americanism. The orators who throughout the summer mounted the exposition's platform reiterated the sentiment, while newspapers and periodicals conveyed the message to their readers. When winter came the Exhibition closed its gates, but celebrations of more local events continued and the theme was repeated with infinite variations.[29] In October 1881 the end appeared in sight as North and South again united to commemorate the surrender of Cornwallis at Yorktown. A representative of the former section, Robert C. Winthrop, was chosen to deliver the oration, while Virginia's unofficial laureate, James Barron Hope, wrote the ode. The address developed the familiar pattern. Winthrop yearned for the restoration of the old relations of amity and good will which were supposed to have existed in the days of the fathers. He eulogized Washington, and he prayed that the present occasion would aid in the work of reconciliation. So too the former Confederate, Hope, pleaded in typical reconciliation verse:

> Give us back the ties of Yorktown!
> Perish all the modern hates!
> Let us stand together, brothers,
> In defiance of the Fates;
> For the safety of the Union
> Is the safety of the States![30]

The centennial celebrations were not significant for what they accomplished so much as for what they illustrated. The yearning for peace broke out in open emotion in which North

[28] "Letters of Sidney Lanier" (New York, 1899), II, 28-29.
[29] The ceremonies at Philadelphia are fully described in U. S. Centennial Commission, *International Exhibition of 1876, Reports* (Washington, 1880-1884). For a typical address at one of the lesser centennials see Curtis, *Orations*, II, 168.
[30] R. C. Winthrop, "Addresses and Speeches, 1878-1886" (Boston, 1886), 297-348; J. B. Hope, "Arms and the Man," in "Poems of James Barron Hope" (Richmond, 1895), 89-131.

and South expressed their attachment to the Union and medi-
tated on its value. Once expressed the phenomenon assumed
greater strength. Consequently the long cycle of observances
with its repetition of a simple truth left stronger in the end
the force which first had called it into being. Nor would the
old reports of sectional hostility ever again sound quite so
plausible to men who had relished a feast of love where words,
at least, of peace had gone the rounds.

The nightmare of Reconstruction was still fresh in mind,
its legacy of discord lingered, when tragedy again revealed
this bond of sympathy underlying the hostility of the divided
sections. During the summer months of 1878 yellow fever
obtained a foothold in the lower Mississippi Valley and developed into an epidemic of unprecedented malignity and duration. The fever raged with especial virulence in New Orleans
and Memphis. Cities along the Gulf from Mobile to Galveston were placed under quarantine. Steamship transportation
on the Mississippi was paralyzed and the operation of railroads entering New Orleans discontinued. A state of panic
prevailed which together with the bereavement of widespread
death and the impoverishment resulting from disrupted industry made the epidemic one of the major misfortunes of
the decade.

Thus an opportunity appeared for the American people to
apply in peacetime the lesson they had learned during the
Civil War in regard to organized relief work on a large scale.
No sooner had the appeal for aid been issued than communities throughout the North responded. Editors and clergymen
urged the necessity of liberal contributions. Organizations for
the collection, distribution, and administration of materials
were formed. Nurses and physicians were marshaled. Such
activity is the normal accompaniment of disaster nowadays.
In 1878 it was a revelation of humanitarian energy. And it
came from a people who had recently been at war with those
befriended.

So prompt and sincere a demonstration of sympathy on
the part of the North went far in convincing the South that
something else than sectional antipathy thrived in the land of
"Black Republicanism." Jefferson Davis wrote privately from

his retirement in Mississippi, close to the center of the fever district, that the "noble generosity of the Northern people in this day of our extreme affliction has been felt with deep gratitude and has done more for the fraternization of which many idly prate than would many volumes of rhetorical assurance." [31] He expressed well the general sentiment of his people. The Southern members of the Board of Trustees of the Peabody Education Fund presented a paper at the annual meeting of that body in October 1878 testifying to the better understanding promoted in the South by this object lesson of Northern kindness. More sentimental and perhaps for that reason more representative of the common run of people was the "yellow fever verse" which was published in startling quantities. Virtually every Southern poet of prominence, as well as most of the local laureates who sent their verse to the newspapers, wrote of the sections at last united and truly reconciled by the generosity of deed and attitude of the North.[32]

Sorrow again a few years later revealed a national heart throbbing in the South as well as in the North. On the second of July 1881 President Garfield was shot by an assassin. A long painful struggle with death resulted as the poison of the bullet slowly wore down the resistance of a strong physique. For eleven weeks the country stood watch over the bed of the sufferer, noting every fluctuation in his condition. Newspapers printed daily reports which frequently occupied an entire sheet. When the contest drew to a close on the night of September 19–20 the death was attended by a grief as universal as any that had ever attended an American.

It was a united people that mourned. The poet Whittier was one of many who noted that "the solemn tragedy . . . was drawing with cords of sympathy all sections and all parties nearer to each other." [33] The penetrating observer who edited the *Nation* believed that the common grief had been conducive to a better understanding, North and South, inasmuch as it

---

[31] Rowland, "Davis," VIII, 283.
[32] Among such poems are Paul Hamilton Haynes' "The Stricken South to the North," Father Ryan's "Reunited," and Maria Louise Eve's "Conquered at Last."
[33] Letter to W. H. B. Currier, Sept. 24, 1881, "Prose Works of John Greenleaf Whittier" (Boston, 1889), II, 284–285.

had "disclosed to view a genuine patriotism where only evil
had been looked for." [34] Nowhere than in the South were manifestations of sorrow more sincere and unreserved.[35]

The proceedings of the city council and the citizens of
Charleston, South Carolina, were representative of the Southern attitude. In the years before the war it had been usual for
the people of Charleston to give communal expression to their
sentiment on occasions which were common to the nation.
Now that the tragedy of Garfield's death had "had the effect
of reuniting the distant sections of our common country in a
common grief," the city assembled for the first time in the
postwar period "as in olden time, to join our sister cities of
the Union in the expression of our sympathies at a calamity
common to the whole country." The nature of the resolutions
and speeches is sufficiently indicated by nothing the recurrence
of such phrases as "common nation," "common grief," "our
Union," "Americans," and "President of the whole People."
The South was realizing its share in the emotional life of the
nation.[36]

What more do these disconnected episodes reveal than that
the popular inclination was to forgive, to stress the things that
made for peace, and to forget the unpleasant features of the
past? The yearning for peace could not in itself, however, effect
release from the hostility that divided North and South. A
void existed, and no one was more conscious of it than the
peacemakers. We have seen Lamar carefully choosing his
words, Lowell avoiding "more recent graves," and Hope
pleading for the earlier "ties of Yorktown." They were reaching "hands across the chasm." The very act was a fatal admission that reunion was not a fact but a pious wish. "Let us
have peace" was primarily an emotion impossible of realization
in this period because it rested upon uncertain foundations.
There was not enough in common in the social and economic
structures of the sections to permit a true integration of interests and attitudes. Yet premature and self-conscious as was

[34] *Nation,* Sept. 1, 1881.
[35] *Charleston News and Courier, Atlanta Constitution,* July 3–Sept. 20,
1881.
[36] *Proceedings of the City Council and the Citizens of Charleston, South
Carolina, upon the Death of President Garfield* (pamphlet).

the early quest for peace, it had its significance in results achieved. Much of the old suspicion and recrimination was removed or discredited. More important, sentiment North and South had turned definitely toward reconciliation. It could be said at last that popular predilection favored the closing of the chasm. Whether the hope would be fulfilled depended largely upon forces beyond the power of individuals to direct.

CHAPTER VI

ECONOMIC AND SOCIAL CONTACTS
1865–1880

IN most respects the South that had sought independence had been attuned to ideals that sharply diverged from Northern aspirations. The agriculture of great estates, staple export crops, and enslaved labor had developed antagonisms with both the homestead farming of the Northwest and the business enterprise of the Northeast. Planters had waged war on one front against free homesteads of the new agricultural domain of the Mississippi Valley, while on another they contested with bitterness and suspicion the demands of industrialists for protective tariffs, centralized banking institutions, and subsidies for commerce. Moreover, the predilections of an aristocratic society for stability had not harmonized with Northern inventiveness and social experimentation. In the prewar South a favored oligarchy rested upon a basis of Negro slaves and an acquiescent and unprosperous white farming class. In the North politics had been democratized, humanitarian reform had improved the condition of the unfortunate, and systems of free and tax-supported education had been established. The life of the Southern gentleman, whose occupations centered in planting, politics, and the army, had stood in sharp contrast to that of leaders of Northern society, who had plunged into the money-making activities of trade and industry. The South had clung to an older trilogy of agriculture, aristocracy, and decentralization. The North had placed its future in a rapid and revolutionary progress toward machine industry, democracy, and a centralized nation. Basically the War for Southern Independence was the armed phase of an "irrepressible conflict" between these divergent objectives. More than any other factor they had constituted the most potent influence in widening the chasm between North and South.

The destruction of slavery, the humbling of the planting aristocracy, and the unimpeded sweep permitted Northern enterprise as a consequence of the war seemed to presage the removal of the major cause which had made for separateness. Many expressed the belief that the centrifugal force had been destroyed and now the centripetal force would operate unimpeded to unify the nation. It was obvious that the South faced an economic and social, as well as a political, reformation as a consequence of its defeat. A possible outcome might well be a greater approximation of Southern conditions to the Northern pattern.

The revolution was not slow in materializing. Emancipation of the Negro removed the cornerstone of ante-bellum Southern society. This in itself had far-reaching consequences. The small, rich landowning aristocracy in whose interest so much of Southern energy had been expended was deprived of its privileged position. Southern opinion was emancipated from the warping necessity of defending a peculiar institution from the attacks of Northern and European criticism, a necessity which before 1860 had led Southerners into a general contempt and suspicion of all things labeled free. But most significant, an economy of free labor proved incompatible with the maintenance of great estates. Almost immediately the plantation disintegrated into a system of small holdings. Farms scattered over the countryside took the place of the older centralization in plantation quarters. The individual working his tract and directing his own activity replaced the slave system of labor in gangs directed by overseers. "The quiet rise of the small farmer" became, as Sidney Lanier observed, "the notable circumstance of the period, in comparison with which noisier events signify nothing." [1]

In spite of the low price of land and the small acreage in which it could be acquired, few Negroes or white farmers were financially capable of purchasing farms and becoming actual

[1] Lanier, "The New South," *Scribner's*, XX (1880), 841. See also Henry Grady, "Cotton and its Kingdom," *Harper's*, LXIII (1881), 719–734.

owners. The split-up of the plantation did not result in a land-owning, independent and sturdy yeomanry. A system of tenancy, in which the laborer worked assigned tracts and shared the produce with the owner, developed and became permanent. It can be demonstrated that the increase in the number of small farms was a barometer for measuring the increase in tenantry. By 1880 forty-five per cent. of all the farms of Georgia were operated by tenants.

As far as the landlord was concerned the resort to tenancy was a necessary evil rather than a deliberate choice. He was in no position to control the agricultural reformation. Not only had his property resources been largely destroyed by emancipation, but frequently he was burdened by debt, and he was further crippled by a fall in land values of some forty-eight per cent. between 1860 and 1870. He was without liquid capital to finance, or experience to direct, a wage system by which alone the plantation could have been kept intact. Instead of a docile labor class he found the freedmen rebelliously independent and insistent upon greater exemption from control. Poverty and urgent necessity compelled him to salvage what he could from the débâcle. Tenancy seemed the only way by which the inefficient elements of Southern agriculture — an ignorant, unpropertied labor force and a landowning class without capital or authority — could be fused into a productive combination. It at least permitted life.

At best, however, the situation was not an attractive one for the planting aristocracy. Many threw their lands upon the market for sale and sought other means of livelihood. Others moved into the cities, and absentee landlordism took its place among the ills from which the South suffered. The agricultural well-being of the South rested in the hands of the Negroes and the small white farmers. On the one hand this gave the energetic and capable poor men of both races greater opportunity for progress. But it also meant a weakening of intelligent control. The poverty and ignorance of the farming classes were soon reflected in a steady decline in the efficiency of Southern agriculture, especially in the more fertile areas where slavery had planted the Negroes in largest numbers. Even from this misfortune, however, came some good. Need for better educational facilities became a pressing problem now that it affected the economic welfare of the section. Ere long a common school movement would sweep the South in much the same manner the North had experienced a generation earlier.

The abounding poverty depressed the tenant into a status approximating peonage. Lacking sufficient savings to live through a season of growing crops without borrowing, he discovered that credit was an expensive luxury. Banking facilities in rural areas fell sadly short of the demand. Even where they existed, the only security the tenant had to offer the bank was a lien placed on his share of the anticipated crop. The village merchant with whom he traded for food, clothing, and other supplies perforce became his banker, giving credit in return for a crop lien. By 1880 approximately three fourths of the agricultural classes in the South were chronic debtors, and the merchants through their control of credit were the dominant factor in the new economic structure.

With all its faults, the decentralization of Southern agriculture involved a social revolution that brought the section nearer to the Northern way of life. The center of gravity in rural areas became the common man. Tenancy, low crop prices, debt, poor educational facilities, and other similar problems that pressed on the dirt farmers assumed the place in Southern thought once occupied by the defense of slavery and the interests of a favored gentry. A community of interest was thus established with the farmers of the West who were also vexed with falling prices and rising debts. In time common needs would operate as a bond of union.

New ties were also established with the commercial centers of the Northeast. The *Commercial and Financial Chronicle* noted as early as 1869 that marked changes of doing business had taken place in the South. No longer did the proprietors of large estates make wholesale purchases for their dependents. The planter had formerly been a sort of small jobber, buying in large quantities from the dealer in the large cities or from the neighborhood merchant who kept a large stock. The middle class of small merchants in the Old South had found little profit in this arrangement and consequently had not thriven.

Now, however, the planter no longer had dependent workers. He purchased only for his household. Former slaves, grouped in families, made their own purchases. Likewise the more progressive status of the white farmer made for a larger market. Retail trading grew up where wholesale trading had prevailed.[2]

In direct ratio as the number of farms increased, villages of retail stores grew up to serve the needs of the small farmer. In this sense the rural South came daily to approximate more nearly the countryside of a Middle Western State. Moreover, a type of Southern buyer previously unknown to Northern markets made his appearance, and to meet his needs the great commercial houses of New York, Philadelphia, Baltimore, Cincinnati, Chicago, and St. Louis sent traveling salesmen into the deepest recesses of the South. A more intimate nexus of trade was thus woven into the fiber of national life.

If the majority of Negroes sank deep into peonage, the tenant system was nevertheless a means by which a low grade of unskilled labor could enter agriculture, and incidentally bring profit to the section. Socially it brought discipline into the chaos of race relationships and in this respect proved the first constructive step in removing the Negro problem from the arena of sectional controversy. At the same time it permitted the more enterprising and capable Negro to progress to the higher level of ownership. Finally it presented concretely to the South the need for Negro education. Soon appeared the Hampton idea of industrial education. This, as we shall see, served as a bridge of better understanding between North and South.

So far as the white farming classes were concerned, the breakup of the plantations destroyed the major force which had repressed their development. Steadily they assumed a more significant rôle in the productive economy of the South. Their gain was in part the Negroes' loss. Whereas in 1860 there had been eight blacks to every white in the cotton fields, by 1876 two out of every five cotton farmers were white.[3] If shiftlessness characterized the bulk of such workers, there was

[2] *Commercial and Financial Chronicle*, Oct. 23, 1869.
[3] M. B. Hammond, "The Cotton Industry" (New York, 1897), 129.

a minority of progressive men who found in the new conditions opportunity for advance. If the crop lien made for single crop agriculture this group nevertheless developed such diversification as the South achieved, notably the later truck farming for Northern markets. If poverty was their lot, it was from the small savings of many farmers that the financing of Southern manufactures was in large part to be accomplished. Where the plantation system had operated to rend asunder the economic life of North and South, the small farm worked in countless ways to bring Southern life into closer harmony with the major trends in national life.

Meanwhile a remarkable modification of Southern opinion in regard to economic matters was taking place. The traditional loyalty to agriculture was not repudiated. But the old boasts of cotton supremacy and the glorification of slave institutions that had filled the air in 1860 were silenced. The disasters of the war, affirmed F. W. Dawson, editor of the *Charleston News,* "have taught the Southern planter that he cannot live by cotton alone." [4] The tendency was to blame slavery as "the cause of all [our] evils — the backwardness and stationariness of the South; a wasteful husbandry, without other industries; the instability of her wealth; . . . her neglect of common schools; the absorption of all her intellectual energies in feverish and revolutionary politics; and, finally, secession and the reddened ground of a thousand battle-fields." [5] By 1880 those who were concerned with the industrial renovation of the section had made a commonplace out of the observation that "it is the white man of the South more than the black that has been freed by the civil war." [6]

Material interests commanded the respect and energy politics had once received. A man prominent in business was listened to with more attention than a statesman. Dawson wrote the creed of the new order in his editorials: "Restoration of the material prosperity of the South should be the chief object and the untiring effort of all her sons, . . . improvement of

[4] *Charleston News,* Jan. 4, 1868.
[5] Reed, "Old and New South," 11.
[6] W. F. Tillett, "The White Man of the New South," *Century,* XXXIII (1887), 769–776. See also *Land We Love,* III (1867), 29; and A. G. Haygood, "Our Brother in Black" (New York, 1881), 27.

her lands, . . . development of her manufactures, . . . extension of her railroads, . . . growth of her cities and towns, . . . gradual education of her people." Repeatedly he preached the doctrine of work: "The surest way of improving the labor of the country is by going to work ourselves. . . . We must adapt ourselves to the new order of things or we are lost. . . . The salvation of the State depends upon every man going to work." On another occasion he wrote, "We are sick of the everlasting humbug that talks and does nothing. The time has passed when men can prop themselves solely on the reputation of their forefathers. Brain and brawn nowadays are the weapons of the world's struggle." Editorials of this sort published in the most influential newspaper of South Carolina gave evidence of the extent to which the South was altering its views on life. "If the Old South had a contempt for the worker," observed an educator at Vanderbilt in Tennessee, "the New South has a greater contempt for the do-nothing and the idler." [7]

The period was one of self-appraisal. In place of the earlier confidence in the self-sufficiency of the Cotton Kingdom there was at times a tendency to grow too pessimistic in viewing the inadequacies of Southern industry and agriculture. The section surrendered, momentarily at least, to a feeling of weakness and despair. On every hand, a reporter of the *New York Tribune* observed, people were endlessly repeating, "This country will never do nothin' till we have some Northern men and capital." [8]

At no time in the postwar period did Southern morale reach so low a level as when the yearning to escape the dire circumstances of defeat led many to expect salvation from the North. Most of the economic plans of these early years were premised upon an expectation that Northern capital would pour into the South to finance its industrial development and that immigrants

[7] *Charleston News*, Feb. 11, 15, 1868, Dec. 20, 1870. See also King, "Great South," 305; J. B. Harrison, "Glimpses of a New Dixie," *New York Tribune Extra Number 81* (New York, 1881), 5; Tillett, *op. cit.*, 769; N. S. Shaler, "An Ex-Southerner in South Carolina," *Atlantic Monthly*, XXVI (1870), 55; T. W. Higginson, "Some War Scenes Revisited," *Atlantic Monthly*, XLII (1878), 8.
[8] Harrison, *op. cit.*, 5.

from Europe and the North would solve the problem of free labor.

In fact, the Southern people without knowing it were re-enacting the experience of the children of Israel in Egyptian bondage upon whom Pharaoh placed the heavy burden of making bricks without straw. The South had the task of re-juvenating agriculture with an inefficient labor supply and to build factories without capital or much mechanical experience. The Hebrews first "cried unto Pharaoh, saying, Wherefore dealest thou thus with thy servants?" and were rebuffed, turn-ing finally to place their trust in Jehovah of their fathers. Southerners in their first despair pleaded for assistance from the North. They, too, were to find no such easy escape, and turned eventually to building upon their own foundations the basis of their salvation.

Yet the clamor for Northern capital and immigrants was characteristic of the period. Editors, planters, real estate men, cotton merchants, railroad officials, and state commissioners of immigration filled newspapers, periodicals, pamphlets, and books with a swelling chorus of appeals for investments and settlers.[9] Immigrants, it was expected, would add diversifica-tion to agriculture and teach thrift and industry to the Negroes. Capital would rebuild and extend the Southern railroad net, develop water power, and boom cotton and iron manufactur-ing. It was not only Southerners who spread this propaganda. Pike found space in his short book, "The Prostrate State," for two chapters on immigration ("the South's greatest need") and inducements for Northerners to venture into this "agricul-tural paradise." King, Somers, and Nordhoff devoted many pages to observations about "the crying need at the South for both immigration and capital." The *Commercial and Financial Chronicle* urged the establishment of emigration companies in the North to establish new settlements in the South. The most publicized document of the period in this respect was a book prepared and freely distributed by a Boston firm of cot-

[9] For examples see *Charleston News,* Dec. 30, 1867; *Nation,* Jan. 6, 1870; and Donoho, Joy and Co., "The Southern States: Their Wonderful Re-sources and Peculiar Advantages" (Memphis, 1870). A recent study is B. J. Loewenberg, "Efforts of the South to Encourage Immigration, 1865–1900," *South Atlantic Quarterly,* XXXIII (1934), 363–385.

ton brokers, Loring and Atkinson. Based upon a questionnaire widely circularized among cotton planters, it indicated a consensus in favor of immigration.[10]

Those interested in the industrial recovery of the South gave little attention to the issues which were keeping alive the sectional conflict. It is an instructive experience to note how Dawson's hopes for an economic union of North and South tempered his editorials on Reconstruction in the harassed State of South Carolina.[11] Southern business men spoke with contempt of the politicians who "used the language of the past to give them, personally, . . . prominence." [12] While the *Southern Review* under Bledsoe's editorship went its vindictive way, another journal was founded in Charlotte, North Carolina, to express a different sentiment. Bearing the sentimental name, *The Land We Love,* and edited by a former lieutenant general of the Confederacy, D. H. Hill, this periodical devoted its chief energies to preaching the industrial possibilities of the Piedmont. With such work to accomplish its tone on sectional issues was distinctly conciliatory.[13]

The North towards which the Southern business man thus cast a wistful eye was a giant growing daily more powerful in economic strength. It may well be true that Northern editors occasionally affirmed that "at this moment there is no more truly patriotic effort than that of promoting the movement of skilled industry toward the . . . Southern States." [14] But actually the North had little energy or money to devote to Southern development. The section was preoccupied with its own tremendous advance — in building its great industries and railroads and extending the empire of business. So far as exploitation of new regions was concerned, the New West of agriculture, transcontinental railroads, ranching and mining, seemed far more remunerative for investment than the har-

[10] Loring and Atkinson, "Cotton Culture and the South Considered with Reference to Emigration" (Boston, 1869).

[11] *Charleston News,* Feb. 2, 1870, April 29, 1871.

[12] President Baldwin of the Louisville and Nashville Railroad, as quoted in B. Mitchell, "The Rise of The Cotton Mills in the South" (Baltimore, 1921), 78.

[13] See as typical *Land We Love,* III (1867), 29.

[14] *Harper's Weekly,* April 29, 1871.

assed South with its apparently exhausted fields, its Negro disturbances, and its bankrupt governments.

It was the South's own problem to solve. No lesson was more valuable or more thoroughly learned than that the section's redemption would have to be achieved through the efforts of Southern people. Yearnings for easy escape were frustrated. The amount of immigration proved insignificant. The census of 1880 numbered fewer persons of foreign birth in the South than had been there in 1860. Within the United States, the same authority indicated, the course of migration was mainly westward, and secondarily northeastward to the cities, with the southward trend not appreciable. Nor did the appeal for capital, except in cases about to be noted, meet with greater success. Southern pleas for men and money aroused a counter propaganda in the North which pointed to disturbed political conditions, the presence of the Negro, and the general uncertainty of the Southern future as reasons why moneyed men and homeseekers should shun the unhappy section.

Economic contacts between the sections revealed the uncertainties and maladjustments natural to imperfect integration. Business men in quest of profits found the same embarrassment that had handicapped the reconcilers of the centennial celebrations. Enterprising plans, hopefully conceived and involving friendly intercourse between the sections, too frequently came to grief. "Every consideration of national interest and national pride," the ordinary man of business was apt to say, "requires the prosecution of a more generous policy" of Reconstruction "in order that we may develop the wealth of the South." [15] But timidly he waited for greater security. The editor of *Hunt's Merchants' Magazine* observed that business men were apprehensive and deemed it prudent to wait until political affairs became more settled.[16]

It was this attitude, resulting in procrastination, rather than the hostility of the business classes, that retarded the unifying influence of economic activity. Opinion in the business world varied as it did in the field of politics. One student has pre-

[15] *Hunt's Merchants' Magazine*, LIV (1866), 170–172.
[16] *Ibid.*, LV (1866), 309–310. See also *Commercial and Financial Chronicle*, Oct. 6, 1866.

sented the thesis that certain Radicals in New England interested in tariff protection were hostile to the restoration of
friendly relations with the South.[17] It has also been maintained
that some powerful politicians of the East were inimical to
the South because they saw the opportunity of entrenching
"big business" in the phraseology of the Fourteenth Amendment.[18] A reading of contemporary documents and business
periodicals, however, would seem to indicate that the more
vocal groups of Northern business favored moderation as the
more effective means of effecting a rapid economic recovery
of the South. This was especially true of merchants, cotton
manufacturers, financiers, and railroad executives.

The leading business journal of the country, the *Commercial
and Financial Chronicle,* consistently advocated a policy of
leniency towards the South. It assailed as unstatesmanlike the
program of Radical Reconstruction and reported conditions
in the South in a manner that contradicted Radical propaganda.
It advised Northern investments in the defeated section and
sought to divert Southward a portion of the immigration tide.
It worked avidly for the upbuilding of Southern agriculture,
mining, and manufacture. Its eyes were directed to a future
South of prosperity that might become a lucrative market for
Northern goods. To reunite the Nation economically seemed
to the *Chronicle* a far more patriotic course than to perpetuate
division by agitating impossible ideals of Radical inception.

Cotton brokers of New York and Philadelphia, and cotton
manufacturers of New England, apart from what views they
entertained in regard to a protective tariff, had an immediate
interest in seeking the restoration of friendly relations with
the South. The cotton trade knew full well the importance of
bringing discipline to the Southern labor force. When theories
of Negro equality resulted in race conflict, and conflict in
higher prices of raw cotton, manufacturers were inclined to accept the point of view of the Southern planter rather than that
of the New England zealot. There is sufficient evidence in the
activity of the Boston firm of Loring and Atkinson to war-

[17] H. K. Beale, "Tariff and Reconstruction," *American Historical Review,*
XXXV (1930), 276–294.
[18] Charles and Mary Beard, "Rise of American Civilization" (New
York, 1927), II, 113.

rant this observation. When the National Association of Cotton Manufacturers and Planters was organized in 1868, the larger Northern membership was especially concerned in increasing the Southern representation, and indicated that a prime purpose of organization was to establish more harmonious contact between the raisers and manufacturers of cotton.[19]

Another problem for the cotton trade to solve was to adjust marketing to the changed conditions of production. Small farmers sold their crops in small quantities to local dealers, whereas the prewar organization had been adjusted to the larger outputs of plantations. New practices in grading and collecting had to be devised. Quietly through these years was perfected a network of relationships that integrated nationally one of the nation's greatest economic activities. Even the speculators in cotton futures found it imperative to organize more intimately their Southern contacts. The decentralization of Southern agriculture made more difficult the task of estimating the probable size, condition, and price of crops. This difficulty could be solved only by closer contact with the cotton fields. The Federal government was urged to enlarge its activities in crop reporting. Cotton exchanges were organized in New Orleans, New York, and a number of lesser cities. A convention of all the cotton exchanges met in Augusta, Georgia, in 1874, and organized a National Cotton Exchange. This body had a checkered career, but the New York and New Orleans exchanges continued active in promoting uniformity in trading practices.[20]

Because of the insecure agricultural and industrial future of the South, the interest of Northern banking houses in the section during the fifteen postwar years was limited primarily to financing railroad securities and issues of State bonds. Until 1873 the situation was favorable for promoting railroads wherever located if the slightest promise of eventual profit could be shown. The North was in the midst of a great industrial boom the chief feature of which was the construction of

[19] *National Association of Cotton Manufacturers and Planters, Proceedings,* New York City, April 29, 1868 (pamphlet).
[20] G. W. Neville, *New York Cotton Exchange in Its Relation to Merchandising Cotton* (pamphlet, Boston, 1912), 12–13. See also C. W. Burkett and C. H. Poe, "Cotton" (New York, 1906), 72.

railroads in all parts of the United States. The ten thousand miles of track possessed by the South in 1861 had been largely destroyed or placed in bad condition by the wear and tear of war. By 1873 this original mileage was rebuilt and an additional eight thousand miles constructed. This progress was halted by the depression which began in 1873, but by 1880 the South had a modern railroad system of twenty thousand miles which gave it better economic unity than it had ever previously possessed.

If the improvement of the railroad facilities of the South was primarily the work of Southern men, the money which financed it came from the North. Brokerage houses in New York specialized in Southern rails. The officers and directors of nearly every important Southern road included Southerners active in management and Northern capitalists interested in investment. The Adams Express Company (itself a factor in the integrating influence of business) acted through its subsidiary, the Southern Express Company, in loaning money especially to the weaker roads in return for a monopoly of express business. The Louisville and Nashville Railroad may serve as an illustration of the sectional coöperation implied in this activity. The president of the road was E. P. Alexander, a young Georgian with a noteworthy military record in the Confederacy and the title of general. Under his direction the road expanded into a system operating more than two thousand miles of track connecting Cincinnati and Louisville on the Ohio with Mobile and New Orleans. The capital which made Alexander's work possible was furnished by such New York investment houses as Drexel, Winthrop and Company, J. B. Alexander and Company, and John J. Cisco and Sons.

Of more permanent value to national integration was the fact that this railroad-building tended more than ever to absorb the South into the transportation system of the country. Shorter and weaker lines were acquired by the stronger, and the consolidated roads built new track to reach more distant terminals, usually a contact with some important Northern point. The extension of the Louisville and Nashville has been noted. The Chesapeake and Ohio by 1873 vindicated its name by completing a track from White Sulphur Springs to the Ohio. The Richmond and Danville, aided financially and controlled by the Pennsylvania Railroad, consolidated by 1881 a line connecting Richmond and Atlanta with branches that linked together the commercial centers of the Atlantic seaboard. The Norfolk and Western penetrated the Appalachian mountains of western Virginia and eastern Tennessee, opening a new mining empire. The Mobile and Ohio and other roads between the mountains and the Mississippi were undergoing changes that would result in the eighties in consolidation under the Illinois Central system. By 1880 the transportation system of the South joined it far more effectively to the North than previously when few Southern roads had been built with a Northern contact in view. Regardless of what politicians were thinking, railroad builders were proceeding on the assumption that the movement of freight and passengers would know no section. Much of importance in the later wedding of the sections — tourist travel, truck farming, grain shipments from the upper Mississippi Valley to the Gulf, cotton shipments by rail, as well as a greater interchange of articles of every sort — was to proceed from this railroad activity and its continuance.[21]

Northern investment in the bonds of Southern states was to have no such happy consequence. Owing to the wild extravagance of the carpetbag governments which issued them, the securities were never better than dubious speculative ventures. This, however, was not appreciated by the Northern purchasers, partly because the country was in a frenzied boom of industrial activity and partly because the practices of the Northern brokers were at a very low ethical level. The extravagance and corruption of the Southern governments under Radical control necessitated borrowing far beyond the capacity of the impoverished States to repay. The credit of the State was pledged to any wild scheme for which a sufficiently powerful political support could literally be purchased by those seeking the support. A large proportion of the issues represented corrupt aid to railroads, canals, and levees. Even before the carpetbaggers were driven from office, their weird financial

[21] I have relied chiefly upon the *Commercial and Financial Chronicle* for this account of Southern railroads.

structure began to topple. By 1872 a "scaling down process" had begun. By 1880 a wholesale repudiation had taken place. Every Southern State except Texas was implicated.[22]

It would be difficult to see who profited from this unpleasant business except the Radical politicians and the brokers who marketed the securities. A very small proportion of the money was ever used in honest construction or legitimate purposes of government. Radicals controlling the Southern legislatures operated in open connivance with Northern banking houses. The former printed the bits of paper which pledged the honor of a State; the latter found the purchasers in Europe and the North. Possibly the most active alliance resulted from the support given by the prominent New York firm of Henry Clews and Company to the Stanton brothers of Boston for corrupting the Alabama legislature. Clews, whose agents were not always above resort to bribery, and whose own practices left much to be desired, had similar contacts in the Carolinas and Georgia. It is not known how many millions of dollars' worth of bonds the firm sold, but Clews himself stated that he invested (possibly it was his share of the profits) more than three and a half million dollars of his own fortune in Southern State securities.[23]

Ugly scars were left in both North and South. During the long years of saving and skimping that followed the carpetbag orgy, the latter section remembered the extravagance. From the day in 1868 when Dawson wrote that the South would never feel in honor obligated to respect "bayonet" bonds, Southerners always felt justified in repudiating the issues.[24] But both the credit and the reputation of the South severely suffered. Not only did business in Southern State securities virtually cease, but a general suspicion was aroused

[22] Excellent accounts of this subject are found in W. L. Fleming, "Civil War and Reconstruction in Alabama" (New York, 1905); F. B. Simkins and R. H. Woody, "South Carolina during Reconstruction" (Chapel Hill, 1932); and W. A. Scott, "The Repudiation of State Debts" (New York, 1893). See also *Commercial and Financial Chronicle*, Jan. 27, 1877; and R. P. Porter, "State Debts and Repudiation," *International Rev.*, IX (1880), 556–592.
[23] Fleming, "Alabama," 582–585, 591–603; Simkins and Woody, "South Carolina," 213–214; "South in the Building of the Nation," VI, 307; Henry Clews, "Fifty Years in Wall Street" (New York, 1908), 551.
[24] *Charleston News*, Aug. 17, 1868.

as to the financial trustworthiness of the section in other respects. This was a major factor in explaining why in the early period of the development of Southern manufactures, just beginning, so little Northern capital was attracted to the South.

Repudiation met with a storm of denunciation throughout the North. Those who were left holding the worthless paper had for the most part purchased it in good faith. Their voices were now raised in condemnation of "these Southern States, with their solemn promises broken and their plighted faith disregarded." [25] Repudiation brought criticism from some of the most friendly supporters the South could claim in the North. Thus the *Nation* asserted:

It ought to be known by every one who has a dollar to invest, and by every emigrant who thinks of seeking a new home . . . , that in addition to the usual risks he runs, there is in such States as these one more — that the sense of good faith is benumbed, if not dead, and that he is making himself one of a community of swindlers.[26]

The *Commercial and Financial Chronicle* was shocked into delivering a continuous lecture of many years' duration on the importance of honorable financial conduct. Even Henry Clews was discovered to possess a moral sense, making speeches and writing articles that burned with righteous indignation at the spectacle of "Southern robbery." [27] Public opinion seemed prone to moralize on the general weaknesses in Southern character. As late as 1893, when a candidate for the degree of doctor of philosophy published an historical examination of the cantankerous subject, he felt it necessary to probe "the fundamental differences of character between the Northern and Southern people," to ascertain whether "in the course of these debt controversies the Southern character was unreliable." [28]

Where economic interests jibed, however, men of business

[25] Porter, *op. cit.*, 585.
[26] *Nation*, Aug. 16, 1877.
[27] Clews, "Fifty Years in Wall Street," 255–288.
[28] Scott, "Repudiation of State Debts," 233–237.

were men of peace. The Great Plains of the West, last frontier of the expanding Union and an area over whose destiny as free or slave territory the sectionalists of the fifties had wrangled the nation into war, gave opportunity for the rise of a new industry that first foretold the ultimate economic integration of the North and South. Texas had cattle and needed money. The North had money and needed meat for its growing urban population. The Great Plains, over whose free grass cattle, grazing and fattening as they went, could be driven to market, became the nexus. Within fifteen years after the close of the Civil War, four million Texan cattle were driven across the Great Plains to some railhead in Kansas whence they were shipped to Northern markets.[29]

It was historic justice that this earliest economic reunion of the sections occurred in that state where the first blood of civil conflict had been shed. Abilene, Kansas, was the first cowtown at whose market Southern ranchers met Northern buyers. Here, on September 5, 1867, amid the crude surroundings of a frontier settlement, men who had worn the blue and men who had worn the gray sat down together at a banquet celebrating what they had done in erecting a bond of union between the sections. In the South Federal troops were busily engaged in executing the will of Thaddeus Stevens. In the North the Radical spirit was dominant. Nevertheless the future was with Abilene. Where its sister town of Lecompton had pointed the way to blood and tragedy, Abilene was a signpost to reunion.

While business men were seeking profits and financiers were wrangling over securities, another economic contact was made by Northerners who sought in the mild winter climate of the South resorts for relaxation and health. The White Sulphur Springs of Virginia was possibly the only Southern resort much frequented by Northerners in the ante-bellum period. But the extension of railroad facilities opened to ready access before 1880 points in northern Florida, the Asheville country of North Carolina, the Aiken region of South Carolina, the Gulf coast, and the Hot Springs of Arkansas. An increasing number of Northern visitors patronized these communities,

[29] W. P. Webb, "The Great Plains" (Boston, 1931), 205–269.

and some purchased property to establish permanent winter homes.[30]

The economic importance of this development was appreciated by the editor of the *Virginias Magazine,* who commented on the opening of the Luray Caverns as follows:

This also suggests that Virginia has greatly benefited by the enterprise of the Northern capitalists that has constructed the Shenandoah Valley R. R., by which these wonderful caverns are reached, built the Luray Inn to give first class accommodations to visitors, and converted an undeveloped "hole-in-the-ground" into a thing of surpassing beauty and a mine of wealth. Our people, if they but knew it, get the lion's share of such developments.[31]

It is also expected that an increase of Northern travel in the South would lead to greater social intermingling and advertise the economic possibilities of the section. Whether these expectations would materialize the future would determine. Meanwhile it could be noted that a beginning of tourist travel had been made.

While the census of 1880 did not indicate a numerically important migration of Southerners to the North, it did reveal that the Northern metropolises were beginning to attract Southern youth of exceptional ambition, and that Virginians especially were showing a propensity to try their fortunes in New York and Philadelphia. There seems to be no effective way of measuring the extent or influence of these transplanted Southerners. But one can point to the phenomenon and suggest the careers of John R. Thompson in journalism, George Cary Eggleston in letters, John H. Inman in the cotton trade, and Roger A. Pryor in law, as examples of Southerners in New York during the late sixties and the seventies who rose to prominence and made wide circles of friends. It was maintained both that the émigrés showed too great an eagerness "to crook the pregnant hinges of the knee," and that they "pro-

[30] Typical books and articles are S. Lanier, "Florida" (Philadelphia, 1875); *Nation,* Jan. 20, 1876; *The Mountain Tourist* (pamphlet, Spartanburg, 1878); A. Coffin and W. H. Geddings, *Aiken and Its Climate* (pamphlet); and *Appletons' Handbook of American Travel, Southern Tour* (New York, 1869, 1874, 1880).
[31] *The Virginias,* VI (1885), 33.

moted the solidarity of the country" by "utterly destroying" the "preconceived erroneous ideas" of the North toward Southerners.[32]

Contacts in the field of humanitarian endeavor between 1865 and 1880 formed also a story of gains and losses. One of the greatest disparities between North and South when the war ended was the status of elementary education in the respective sections. The Northern States had well-established tax-supported public schools. Public opinion was thoroughly informed as to the value of such a policy. The Southern States had made a start before the war toward establishing general systems. But attendance had not been made compulsory, taxation had been inadequate, a charity aspect associated with public schools had handicapped the movement, and public opinion had been extremely conservative in regard to the State's duty of public education. The Southern educational system had been adapted to perpetuate an aristocratic structure of society with the result that the training of the upper classes had been stressed while the great bulk of the Southern whites had been unreached by formal education and the Negroes had received no other training than the discipline of slavery. Impoverished by losses of life and property in the war, confronted by the extravagant and fraudulent spending of the Reconstruction governments, the South seemed to face an impossible task in the reorganization of its school system on a basis similar to the North and the inclusion within it of the mass of Negroes and hitherto unschooled whites.

Southern historians are divided in regard to the contributions made by the Reconstruction governments established by the bayonet policies of the North. On the one side it has been maintained that, "When the reconstructionists surrendered the government [in Mississippi] to the democracy, in 1876, the public school system which they had fathered had become firmly established, its efficiency increased, and its administration made somewhat less expensive than at first." [33]

[32] H. I. Brock, "The South in Northern Culture," in "South in the Building of the Nation," VI, 280; N. K. Davis, "The Negro in the South," *Forum,* I (1886), 130.
[33] J. W. Garner, "Reconstruction in Mississippi" (New York, 1901), 370–371.

A second student, especially well informed on North Carolina, affirmed that "the principle of direct taxation was undoubtedly the most important contribution of the Reconstruction regime to the public school movement in the South." [34] A third investigator discovered that none of the first eight constitutions of South Carolina had mentioned education. The constitution framed by the Radicals in 1868, however, made mandatory a complete system modeled on the best practices of the Northern States. When the Democrats came into control of South Carolina they built directly upon the foundations laid by their predecessors.[35] So also Bishop A. G. Haygood, of Georgia, noted that Reconstruction brought the common school to the South much sooner than natural evolution would have developed it.[36] On the other hand, E. W. Knight, the leading authority on education in the South, is unwilling to admit that the section owed much to the carpetbag governments. He pointed to the looting and misappropriation of public funds and the piling up of colossal debts as permanent impediments in the way of a later taxing program adequate for the needs of public education. He also saw in the efforts to force Northern conceptions upon the South without sufficient allowance for local differences an influence which alienated Southern opinion on schools in general. Knight was so confident that the white people of the South, if left unmolested, would have solved more easily and readily the problem of education, that he was inclined to view pessimistically all that the carpetbaggers attempted as less good than what might have been.[37]

Yet it seems beyond doubt that, in anchoring the principle of the common school safely in the state constitutions, the carpetbag governments established a principle which henceforth remained unassailable. Especially beneficial was the designation of the sources for school support, uniform systems

[34] W. K. Boyd, "Educational History in the South since 1865," in "Studies in Southern History and Politics, Inscribed to W. A. Dunning" (New York, 1914), 263.

[35] J. A. Stoddard, "Backgrounds of Secondary Education in South Caroline" (Columbia, 1924), 65–68.

[36] A. G. Haygood, "The South and the School Problem," *Harper's Monthly*, LXXIX (1889), 225–226.

[37] E. W. Knight, "The Influence of Reconstruction on Education in the South" (New York, 1913), and "Public Education in the South" (Boston, 1922).

of taxation, and the emphatic injunction that Negroes as well
as whites should be educated. It seems also true that the chief
obstacles in the way of realizing these ideals were not political
so much as they were social — impoverishment, sparseness of
population, and divided races. The task of overcoming these
obstacles had not become less difficult in 1880 than it had been
in 1865, but a clearer understanding of the fact prevailed that
it was a burden and that the South must bear it.

If contention accompanied the Radicals in all that they attempted, there was another agency in the Southern field whose
work in these early years gave promise that ultimately the
program of education would be a narrative of sectional co-
operation. George Peabody, one of the nation's greatest and
wealthiest financiers, had achieved a reputation for wise
philanthropy through endowments which sought the allevia-
tion of poverty in London. As in his gifts to England he had
hoped to link two nations in friendly bonds, now after the
Civil War it seemed to him more imperative to use his bounty
in the restoration of good will between North and South.
In two donations, February 7, 1867, and June 29, 1869, at a
time when the Radicals in Congress were enacting the Reconstruction legislation, he established a trust fund of two million
dollars, the interest of which was to be used for the promotion
and encouragement of common school education in the South.
"This I give to the suffering South," he wrote, "for the good
of the whole country." [38]

The Peabody Education Fund thus established was directed
by a board of trustees, which in itself was an experiment in
harmony and understanding between the sections. On the
original board sat representatives of Virginia and New York,
North Carolina and Ohio, South Carolina and Massachusetts,

---

[38] Peabody also donated $1,500,000 in repudiated bonds of several South-
ern States, but inasmuch as the Trustees never received a return on these
bonds it seems more accurate to give the amount of the Fund as $2,000,000.
The chief source of information on the work of the Peabody Education Fund
is the published "Proceedings of the Trustees of the Peabody Education
Fund," 6 vols. (Boston, 1875–1916). See also J. L. M. Curry, "Brief Sketch
of George Peabody, and a History of the Peabody Education Fund" (Cambridge, 1898). Curry and Barnas Sears delivered many addresses before
Southern legislatures and educational bodies. Most of these addresses have
been published in pamphlet form. Knight, "Public Education in the South,"
devotes a chapter to the Peabody Education Fund.

and Maryland and Pennsylvania. Distinguished men not only accepted membership on the board as an honor; they seriously devoted time and energy to the work. Grant, even in the years of his Presidency of the United States, was faithful in attendance, as was his Secretary of State, Hamilton Fish, of New York. Robert C. Winthrop, of Massachusetts, made service on the board the major interest of his later years, as did ex-Governors William Aiken, of South Carolina, and W. A. Graham, of North Carolina. Admiral Farragut seemed to his fellow trustees as zealous in this work of peace as he had been in running his ships past Confederate batteries. The Virginian, A. H. H. Stuart, was happy in the warm friendships membership on the board developed. The sincere devotion of these men inspired from the start public confidence in the work of the Fund.

There is no need here to retell the history of the Fund's administration in the South. Barnas Sears, a New England educator who at one time had been President of Brown University, was chosen General Agent. His work, which continued until his death in 1880, was one of the most notable services in the history of American education. He cheerfully shouldered the burden of wide travel throughout the South. The necessity of meeting and reconciling all sorts of people was made easy by his warmth of personality, tact, and intelligence. He inspired confidence, removed doubts and suspicions, aroused sympathy, and did much in making "free schools for the whole people" an acceptable slogan for the advance of Southern education. Under his direction the Fund improved the sentiment for education in the South, developed the idea of adequate taxation for public schools, stimulated the establishment of school systems, and helped remove the hostility toward Negro education. Sears properly assessed the nature of this work when in February, 1880 he wrote, "I shall be happy indeed, if after I shall have done some of the rougher work, in sailing near the rocks and quicksands of the coast, my successor shall be sailing in an open sea." The pioneer work had been done, and when in 1881 management was transferred to a Southerner, J. L. M. Curry, of Alabama, the problem was primarily that of using the Fund as a lever to lift Southern education from under its social inheritance of poverty and retardation.

The Peabody Education Fund contributed largely to a better understanding between North and South. Southerners generally approved of the work. The Trustees sought to shape Northern public opinion to a more charitable approach to Southern problems of Reconstruction, the Negro, and education. Not only was the gift of Peabody one of the earliest manifestations of the spirit of reconciliation, but it was also a most effective means of stimulating that spirit in others.

The public school movement in the South was still in its infancy fifteen years after the war had ended. The work accomplished seemed pitiably insignificant compared to the staggering burden which still remained to be carried. Nevertheless a thoughtful observer in 1880 would have discerned a significant portent in the developing sentiment for education. A basic article in the creed of Americanism was faith in common schools. More important than Northern aid was the fact that the South itself was responding to the urge of placing a school house within the reach of all its people.

A brighter side of the activities of Northern church bodies in the South might also be indicated than that which has previously been described. Mistaken, narrow and bigoted as were many of the early missionaries, and damaging as was their muddling in the delicate realm of race relationships, the main source of the work was a purity of devoted self-sacrifice which a later generation can recognize made some contribution of permanent value. Most of the Negroes who received education in the South between 1865 and 1880 were schooled in institutions supported by the charity of Northern churches. The American Missionary Association spent annually an average of $100,000 and maintained eight institutions of collegiate grade, twelve high and normal schools, and twenty-four common schools in which more than seven thousand Negroes and one hundred and sixty teachers were enrolled in 1880. S. C. Armstrong at Hampton Institute was materially aided by this body. Atlanta University, in the Georgia capital, with the best Negro library in the South, and Fisk University in Nashville were the progeny of this Congregational association. The Freedman's Aid Society of the Methodist Episcopal Church and the American Baptist Home Mission carried a large portion of the work, while the Northern Presbyterians, Episcopalians, and Quakers aided to a lesser extent.[39]

The positive contributions were far reaching. S. C. Armstrong, in founding Hampton Institute on the principle of industrial training and agricultural education, developed the most important single idea in the improvement of the Negro race. Teacher training was an important conception stressed at Atlanta and Fisk. Both the plans by which, and the major institutions through which, the later elevation of the Negro was to be effected were given the South in these years by the endeavor of Northern churches. Progress in the future depended largely upon the white South's acceptance of this work and building upon its foundation.

Even in this respect there was reason for optimism. Gradually the possibilities of common work on common ground were being recognized. It would be an exaggeration to say that the Northern workers in the South were adjusted to their environment by 1880, or that Southern opinion accepted them in intimate communion. But it is true that the trend was toward improved understanding. Better-minded Northerners were beginning to realize that their work must be subordinate and supplementary to what the white South did, that they were henceforth to assist rather than to direct. New efforts were being made to effect a closer harmony. Likewise Southerners were showing less suspicion of schools for Negroes, and in places there was actually developing a sustaining public opinion for Negro education. With this better basis established the activity of Northerners like A. D. Mayo and Southerners like A. G. Haygood during the eighties and nineties would proceed on easier terms of coöperation.

The fifteen years after Appomattox had thus constituted a period of diverse and contradictory lights and shadows. The confusion of Northern attitudes had found expression through varied outlets that ranged from extreme vindictiveness to sur-

[39] A. D. Mayo, "Work of Certain Northern Churches in the Education of the Freedman, 1861–1900," *Report of the United States Commissioner of Education for 1901–1902* (Washington, 1902), I, 285–314; Haygood, "Brother in Black," 170–181.

prisingly generous acts of charity. Uncertainty as to what the North would do and could do in the South had prevailed, making for trials and errors and then resulting by 1880 in a general cessation of Northern attempts at positive conquest of Southern culture. Political Reconstructionists retired, leaving the South to its own devices. Northern churchmen and charity workers beat a retreat, from the confident crusade of remaking Southern society, to the humbler attitude of giving aid where aid was acceptable. Boosters were still predicting a boom in Southern industry, but the Northern attitude had grown cynical of expecting progress from what it was convinced was the most economically backward section of the country. In fact the North by 1880 was willing to retire from the field of combat, no longer apprehensive of the Union or zealous for the rights of Negroes, and confident in its own political and economic dominance. The North was willing to let the South solve its own destiny. Whether the proud foe of earlier days, now reduced to a humble state of impotency, would beat down its traditions of gentility and agriculture and adjust itself to the newer age of business exploitation and common man standards in society was henceforth a decision for the South to make.

The South had within itself all the elements for deciding whether it would merge its future in a common Americanism or remain aloof, loyal to a tradition which seemed discarded and destroyed by the remainder of the world. Bledsoe or Dawson, Dabney or Curry, each a Southerner — which was the wiser prophet? Evidence as to conditions in the South was presented in such bewilderment of contradiction as to make difficult for Southerners an answer to the question. The rural South seemed a community of impoverished aristocrats and debt-ridden tenants, yet in apparent inconsistency more people were at work than ever before and census figures revealed that they were raising more crops than in the good old prewar years. While gentle ladies and gallant heroes filled pages of unreconciled reminiscences about the horrors of Sherman's march, other Southerners who had worn the gray uniform of the Confederacy boasted of the returning prosperity in such citadels of Southern tradition as South Carolina and Virginia.

If many were bitter over Reconstruction memories there was in contrast the accomplished fact of Southern restoration to full political rights within the Union to take off the edge of bitterness. If pessimism prevailed in some quarters in regard to race relations, there was also optimism in the observation that the system of free labor was meeting with an unexpectedly high degree of success and that the abolition of slavery had destroyed a provincializing influence.[40]

The Old South had had DeBow and William Gregg to champion manufactures and to urge diversification of agriculture. The Old South had also had land for yeoman farmers and resources of raw materials, water power, and potential labor supply. All the seeds for its own eventual destruction had been planted in Southern soil before the War for Southern Independence had begun. Yet their germination had been retarded by the presence of the hardier growths of slavery and the plantation system. These latter plants were now uprooted and the seeds of a New South were beginning to sprout. Historians will probably always disagree as to which was the lovelier bloom, the Old or the New.[41] But two things seem beyond dispute. The New South was the South's own responsibility, and it was built upon inbred Southern traits that approximated Northern characteristics far more completely than did the distinctive qualities of the ante-bellum South.

One thing was still required for the revolution in Southern attitude to be complete. The New must breed a faith and confidence in itself. That faith and confidence was the contribution of young men growing up to manhood in the eighties, young men demanding the right to live a life of action and fulfillment rather than a life of wearing sackcloth amid the ashes of past grandeur.

[40] For various shades of Southern opinion see Charleston Chamber of Commerce, *The Trade and Commerce of the City of Charleston* (pamphlet, Charleston, 1873); *Virginias Magazine*, II (1881), 12; E. DeLeon, "The New South," *Harper's Monthly*, XLVIII (1874), 270–280, 406–422, XLIX (1874), 555–568.
[41] The disagreement among Southerners can be shown by comparing Twelve Southerners, "I'll Take My Stand" (New York, 1931), and Stark Young, "So Red the Rose" (New York, 1934), with R. H. Edmonds, "The South's Redemption from Poverty to Prosperity" (Baltimore, 1890), and Broadus Mitchell, "The Industrial Revolution in the South" (Baltimore, 1930).

CHAPTER VII

YOUNG MEN GROWING UP

THE young men of the postwar South were sired by an Old South disciplined in war and revolutionary Reconstruction. Virtually every tenet of the new creed of life was a lesson seared deep into the minds of the older generation by painful experience and exacting necessity. No later politician was to plead more eloquently for peace between the sections than had Wade Hampton, John B. Gordon, and L. Q. C. Lamar in the seventies. No journalist after 1880 added an idea or a word to the preachments of F. W. Dawson on the gospel of labor, the need of manufactures, and the desirability of agricultural diversification. The industrialists had little more to do than to follow the trails blazed before 1880 by such pioneers as John T. Milner and Henry P. Hammett. In the field of education men of the war generation like J. L. M. Curry and William Preston Johnston had fully developed the dogma of public schools and were engaged in the campaign for its attainment. The language and much of the equipment of the coming order were the Old South's transmittal to the New.

Young men, growing up in an age of war and Reconstruction and compelled to adapt themselves to the altered conditions of life which these struggles created, revealed a strong predilection to follow the teaching of those members of the older generation who were loudest in disavowal of "the mythic beauties of a mythic past." [1] To adherents of the tradition of departed grandeur it seemed as though the young men

[1] John Hampden Chamberlain, Confederate veteran and editor of the *Richmond Whig* in an address to the student body of Randolph-Macon College in 1875, as quoted in Hendricks, "Training of an American," 57. See also W. P. Johnston, *Commencement Address, South Carolina College, June 25, 1884* (pamphlet).

were bowing "the knee to expediency, ignoring or forgetting principle." [2] But actually it was the impulse of youth which, conscious of the suffering through which the South had passed, nevertheless preferred to welcome the herald of hope and ambition rather than abide the prophet of despair and disaster.

To equip themselves for life in the future rather than for defense of the past, the young men accepted and made basic in their creed the revised judgment of Southern history which the more progressive of their elders had so painfully elaborated. Typical of the prevailing opinion was the speech made by a twenty-four year old Virginian whose boyhood had been spent in South Carolina. "I yield to no one precedence in love for the South," asserted Woodrow Wilson in 1880. "But *because* I love the South, I rejoice in the failure of the Confederacy. . . . The perpetuation of slavery would, beyond all question, have wrecked our agricultural and commercial interests, at the same time that it supplied a fruitful source of irritation abroad and agitation within. We cannot conceal from ourselves the fact that slavery was enervating our Southern society and exhausting to Southern energies. . . . Even the damnable cruelty and folly of reconstruction was to be preferred to helpless independence." [3]

Others were eager to demonstrate that the new creed was in harmony with the best traditions of the South. Edgar Gardener Murphy went so far as to maintain that the New South was only "a story of reëmergence" of the finest traits in Southern character.[4] Richard H. Edmonds, the founder, editor, and manager of the *Manufacturers' Record,* found justification for his determined boosting of Southern industry in what he asserted to be the amount of manufactures and the extent of mechanical skill in the Old South.[5] Walter Hines

[2] William Barnes to Jefferson Davis, June 26, 1882, Rowland, "Davis," IX, 174.

[3] Woodrow Wilson, "Oration on John Bright," delivered before the Jefferson Society of the University of Virginia, R. S. Baker (ed.), "Public Papers of Woodrow Wilson, College and State" (New York, 1925), I, 43–59.

[4] E. G. Murphy, "Problems of the Present South" (New York, 1904), 10–11, 97.

[5] Edmonds, "South's Redemption"; *Manufacturers' Record* (Baltimore), I–X (1882–1892), *passim.*

Page, looking to the remoter past, assailed the "mistaken leadership" of the prewar and war period for departing from the true Southern mission, established by Jefferson, of uplifting the "forgotten man," and for plunging the section into the fatal consequences of the Civil War. To Page the "submerged people," that is the rural population of "sturdy fiber" and "robust vigor" of which he himself was a representative, was the true South upon which future greatness must be built.[6]

Most persuasive of all the historical revisions was that made by D. A. Tompkins, possibly the most energetic of all the promoters of the cotton mill campaign. He pictured the early nineteenth century, before the institution of slavery had become the dominant economic force in Southern life, as a golden age when Southern manufacturers had been more prosperous than those of any other section, and when Southerners had shown greater mechanical aptitude than Yankees. The "revolutionary growth" of the slave plantation system was, in Tompkins' exposition, both a break in Southern tradition and a fatal diversion of Southern energies into a form of agriculture which ruined manufactures, depressed the white wage-earning classes, and impoverished the section. Consequently the war which removed the incubus, in spite of the sufferings it entailed, proved not a tragedy but a blessing. Henceforth a greater future was in store when Southerners could prosecute to a happy completion the industrial development which "an excess zeal for slavery" had previously prevented.[7] If Tompkins' thesis rested upon shaky historical evidence it seemed plausible to the supporters of the new régime and permitted them to claim that they were patriotic Southerners working in loyalty to the Southern past.

At times the more impetuous of the young men indulged in harsh strictures of those members of the older generation

---

[6] Hendricks, "Training of an American," *passim.*

[7] Tompkins expressed these opinions on many occasions in speeches, some of which were published in pamphlet form, in editorials of his newspaper, the *Charlotte Observer,* and in several books, more notably, "Cotton Mills" (Charlotte, 1899), "Cotton and Cotton Oil" (Charlotte, 1900), and "History of Mecklenburg County and the City of Charlotte," (1903). See also G. T. Winston, "A Builder of the New South" (New York, 1920).

who held tenaciously to the beliefs of antebellum days. This was notably true of Walter Hines Page who spoke contemptuously of "mummies," "ghosts," and "Bourbons," and on one occasion arrogantly asserted that "What North Carolina most needs is a few first-class funerals."[8] But more normal was the practice of idealizing the past without permitting it to interfere with the practices of the present. Youth needed courage to stifle the feeling of inferiority that arose out of the South's defeat. This, too, they received from the Old South by boasting of the greatness of their fathers. They made a golden age of the plantation era and a heroic epoch of the Confederate War. In doing so they equipped themselves with strength to face the future.

The idealization of the past arose naturally from boyhoods spent in the exciting days of war and Reconstruction. Too young to comprehend the full significance of the events that occupied the lives of their parents, the children who formed the new generation were deeply impressed that the period had been one of great fortitude and devotion. Joel Chandler Harris and Thomas Nelson Page were imbued with a sense of reverence toward the Old South and urged the New to emulate its virtues. Henry W. Grady gloried in the bravery of the Confederate soldier. Tompkins, while attacking the economics of slavery, defended the humanity of the system, and wrote idyllic pictures of "Life in the Old South." Woodrow Wilson, after condemning the institution of slavery and the policy of Southern independence, paid "loving tribute to the virtues of the leaders of secession, to the purity of their purposes, to the righteousness of the cause which they thought they were promoting — and to the immortal courage of the soldiers of the Confederacy."[9] Even Walter Hines Page wanted to combine the best features of "two distinct civilizations," so as to move forward without repining but with a reverential respect for the past.[10]

[8] Hendricks, "Training of an American," 168. See also the "Mummy Letters," ibid., 176–189, and Nicholas Worth (pseud. for W. H. Page) "The Southerner" (New York, 1909).
[9] Wilson, op. cit., 57.
[10] W. H. Page, "Story of an Old Southern Borough," Atlantic, XLVII (1881), 658.

Yet there was a distinction in the experiences of the two generations which set them apart and prevented complete understanding. Old and new alike had known impoverishment and sacrifice, stinting economy and relentless toil, fear of race conflict and the humiliation of Reconstruction. But to one the trials and discipline had come in the evening of life after a full day of sunshine and laughter. To the other there had never been a sunrise. Life itself had begun in darkness. The older generation was warmed by the mellow recollection of the past. But tales of departed grandeur could only arouse the younger into restless yearning for a better life of its own. "The elders had had their day," wrote one of the growing generation, "and had had acquaintance with achievement and sadness and defeat." Youth now demanded the right to live unencumbered by the legacies which chained their parents to the past.[11]

Another distinction between the generations was to be found in the origin and training of their leaders. Men to the gentry born had for the most part been accepted as the natural spokesmen of the Old South. Men of the same class, Curry and Lamar, Hampton and Johnston, had assumed the direction of the South's first adjustment to the new way of life. But birth, privilege, gentility of training, were of little aid in climbing the steep and rocky path that lay before the young men growing up. Sturdiness of fiber, persistence of morale, and quickness of wit became the necessary equipment for leadership. The new men who began to emerge at the top in the eighties revealed a background somewhat novel in the annals of the South. Their life stories were told in anecdotes which duplicated the "success pattern" so familiar to the North and West. It seemed to Henry Watterson as though a Yankeedom had arisen from within the South, with every Southerner emulating traits which the Old South would have contemptuously associated with shop-keepers.[12]

Even Horatio Alger could not have improved upon the

[11] E. A. Alderman, *J. L. M. Curry: A Memorial Address* (pamphlet, Brooklyn, 1902), 9–10.

[12] Henry Watterson, "Oddities of Southern Life," *Century.* XXIII (1883), 895.

story of Joel Chandler Harris's rise from obscure poverty to fame as "Uncle Remus." [13] The epic of Charles D. McIver, who began his teaching career in 1881, was that of the raw, eager, and resolute country boy, who, working his way through college, found a broader life, the benefits of which he henceforth sought to give to others. [14] The anecdote of his boyhood most repeated by Charles B. Aycock, one day to be known as the "Education Governor" of North Carolina, was the impression he received when seeing his mother make her mark when signing a deed. [15] The career of Booker T. Washington, who in 1881 founded the great New South institution at Tuskegee, was a narrative of overcoming obstacles, discouragements and temptations, the most colorful incident of which was the poor boy sleeping under a board sidewalk to save pennies that might be devoted to his education. [16]

Inevitably the gentler attributes of aristocratic leadership disappeared. "The very life which made them possible is gone," wrote Watterson. [17] Crude energy and calculating shrewdness were more essential to the new age. Here and there a scion of the gentry, like Thomas Nelson Page, achieved prominence without seemingly to depart from the tradition. But more frequently, as in the cases of Tompkins and Grady, birth on a plantation or education in a university did not remove the necessity of "paddling one's own canoe." If leaders furnished by the gentry donned the appurtenances of "self-made men," it was even more true of the larger number who emerged from the farming and merchant classes into positions of prominence. [18] Struggle for material achievement, whether it was to gain wealth, build a factory, or plant a school, was the major characteristic of the new leadership. Success was measured largely in terms of the extent to which

[13] Julia Collier Harris, "The Life and Letters of Joel Chandler Harris" (Boston, 1918), chs. i–ix.

[14] E. A. Alderman, "Charles D. McIver of North Carolina," *Sewanee Review*, XV (1907), 100–110.

[15] R. D. W. Connor and C. Poe, "The Life and Speeches of Charles Brantley Aycock" (Garden City, 1912), 7.

[16] B. T. Washington, "Up from Slavery" (New York, 1901), chs. i–iii.

[17] Watterson, *op. cit*, 895.

[18] A. M. Schlesinger, "The Rise of the City," 1878–1898 (New York, 1933), 15.

the individual beat down and escaped the menace of poverty. If such efforts narrowed the spirit and sharpened the acquisitive traits, it must also be apparent that they required a ruggedness of moral force few people have ever surpassed. If life in the New South seemed less pleasant, there was in compensation a strength of character not unworthy of a section which had produced the Washington of Valley Forge and the Lee of Appomattox.

It was inspiring to see the spirit of youth rise triumphant over the primitive postwar conditions of the South and to replace the "mournful threnodies" of Father Ryan's "Conquered Banner" with songs of hope.[19] The older generation might beget the creed, but it remained for youth to contribute the faith and optimism that made the conception of a "New South" a positive agency for change. It was youth which read into the many inadequacies in Southern life not defeat but opportunity. "The South" wrote Woodrow Wilson in 1881, "has just begun to grow. . . . There appear to be no limits to the possibilities of her development; and I think that to grow up with a new section is no small advantage to one who seeks to gain position and influence." [20]

The voice of ambition was heard again in the early eighties as a reviving prosperity seemed to spread over the South. The day of narrow, local prejudice had passed away, noted one observer, "and we are now about to enter on the career of progress which ought to have commenced half a century ago, but which we believe will now advance with accelerated speed." [21] The New South was more than the sum total of changes that the war had effected. Its spirit was one of optimism, a belief in progress, a faith in Southerners. If this proceeded from purely Southern conditions, it was an expression of those traits in Southern character which most nearly approximated the attributes of Northern and Western life and lay basic in the American character.

The new spirit and the new energy found complete expression

[19] Alderman, as quoted in Connor and Poe, "Aycock," 22.
[20] R. S. Baker, "Woodrow Wilson, Life and Letters" (New York, 1927), I, 143.
[21] A. H. H. Stuart, "Facts Worth Thinking About," *Virginias*, II (1881), 51.

in the industrial transformation of certain areas of the South during the decade of the eighties. So rapidly did manufactures develop that it seemed as though the South was undergoing a complete economic revolution. Yet the roots of the movement rested deep in the Southern past. For at least half a century before 1880 the obvious advantages the South possessed in raw materials, water power, and potential labor had been fully known. Individuals had ventured profitably in cotton, iron, and tobacco manufactures, and a powerful propaganda had been urged to demonstrate the advantages of adding a partial industrialization to complement Southern agriculture. If first the slave economy and then the impoverishment and disorder of Reconstruction had operated as impediments, the one was destroyed by the war and the other proved to be not an unmixed evil. Mills had been rebuilt, and, even in the darkest days of Reconstruction, made profits large enough to discharge indebtedness and still yield dividends which in certain instances amounted to twenty-five per cent. and more.[22] By the early seventies the South had recovered all that it had possessed industrially in 1860.

Meanwhile the altered life of the postwar South revealed conditions far more favorable to factory expansion than had previously existed. The influence of the war blockade in demonstrating the section's lack of self-sufficiency, and the overthrow of the planting aristocracy made popular the propaganda of diversification and weakened the appeal that agriculture once had exercised as a road to wealth and social prominence. Where planters had formerly reinvested profits in land and slaves, the merchants and farmers who made money in the new regime could be tempted to place some of their savings in manufactures, and even, if they were ambitious, to launch forth on new careers as industrialists themselves. The recovery of political self-rule gave added confidence, as well as removed the necessity of devoting energy to politics. Even more important was the growing conviction that the South might win back industrially the pride it had lost on the field of battle. No sweeter revenge sug-

---

[22] *Commercial and Financial Chronicle,* Nov. 4, 1871; King, "Great South," 472; E. Armes, "The Story of Coal and Iron in Alabama" (Birmingham, 1910), ch. xiv.

gested itself to Southerners than that of beating the North in
the arena where the latter had always claimed supremacy.[23]

Favorable as the situation was becoming, the actual development of Southern manufactures by 1880 was modest indeed in
comparison with the tremendous strides the North was taking.
The eighties, however, witnessed a growth so remarkable that
all the ancient prejudices and lingering doubts were swept
aside. The number of factories, furnaces, and forges multiplied, giving the South again something to boast about. By
1890 a firm and permanent basis for a variety of manufactures
was established, and the wealth and prosperity of Dixie no
longer depended solely upon agriculture. It proceeded from a
more diversified economy.

The pace of development was sensationally rapid, dazzling
the imagination, and stimulating the enthusiasm of the be-
lievers in the new order. A feebly established, dispersed, and
antiquated iron industry was modernized, centralized in natural areas, and tremendously expanded. The amount of Southern pig iron increased from less than four hundred thousand
tons in 1880 to more than one million seven hundred thousand
in 1890. Even more impressive to the Southern mind was the
growth of cotton mills. The number of spindles trebled in the
ten year period — from slightly more than five hundred thousand to one million six hundred thousand. Not to be outdone by
its rival staple, the tobacco plant yielded increased profits by a
fifty per cent. growth of manufactures, featured by the appearance of larger plants and the mechanization of cigarette
making. The eighties also witnessed the development of a number of lesser industries. Charleston had a momentary boom in
exploiting newly discovered beds of phosphate rock for the
manufacture of fertilizer. Hitherto discarded cotton hulks were
also made to yield fertilizer, while the cotton seed was found
to be a source of wealth by conversion into a marketable oil for
cooking. The amount of timber taken from Southern forests
more than doubled between 1880 and 1890, giving the South
first rank as a source of the nation's lumber supply, besides
making freight for Southern railroads, and here and there, as

[23] Broadus Mitchell, "Rise of the Cotton Mills in the South" (Baltimore,
1921), 90.

at High Point, North Carolina, giving rise to a manufacture of furniture. As new beds of coal were opened, the Southern production increased from six million tons in 1880 to twenty-two in 1890. Keeping pace with the industrial development was the continued extension and consolidation of the Southern railroad system. The twenty thousand miles of new track laid between 1880 and 1890 approximately doubled the total mileage.[24]

Southerners hailed this triumph of enterprise as the greatest achievement of the New South. It inspired confidence and generated pride. Especially was it gratifying to boast that the great industrial progress was the result of Southern resources, capital, and leadership. The entire impulse was Southern in its origin. The cotton mill campaign was waged in the face of Northern predictions of its failure. The energy which developed Birmingham and Chattanooga and modernized the iron industry in Virginia was almost exclusively native born. Nor did the South depend on outside agencies for raw material or labor. All that it needed in the way of cotton, tobacco, lumber, coal, and iron was found in its own fields or mines. Its labor was drawn from its own farms and mountain coves. So far as energy, labor, and raw materials were concerned, the South alone deserves the credit or blame for bringing factory, mill, and furnace into its agricultural domain.

It is also probably true that the South furnished the greater portion of the capital which financed the industrialization of the eighties. Nevertheless important qualifications must be made to this generalization. Southern sentiment remained distinctly friendly toward welcoming investments from the North.

---

[24] *Eleventh Census, 1890, Manufactures, Selected Industries;* Edmonds in the *Manufacturers' Record* gave much space to Southern development, although some allowance should be made for his enthusiasm which led to exaggeration. Statistics in the *Com. and Fin. Chron.* for current movements were also larger than the Census figures, but these were always corrected in later issues. The best secondary accounts are Mitchell, "Cotton Mills"; Armes, "Coal and Iron"; J. C. Ballagh (ed.), "Economic History of the South," in vol. vi of "The South in the Building of the Nation" (Richmond, 1909); P. A. Bruce, "The Rise of the New South" (Philadelphia, 1905); and M. Jacobstein, "The Tobacco Industry in the United States" (New York, 1907). See also B. W. Arnold, "History of the Tobacco Industry in Virginia from 1860 to 1894" (Baltimore, 1897); A. Kohn, "The Cotton Mills of South Carolina" (Columbia, 1907); S. D. Lee, "The South since the War," *Confederate Military History* (Atlanta, 1899), XII; and H. Thompson, "From Cotton Field to Cotton Mill" (New York, 1906).

Henry W. Grady expressed the prevailing opinion when he said that the South had hung out the latchstring and hoped the North would freely enter. The *Charleston News and Courier,* the *Manufacturers' Record,* and the *Virginias Magazine* actively solicited Northern capital, and reported a generous movement of money from the North to the South.[25] But no one seems ever to have gone beyond vague expressions of opinion into a presentation of concrete evidence.

The North, as has been noted, felt no hesitance in investing in Southern railways. The extension of the eighties was financed by Northern banking houses in the same manner as that of the seventies. By 1882 it could be said that a few great syndicates, located chiefly in New York and Philadelphia and representing Northern and English capital, controlled most of the railways of the South, and this fact became increasingly true as the tendency was toward ever greater combination and integration.[26] Investments in railroads led naturally to an interest in a general development of the section in which the lines were located.

Nowhere was this better illustrated than in the development of the coal and iron industry of Virginia and West Virginia. Southern enterprise supported by Northern capital provided the transportation facilities by creating the two great systems, the Chesapeake and Ohio and the Norfolk and Western, which opened the region and gave it access to national markets. But the field of investment widened far beyond the financing of railroads. Coal lands and mineral beds were purchased and developed. Old furnaces were modernized and new ones constructed. Rolling mills, nail works, and foundries were established. Especially active in this financing were A. A. Low, of New York, George W. Perkins, of New York, Theodore Dwight, of Philadelphia, Samuel Coit, of Hartford, Connecticut, and H. C. Frick, of Pittsburgh. Such important properties as the Clyde syndicate, the Crimmora manganese mines, the Pocahontas mines, the Shenandoah iron works, the Lowmoor iron works, the New Castle slate quarries, the Old Dominion

---

[25] *Charleston News and Courier,* March 14, 1881; *Manufacturers' Record,* July 1, 1882; *Virginias,* I (1880), 1–15, II (1881), 109, V (1884), 27.
[26] *Manufacturers' Record,* March 18, 1882.

Land Company which developed properties along the route of the Chesapeake and Ohio and built up the city of Newport News, the James River Steel Manufacturing and Mining Company, the Fayette Coal and Coke Company, the Coral Marble Company, the Holston Salt Works, the Great Kanawha Coal Company, and the Virginia Beach development were all projects financed by Pennsylvania, New York, New England, and other Northern capital.[27] The economic life of Virginia was not only invigorated, but the industrial future of the State was linked with business interests resident in the North.

The capital as well as the enterprise which carried Chattanooga and Birmingham through the precarious period of beginnings was more largely Southern in origin. Nevertheless some of the pioneers like W. S. McElwain secured capital from the North as early as 1865 to reconstruct furnaces destroyed in the war. Moreover individual Northerners made important contributions both in management and finance. General John T. Wilder, of Ohio, who first learned of the possibilities of Chattanooga in 1863 while campaigning in the Union army, established in 1867 what was then the largest iron works in the district with capital raised in Ohio and Indiana. Likewise David Thomas, a veteran of the Pennsylvania field, with his son Samuel and grandson Edwin, removed to Alabama in the late sixties, and coöperated with natives in initiating undertakings which later proved significant. Even more outstanding was Truman H. Aldrich, of New York, who, entering the Birmingham district in 1872 with Northern capital, joined his energies and resources with the Alabamans, Sloss and De Bardeleben, to become with them the key men of the industry. When the period of expansion and combination came in the years around 1886 and 1887, the Birmingham-Chattanooga area had so demonstrated its ability to produce pig iron profitably that the great promotions of De Bardeleben and Aldrich were readily financed by Northern bankers. In the same period (1886) the Tennessee Coal, Iron, and Railroad Company acquired its first properties in Birmingham, initiating a policy of expansion which in the nineties would lead to a complete absorption of Southern iron and steel into a national integration.

[27] *Virginias*, I-VI (1880-1885), *passim*.

Even before this occurred, however, the Southern producers realized that the major portion of their iron must be marketed outside the area. The middle eighties saw an increasing tonnage passing through Birmingham and Chattanooga to the North and West.[28]

Northern capital was far more reluctant to give support to the building of cotton mills in the South. In fact, the established textile manufacturers of New England did much at the start in spreading the impression that Southern mills could not operate with profit.[29] Occasionally direct solicitation for Northern capital met with success, as was true in the case of the Graniteville, South Carolina, factory which in 1867 was reorganized and expanded with Northern money.[30] But in the large majority of cases the promoter had to rely upon domestic resources.

The result was that the cotton mills were financed through appeals to local patriotism. Campaigns were waged to enlist every community interest in support of the new enterprise. Village merchants were convinced that a factory population would increase the demand for their goods. Preachers were told that labor for idle hands would encourage sobriety and thrift. Local bankers were led to expect an increase in savings deposits. Farmers were told that the mills would consume their cotton, the factory hands would buy their food crops, and their wives and children find employment in the mills. If appeals to interest failed, pride was stimulated by slogans which urged the men of Dixie to gain industrial emancipation from the Yankees. The promoters were also favored by the change of attitude, already noted, which had convinced Southerners that economic redemption depended upon an extension of manufactures. The varied sources of the movement were woven together in a fervent crusade to "bring the cotton mill to the cotton field." In such a manner it was possible to scrape together the small savings of many investors, and the mill thus became a reservoir of local savings and a symbol of community progress, as well as a purely business enterprise.

[28] Armes, "Coal and Iron," 196–197, 212, 266–274, 332, 339–349, 361–362; King, "Great South," 212.
[29] See as typical, Edward Atkinson, *Address Given in Atlanta, Georgia, in October, 1880* (pamphlet, Boston, 1881).
[30] Kohn, "Cotton Mills of South Carolina," 19.

It remains to be pointed out, however, that local capital thus painfully collected was supplemented by important contributions from Northern sources. Northern manufacturers of mill machinery usually accepted stock in the mills they equipped in part payment of the machinery purchased from them. Northern commission houses also purchased stock, and contributed cash for working capital, in return for the privilege of marketing the output. A real integration of interest was thus established. The commission houses were located almost completely in Philadelphia and New York. The market for the Southern product therefore lay outside the section. If the Southern factory owner was interested in making a profitable Northern connection, it was equally in the interest of the commission house to do all that it could to make prosperous the mill whose goods it marketed.

The Southern mills during the eighties specialized in the manufacture of coarse yarn and cloth. Almost from the start the majority of the mills, favored by local enthusiasm, a cheap and amenable labor force, efficient new machinery, and low cost water power, made net profits which frequently reached from forty to sixty per cent. and averaged around fifteen. It was then that New England spinners began to show an interest in the Southern field. Branch mills to manufacture the coarser products were acquired in the late eighties by several established New England corporations.[31] Possibly the first migration of an entire cotton mill from North to South occurred in 1889, when the Providence, Rhode Island, firm of Lockwood, Greene, and Company closed their Newburyport, Massachusetts, mills and moved the machinery to Spartanburg, South Carolina. Within the next decade this firm was to build mills that added two million spindles to the South, more than the entire section had possessed when the migration began.[32]

It seems a paradox that the South became more nationally minded in direct ratio to the extent it achieved a degree of in-

[31] The Dwight Manufacturing Company, of Chicopee, Massachusetts, established a profitable branch at Alabama City, Alabama, while the Goff interests, which had mills in Massachusetts and Rhode Island, purchased the Riverside Mills of Augusta, Georgia, in 1887. "Lamb's Textiles," II, 47, 337–338.
[32] "Lamb's Textiles," I, 339–340.

dustrial self-sufficiency. In the ante-bellum South the lack of diversification had generated sectional animosity. The new age was premised upon a conviction that material prosperity and sectional harmony went hand in hand. The business brains, capital, and technology of North and South found a community of interest politicians had never known. It seemed as though a vast wall of misunderstanding had fallen, destroying the isolation of the earlier years.

The industrial expansion appeared all the more revolutionary because it was concentrated in well-defined areas. The iron industry was localized in two centers, the Virginias and the Birmingham-Chattanooga district. Cotton mills clustered in a belt that followed the Piedmont crescent through the Carolinas into Georgia and Alabama. Tobacco manufactures were restricted largely to cities like Richmond, Durham, and Louisville, in the three states of Virginia, North Carolina, and Kentucky. The economic life of such regions was completely altered. But in contrast the greater portion of the South remained the most rural part of the United States, seemingly unaffected by the vigor and prosperity of the changing order. The growth of manufactures made no appreciable conquest upon the dominant hold agriculture exercised upon the South, although for the moment it was the booming, confident voice of the business man which sang the pæans to a New South. The coming of industry to the South did, however, disrupt the section's economic unity. A divided Dixie would prove a weaker resistant to the advancing forces of nationalism.

One of the newer formative influences which accompanied the expansion of manufactures was the growth in urban population. In certain instances the development of manufactures acted directly to create new cities or to multiply the inhabitants of others. This was notably true of Birmingham, the site of which was a cotton field in 1869, and which grew from three thousand in 1880 to twenty-six thousand in 1890. Durham, North Carolina, was converted from an insignificant village into a thriving center of tobacco manufactures. Older cities like Chattanooga, which increased one hundred and fifty per cent. in the eighties, and Richmond, which witnessed a twin development of iron and tobacco, were remade into boom cities of the New South. Columbia, South Carolina, "rose from her ashes" to exclaim, during her centennial celebration in 1891, that prosperity had dried all her tears. Norfolk was greatly invigorated by the industrial development of the Virginias, while an adjacent tidewater plantation was converted into the city of Newport News by the hand of Collis P. Huntington, who there developed one of the greatest shipyards in the United States. More typical than the larger cities, however, especially in the cotton mill belt, were a number of smaller places like Lynchburg, Virginia, Charlotte, North Carolina, and Greenville, South Carolina. Such a town had within its limits a cluster of mills or furnaces, but its life was composed mainly of the activities of merchants, bankers, and professional men who served the needs of the neighboring villages and farms.[83]

The extension of the railway system into all parts of the South likewise fostered the rise of cities. Richmond, served by the Chesapeake and Ohio, the Atlantic Coast Line, the Seaboard Air Line, and the Southern Railway, became an important distributing center of the Upper South. West of the Alleghenies, Louisville, Knoxville, Nashville, and Memphis felt the same invigorating tonic and grew rapidly in population and wealth.

Most energetic and alert of the new cities was Atlanta, which grew from thirty-seven thousand to sixty-five thousand in the ten-year period. Favorably situated and admirably served by a network of railways, the Georgia capital forged ahead as the chief distributing center of the Southeast. To observers there seemed little of the Old South about it. Many described it as a Southern Chicago.[34] But the model city which all Atlantans hoped to pattern after was New York. Actually Atlanta was "a new, vigorous, awkwardly alert city, . . . modern and unromantic," with much of the crude energy and soaring ambition typical of the Middle West in the same period.[35] If Atlanta epitomized the spirit of the New South, it was still, in spite of

---

[33] *Eleventh Census, 1890, Population,* 379–380; W. K. Boyd, "Story of Durham" (Durham, 1925); Bruce, "The New South," 222; *Proceedings of the Centennial Celebration of Columbia, S. C.* (Columbia, 1891).

[34] A. K. McClure, "The South" (Philadelphia, 1886), 58–60; Ernest Ingersoll, "The City of Atlanta," *Harper's Monthly Magazine,* LX (1879), 30–43; H. M. Field, "Bright Skies and Dark Shadows" (New York, 1890), 102.

[35] King, "The Great South," 350; M. J. Verdery, "The New South," *North American Review,* CXLIV (1887), 117.

its proud pretense of being a metropolis, like Chattanooga and Birmingham, little more than an overgrown town. Nor could it claim to be as typical of the section as the sleepy cotton markets like Augusta, Savannah, and Mobile, "whose growth, if they have any, is imperceptible, and whose pulse beats with only a faint flutter." [36]

Yet these new cities were dynamos generating energy to beat against the inertia of the old traditions. They fostered, for one thing, newspapers whose editors were imbued with the restless spirit of progress. Dawson had already shown what a brilliant and courageous journalist could do even when surrounded by the mellowed traditions of Charleston. Until his death in 1889 he continued to fight hard for the industrial awakening of the South. Likewise the old city of Mobile sheltered the *Register,* edited by John Forsyth, a Georgian born in 1853, which pleaded for a united nation, progressive industry, and agricultural diversification. In Louisville the redoubtable "Marse" Henry Watterson made the *Courier Journal* an influential newspaper which was accepted in the North as an oracle of Southern opinion. D. A. Tompkins purchased the *Charlotte Observer* and placed in its editorial sanctum Joseph P. Caldwell, a man who spoke the language of industrialism. But again it was Atlanta which took the leadership. The *Atlanta Constitution,* edited by Henry W. Grady and Joel Chandler Harris, both young men of the New South, rose to primacy as the South's leading advocate of business enterprise and of friendship with the North. [37]

Whether or not this journalism accomplished much in penetrating the rural aloofness of the South, it did reveal anew that the young men rising to leadership were governed by the desire to harmonize Southern regionalism and American nationalism. Possibly the chief influence of their activity was to advertise a New South of progress and reconciliation. No concept was more often transmitted to the North in the eighties than that the South had buried its resentments and had entered

---

[36] Ingersoll, *op. cit.,* 33.
[37] J. C. Harris, "Life, Writings, and Speeches of Henry W. Grady" (New York, 1890); Julia Collier Harris, "Joel Chandler Harris, Editor and Essayist" (Chapel Hill, 1931).

a new era of good feeling based upon an integration of material interests.

Contributing greatly to the spread of this propaganda was a series of expositions held in Southern cities during the decade. Atlanta held an International Cotton Exposition in 1881, Louisville a Southern Exposition in 1883, New Orleans a Cotton Centennial Exposition in 1885, and Richmond an Exposition in 1888.[38] The motive for these displays was to remedy the inadequate representation of Southern industry in the Philadelphia Exhibition of 1876, to advertise Southern resources, and to demonstrate the national patriotism of the New South.

The expositions were built upon a generous coöperation of North and South. Northern manufacturers willingly sent their fabrics and machinery to Atlanta and New Orleans to complement the Southern displays. General Sherman contributed two thousand dollars to the former exposition to begin a liberal subscription raised in the North. Congress appropriated a million dollars to the general fund of the New Orleans Exposition and an additional three hundred thousand dollars for a national exhibit. Northern States likewise took prominent parts in displaying their resources, contributing their share to establishing a sentiment of friendliness between the sections. The usual fraternizing of individuals representing Union and Confederate backgrounds occurred, and the "late unpleasantness" was interred beneath the oratory of reconciliation. There was little new in these felicitations, not even the many naïve assertions that "now, at last, we are one country." But it does seem true, as the editor of *Harper's Weekly* observed, that the "pocket nerve" was more intimately affected, and that "men do not easily quarrel who are engaged in prosperous business one with another." [39]

[38] *Appletons' Annual Cyclopædia* (1881), 260–271; (1883), 464–465; (1884), 573–579; *Commercial and Financial Chronicle,* Jan. 7, 1882; *Century,* XXIII (1882), 563–574, XXX (1885), 3–14; *Lippincott's* XXXIV (1885), 275–285, 408–417; *Harper's Weekly,* Jan. 3, 10, 17, 24, and 31, 1885.
[39] *Charleston News and Courier,* May 3, 1881; *Appletons' Annual Cyclopædia* (1884), 574; B. E. Mahan, "Iowa at the New Orleans Fair," *Palimpsest,* VI (1925), 77–94; Maud Howe Elliott, "Three Generations," 204–216; *Harper's Weekly,* Aug. 4, 1883; R. Brinkerhoff, "Recollections of a Life Time" (Cincinnati, 1900), 281–284.

The note of optimism struck by the boosters and builders of the New South met a cordial response in the North. Edward Atkinson, a distinguished New England cotton economist, who expressed skepticism in regard to Southern success in textile manufacturing and attempted to discourage the cotton mill campaign, nevertheless believed that a closer union should be established between the business interests of the North and South, and worked persistently through speeches, magazine articles, and personal contacts to establish a greater cordiality of sentiment. The keynote of his message was stated in an article published in the *International Review* for March 1881.

The old "Solid South" of slavery and Bourbonism is dead. A new South is rising from the ashes, eager to keep step with the North in the onward march of the Solid Nation.

It is significant that Atkinson, in spite of his hostility to Southern textile manufactures, always received a hearty welcome in the South, especially at Atlanta.[40]

It was this note which became the dominant theme in the Northern reporting of the South during the eighties. The output was far greater in quantity than that of the seventies, but it was not so high in quality. Enthusiasm took the place of scholarship, while boosting seemed more in vogue than analysis. Actually there was little new that could be said in description of the South that had not been said by King and Nordhoff. But every newspaper and periodical felt it necessary to send correspondents into the section on annual tours of observation, while politicians and industrialists as well as casual observers rushed into print to tell again the familiar story.

The reporter who achieved the greatest fame in this respect in the eighties was J. B. Harrison, whose letters, first printed in the *New York Tribune* in 1881, were repeated with little change in the *Atlantic Monthly,* and republished in a widely disseminated pamphlet.[41] The North uncritically accepted Harrison's book as the best account of the South since Olmsted —

[40] Edward Atkinson, "The Solid South?", *International Review* (1881), 197–209. See also H. F. Williamson, "Edward Atkinson" (Boston, 1934).
[41] "Glimpses of a New Dixie," *Tribune Extra No. 81;* "Studies of the South," *Atlantic,* XLIX–LI (1882–1883), serially in eleven instalments.

certainly an undeserved encomium — while Joel Chandler
Harris hailed it as the most just and impartial record of observation since the war.[42] Harrison, in fact, traversed familiar
ground. But he did present effectively, through the columns of
a great Northern newspaper and a staunch Yankee periodical,
a popular narrative which portrayed a reconciled South, indifferent to partisan controversy, and devoting its strength to
work, education, and the improvement of race relations.

Carl Schurz likewise repeated the sterotyped pattern in a
book published in 1885 with the now hackneyed title of "The
New South." But because of the prominence of its author, and
the fact that Schurz's report on Southern conditions twenty
years earlier had been a mainstay of Radicalism, the book is
worthy of comment. In a sense Schurz was merely justifying
his recent political career as a Liberal Republican and a re-
former in the Hayes administration when he described a
South "as loyal to the Union as the people of any part of the
country"; one that was quietly solving its race problem, and
developing its resources in harmony with "a great, strong,
prosperous, and united country." Schurz even justified the
affection Southerners entertained for Jefferson Davis, and explained how natural and proper it was for the section to elect
to high office its former Confederate leaders.[43]

The prolific pen of Charles Dudley Warner, a writer much
in vogue in the North, produced a book of "Studies in the
South and West." Warner, too, discovered "that the war is
over in spirit as well as in deed," and that "the thoughts of the
people are not upon . . . the past at all, . . . but upon the
future, upon business, upon a revival of trade, upon education,
and adjustment to the new state of things." [44] Periodicals and
newspapers reiterated the observation until it seemed as though
every one with literary or journalistic aspirations had made a
friendly raid or two into the South. Even casual tourists, un-
blessed by brains or insight, but prompted perhaps with the
pious hope of doing their bit in the swelling chorus of recon-

[42] *Atlanta Constitution*, March 14, 1883.
[43] Carl Schurz, "The New South" (New York, 1885), 14, 15, 18, 29, 30.
[44] C. D. Warner, "Studies in the South and West" (New York, 1889).
Some of the chapters of this book had appeared earlier in *Harper's Monthly*,
LXXI (1885), 546–551; LXXIV (1887), 186–206, 334–354, 634–640.

ciliation, added their observations. Some seemed surprised to find that hotels in Mobile had gas, electric bells, and Grand Rapids furniture just "as though they might have been transplanted from New York." [45] Others became lyrical in relating the heroism displayed by Southerners in rebuilding shattered fortunes at a time when "Great heavens! what injustice we [Northerners] had been doing them!" [46]

The oracle of the commonplace, however, seems to have been an English gentlewoman. Lady Duffus Hardy, who published her "Down South" in 1883, must have worn glasses deeply colored in the propaganda of the day. Her eyes could recognize not "a single feature of its ancient self" in the South. She believed that Northern capital had rehabilitated the section, and that "upon the ruins of a dead past," Southerners had built a life "nobler, far nobler" than that of the "prideful days" before the war.[47] Among the notable conversions of the eighties it is gratifying and somewhat amusing to include the battle-scarred veteran of innumerable "bloody shirt" campaigns, Thomas Nast. A perusal of *Harper's Weekly* would reveal illustrations from this master cartoonist such as the one presenting "Industry, the Real Connecting Link," depicted as a cord of flowers uniting "South," uniformed in gray, and "North," wearing blue, before a sun labeled "patriotism and prosperity." This "looked like business" to Nast, as did "The Queen of Industry, or the New South," where a cotton loom rested upon a somewhat flattened and dismal-looking "arrogant spirit of slavery." Nast attained the climax in an elaborate cover design, "On Earth Peace, Good Will Toward Men," which commemorated the New Orleans Exposition where apparently business enterprise was accomplishing work usually associated with angels.

Possibly the one new element in this reporting was the participation in it of business men and industrially minded politicians. Even before the Southerner R. H. Edmonds had apotheosized the industrial progress of the New South in "The

[45] *Harper's Monthly*, LXXV (1887), 598.
[46] *Ibid.*, 438. See also *Forum*, I (1886), 150; *Atlantic*, LIII (1884), 241–250.
[47] Lady Duffus Hardy, "Down South" (London, 1883), 15, 118–119, 275–276.

South's Redemption from Poverty to Prosperity," published in 1890, two Northerners, A. K. McClure and W. D. ("Pig Iron") Kelley, had anticipated all his choicest superlatives. McClure's "The South, Its Industrial, Financial, and Political Condition" (1886) was a panegyric of Southern achievement which sought to demonstrate how the growing business inter-course between the sections was hastening the restoration of fraternity and enlarging the prosperity of both sections. Kelley was purely and simply a booster who made the pages of his book, "The Old South and the New" (1888), a vehicle of propaganda for industrialization. Yet these two books unquestionably reached the hands of some of the most powerful business men of the North, and possibly they were believed.

Meanwhile prominent financiers and industrialists of the North, like Abram S. Hewitt, Edward Cooper, and Andrew Carnegie, made occasional visits to the South and published comments on their observations. Typical of this group was a letter written by a New York banker, Frederick Taylor, who stated in the *Manufacturers' Record* that "It seemed to me that we traveled through a continuous and unbroken strain of what has been aptly termed the music of progress — the whir of the spindle, the buzz of the saw, the roar of the furnace, and the throb of the locomotive." [48] One wonders what had become of Olmsted's stretches of solitude, or Campbell's vast domains of agriculture, or Walter Hines Page's quiet villages. What Taylor saw, others saw, or at least it was progress that they wrote about. And it is probably true that the North welcomed such reports, especially when it is remembered that news had once come from Atlanta, Richmond, and Chattanooga red with the blood of Union soldiers.

Nevertheless the picture thus presented, much as it might have contributed to reconciliation, was a distortion. To many Southerners the increased friendliness evidenced in the reporting was offset by frequent superficiality and over-simplification which combined to create an image so grotesque as to be unacceptable. Even the most charitably disposed observers were clumsy in their efforts to avoid treading upon the many susceptibilities of Southern pride. Thus one writer seeking

[48] Edmonds, "The South's Redemption," 5.

only to praise the achievement of former Confederates would
write, "Their cause was wrong but their conduct was heroic," [49]
and then wonder why Southerners, who of course would be
more inclined to debate the first half of the sentence than to
accept the praise embodied in the second, put him in the category of those who did not understand the South. Nor can it be
denied that a certain smug Pharisaism underlay much of the
eulogizing. The North took immoderate pleasure in its assumption that the South was taking on Northern ways. Southerners sensed an implied slur upon their past, and, not quite
knowing how to express the sentiment in words, constantly
asserted that the North did not yet know the heart of Dixie.

Consequently when a real grievance arose, the Southern
press was prone to fall back into old habits and angrily protest
against the "wild exploitation" of the South by "Northern
hacks." [50] Such a cause for dissension was created when the
Nation began a campaign to shame the South into doing something about its large number of homicides. Even so friendly
an advocate of the South as *Scribner's Monthly* joined in condemning "these Southern murders . . . as evidence of a
lawlessness and a degraded civilization much more notable
than anything that can be found among the Italian wilds and
mountains." [51] The usual recriminations ensued. Southern
newspapers rose as one in resentment of the "false witness."
Possibly the South was too sensitive as to the honor of its
civilization. But on the other hand it did seem as though the
North was criticizing not a wrong in the South so much as it
was attacking the South itself. Then too the *Nation,* especially
when Godkin was under the full sail of reform, drew so near
to God that normal folk felt an occasional irritation. In any
case, editors North and South found they had stones in their
hands as well as roses. The old bitterness broke out again, and
unhappiest of all was the fact that, in spite of all the invective,
no appreciable diminution occurred in the number of those
unfortunates whose lawless departure from Southern life continued to be an apparently inexhaustible source for debate.

[49] *Forum,* I (1886), 150.
[50] *Atlanta Constitution,* March 14, 1883.
[51] *Scribner's Monthly* (1879), 306–307.

Nevertheless, if occasionally a discordant note was struck, the orchestra of the eighties for the most part played in tune, and before the decade closed found its master conductor in the person of Henry W. Grady. On December 21, 1886, this thirty-six year old editor of the *Atlanta Constitution* addressed the New England Society of New York in New York City. He was not the first prominent Southerner to stand upon a Northern platform and plead for reconciliation. Nor did he have new ideas to offer. The content of his speech was a bundle of platitudes made trite by endless repetition. A "consecrated messenger of peace," he may well have been, but he certainly was not the first to get through the news that the "war was over" and that the erstwhile foes had learned to love each other. Nor was he the originator of the oratorical device of contrasting Cavalier and Puritan, making, through the inscrutable workings of some historical mystery, an English and, it must be said, romantic background responsible for the American Civil War. He could not even claim primacy in his tribute to Lincoln, who was made to embody the virtues of both Cavalier and Puritan, thus becoming an American whom North and South alike could love. The North had heard before descriptions of the beauty of the Old South, and explanations of what the Reconstruction South had suffered, knowing full well that after the heartstrings were touched the orator would describe a New South hard at work, without repining, building a glorious future. Even when the climax was reached and Grady "fearlessly threw" himself upon the generosity of an "untested mercy of a Northern audience," it was readily to be expected from previous experiences that speaker and listeners, some in tears and others on their feet shouting, would find themselves united, in the conclusion, as fellow countrymen who knew and therefore loved each other.

And so they did. Grady was met in Atlanta by a brass band, while North and South, East and West, the newspapers sent his eloquence reverberating through the land.[52] Something

[52] The speech is given in full in Harris, "Grady," 83–93. For editorial comment see *Atlanta Constitution*, Dec. 24, 1886; *New York Tribune*, Dec. 24, 1886; *Public Opinion*, II (1887), 235; *Century*, XXXIII (1887), 807–808; *Nation*, Dec. 30, 1886; *Harper's Weekly*, Jan. 8, 1887; and *Commercial and Financial Chronicle*, Dec. 25, 1886.

great had indeed occurred, but just what, it might be difficult to explain. Artistic as was the speech in its preparation, completely as it answered every Northern apprehension, glowing as was its appeal to patriotic fervor, successfully as it justified the South while at the same time it flattered the North, daintily as it picked its way around possible pitfalls (as for example when it dismissed General Sherman as a "kind of careless man about fire"), it alone could not explain the apotheosis of Grady by North and South alike as the great spokesman of the latter and the reconciler of the former.

Possibly it was the right word spoken at the right time, as the *Seattle Post* believed. Possibly it was the crescendo of emotion reaching its full volume of expression. But probably Joel Chandler Harris, Grady's co-editor on the *Constitution,* found the true explanation when he wrote that Grady was the embodiment of the spirit of the New South. This brilliant young man, whose father had fallen in the service of the Confederacy, whose position as editor of the South's leading newspaper had been won by energy, hard work, and zeal, was made to objectify the new life that had appeared in Dixie. The words that Grady uttered no longer seem important, even as the cotton mills and iron furnaces built in the eighties appear somewhat dwarfed by the growth of later years. Likewise Grady's work can be shown to be the legacy of an older South, as again was true of much of what the New South accomplished. But Grady's faith and Grady's optimism were a living fire peculiar to the New South he served. He became the recognized apostle of the new faith. The three years remaining of his life were devoted to the advancement of reconciliation and the economic upbuilding of the South.

Grady died December 23, 1889, in the thirty-ninth year of his life. Three days earlier he had made his final plea for sectional harmony, dramatically enough from a Northern platform in the city of Boston. Fourteen days before that Jefferson Davis had drawn his last breath of life. The Old and the New thus stood in contrast. Out of the ruins the one had left, the other seemingly had erected a new life of promise, hope, and greatness. The young men growing up had made it easier for

North and South, each cherishing different memories, to press forward in harmony to the ideal of a united nation.

Two years after Grady's death the people of Atlanta erected a monument to his memory, on which was inscribed, "When he died he was literally loving a nation into peace." Whether this be more than sentiment or not, it had been demonstrated by 1890 that a son of the South could, under the new conditions of life, be at the same time a loyal Southerner and a loyal American. This in short was the contribution of the New South to American nationalism. And it was because the young men had grown up under the tutelage of their fathers that some essence of the older Dixie remained to enter into the pattern of emerging Americanism.

CHAPTER VIII

THE SOUTH BEGINS TO WRITE

IN the realm of literature even more than in the field of business the New South demonstrated its capacity to participate completely in the life of the nation. American literature underwent important changes after the Civil War. The novels of domestic manners whose dreamy softness satisfied the taste of mid-century America went into the discard. The Civil War had been influential in broadening interest in American themes and in inspiring a buoyant pride in native life. Fiction became almost a matter of human geography, for the new writers seemed intent upon doing little more than describe in simple language the many local diversities of the national scene. "The everyday existence of the plain people," wrote a contemporary critic, "is the stuff of which literature is made." [1] There is little need for formal training in this type of composition. What was essential was keenness in observing the provincial traits that were described, and a vigorous faith that the province was a part of the awakened nation.

The South was admirably situated to participate in a prose fiction of local types and dialect. No section of America had such an abundance of picturesque detail. Local color was to be found in every corner of Dixie — the romantic Creoles of Louisiana, the droll Crackers of middle Georgia, the many ranges of Negro character, the "contemporary ancestors" of the Appalachian Mountains, the rustic democrat, and the plantation gentry. Moreover these characters acted against a background of rich and varied charm — the bayous of the Mississippi, the white fields of cotton, the humble cabin of the Negro or poor white, the shady verandah of the plantation

[1] Matthews, "Aspects of Fiction," 39.

mansion, the impenetrable swamps of the lowlands, the sea
islands off the coast, the mellow cities of the Old South, the
secluded mountain vales, the deep rusticity of Georgia. There
were currents and counter-currents in class and race relations
that yielded humor or tragedy according to the whim of the
author.

There was also a background of history that offered amaz-
ing contrasts of grandeur and pathos. "Here," wrote one of
the authors, "cavalier and covenanter joined hands to resist
the aggression of monarchy; here was a rampant and raging
love of liberty existing side by side with human slavery; here
was to be found culture, refinement, learning, the highest ideals
of character and conduct, the most exacting standards of
honor in private and official life, and the most sensitive insistence on justice and right, all touching elbows with an ignorance dense and barbarian. Here . . . were to be found aristocracy knocking about the country . . . arm in arm, hail-
fellows well met. Here, too, was the hospitality, hearty, simple
and unaffected, living next door to desperate feud." [2] There
was, finally, the history of the Confederacy, preëminent among
the "lost causes" of American history. A civilization fell with
its defeat, and the contrast of a New South remembering the
heroism of an old furnished an opportunity for pathos unexcelled in literature. It would have been "a miracle of stupid-
ity," as one Southerner observed, "if, in the . . . heyday of
provincial literature the New South had missed [this] golden
opportunity." [3]

Young men growing up without formal training for a literary career were, nevertheless, well equipped by experience to
work in a *genre* which required little more than that the author
"should write spontaneously and simply about those things he
is fullest of and best understands." [4] They set about to exploit
the raw materials of fiction with much the same spirit that
others of the same generation sought wealth in the undeveloped economic resources of the South. Keenness of outlook

[2] J. C. Harris, introduction to Eickemeyer, "Down South" (New York, 1900).
[3] W. P. Trent, "Tendencies of Higher Life in the South," *Atlantic*, LXXIX (1897), 767.
[4] Matthews, "Aspects of Fiction," 39.

and readiness to make the most of every contact were as characteristic of a writer like Harris as they were of a cotton mill builder like Tompkins. To upholders of the tradition of prewar gentility there seemed an element of debasement in this dominant trait of the New South. Charges were advanced that the young men worshiped at the shrine of Mammon, that they were indifferent to the intellectual refinements of an earlier age, that they "lowered the flag of intellectual, moral, and refined supremacy," and that they bowed too readily to flattery from the North.[5] It was, therefore, something of a surprise that the homespun virtues of the New South should give to Dixie a body of literature which the gentility of the Old South had never yielded.

The boast of William L. Yancey — "Our poetry is our lives; our fiction will come when truth has ceased to satisfy us; as for our history we have made about all that glorified the United States" — should not be taken too seriously as representative of the attitude of the Old South. Novelists like Simms, Kennedy, and Cooke, humorists like Longstreet, essayists like William Wirt, and poets like Timrod and Poe were in no sense an insignificant contribution to American letters. Nevertheless the South as a whole was an unproductive literary section before 1860, and slight patronage was extended to the few bold spirits who attempted to make a career by sole dependence upon their pens. The result was, as Thomas Nelson Page bemoaned, that "It was for a lack of literature that she [the South] was left behind in the great race for outside support, and that in the supreme moment of her existence she found herself arraigned at the bar of the world without an advocate and without a defense." [6] The New South was to remedy this defect.

The first preliminary to the triumph of Southern themes in American literature was the destruction of the conception inherited from the antebellum days that Southern writers must

---

[5] C. C. Jones, Jr., *Funeral Oration Pronounced in an Opera House in Augusta, Ga., Dec. 11, 1889, in Honor of President Jefferson Davis* (pamphlet, Augusta, 1889). Jones, an outspoken critic of the New South, delivered many such speeches and orations.

[6] T. N. Page, "The Old South" (New York, 1892), 50. Page was referring to fiction. The Old South produced a superb body of polemic writing.

produce a distinctive Southern literature. The chief output of the late sixties was inspired by the old spirit of Southern independence. Thus Simms with a group of associates founded a periodical in Charleston entitled *The Nineteenth Century* as a vehicle of Southern thought, and Bledsoe established *The Southern Review* to carry on in letters the struggle which, for him at least, had not ended with Appomattox. Another veteran of the old school, John Esten Cooke, wrote many pages of novels and biographies of war experiences that were imperfectly adjusted to the conception of a South within the American union.[7] Cooke illustrated the antagonism of his group toward the North and the Northern reading public when he exclaimed on July 4, 1870, "Grand humbug of celebrations! — in which the South having no independence to celebrate takes no part! Singular how completely we rebellious ones have come to despise the United States, their flag, and all concerning them." [8]

Yet it took a very brief period to demonstrate that Southern writers could not find in Dixie enough patronage to survive, and that unless Southern literature became sufficiently American in tone to appeal to Northern readers there would be no Southern literature. Simms failed as thoroughly after 1865 as he had before 1860 to interest Charlestonians in a native literature. Bledsoe exhausted his ire with the only result that his *Review* expired as a "journal of Southern opinion" and became an organ of the Methodist Church. Cooke, who anticipated Thomas Nelson Page as an idealizer of the life of Old Virginia, sold very few of his novels and was so forgotten by 1880 that Page seemed to be working an unploughed field. So also the publication in 1871 of a Southern edition of "Dukesboro Tales" did nothing in rescuing Richard Malcolm Johnston from his obscurity as a writer.

Through these transition years such poets as Paul Hamilton Hayne and Sidney Lanier received more sympathy and aid from Northern sources than from Southern. Even Cooke prob-

---

[7] "Surrey of Eagle's Nest" (1866), "Mohun" (1869), and biographies of Lee and Jackson.
[8] As quoted in J. O. Beatty, "John Esten Cooke" (New York, 1922), 120–121.

ably received more cash for writing an occasional column for the *New York World* than from the sale of his novels. It is not surprising, therefore, that rancor soon disappeared from the hearts of men who wished to devote their lives to literature. The writer had one of two alternatives. He could follow Bledsoe into the obscurity where restless pens still struggled with irreconcilable emotions. In such a case he would condemn himself to a lack of recognition. Nor would he ever achieve a position where his pen alone could win a livelihood. On the other hand he could follow the example of Hayne, who, courageously turning his back on his native city of Charleston, sought the friendly seclusion of a rural cabin. There he struggled with poverty and, attuning his mind to the newer creed of reconciliation and nationalism, helped pave the way for the triumph of Southern letters in the eighties.

The brief life of Sidney Lanier (1842–1881) bridged the transition and best exemplified the course that Southern literature followed. Raised in the best Old South traditions, Lanier served the Confederacy in the war at the expense of shattered health, and then encountered adversity in Reconstruction so harsh as to justify his own statement that "pretty much the whole of life has been merely not dying." [9] Yet in "Tiger Lilies" (1867) he recognized the futility of the war, in "Corn" (1875) he argued against the tyranny King Cotton had exercised over the South, in the "Centennial Cantata" (1876) he espoused the doctrine of Americanism, and in an article for *Scribner's Monthly* on the New South (1880) he opened his mind to the brightness of the future. It was from Lanier and Hayne that the young men of the new school received the double legacy of respect for the tradition of Dixie and belief in the South as an integral part of the nation.

Meanwhile the basic patterns of the later literature were being fixed. The work was done quietly and imperceptibly as here and there a short story or a poem unobtrusively found its way into a magazine such as *Scribner's Monthly* or *Lippincott's*. The work seemed at first to be little more than reporting. But gradually the familiar types evolved and the basic plots took shape.

[9] Edwin Mims, "Sidney Lanier" (Boston, 1905), 67.

Richard Malcolm Johnston takes high rank among these preliminary writers. His "Georgia Sketches" (1864) and "Dukesboro Tales" (1871) continued the portraiture of the Georgia Cracker started in the prewar years by Augustus B. Longstreet. Life in rural Georgia provided the local color and the dialect that the postwar conception of realism deemed essential. Johnston described a wholesome, simple, and democratic republic of agriculture, rich in humor and sound in character. It was probably Johnston more than Harris who established the convention of considering middle Georgia the seat of a pure American folk — homely in wit, neighborly in customs, and yet rustically independent in conduct — harmonious, certainly not inimical, to the Indiana Hoosier Edward Eggleston was contemporaneously introducing to the public.

Possibly because of the praise liberally bestowed upon him by Harris and Page, Irwin Russell is usually credited with being the postwar discoverer of the Negro character in literature. But before Russell, one could find in the corner of *Scribner's* reserved for "Bric-a-brac," poems in Negro dialect by Thomas Dunn English in 1871 which contained, imperfectly developed, all the elements of droll humor and pathos exploited by later writers. So also Jennie Woodville and Sherwood Bonner used the dialect poem after 1875 to portray the many types of Negro character, from the faithful retainer of the past to the upstart spoiled by freedom. These writers, however, lacked what Russell possessed — a spark of genius and a spontaneity that gave to his work a feeling of intimately sharing the emotions of the black men he described. It was this inner sense rather than the use of dialect or situations that made Russell a true progenitor of Harris.

Russell lived only twenty-six years. He was born in Mississippi in 1853, lived irresponsibly and dissolutely, and died in New Orleans in 1879. Untrained and undisciplined, he reported rather than created the songs and stories of Negro life around him. Russell was as careless with his poetry as with his life. Yet in spite of his wastefulness this spendthrift youth put something of a complete philosophy in his work. "Christmas Night in the Quarters" (1878) stands on the threshold of greatness. Certainly Russell's Negro is the type familiar to

Harris and Page — the superstitious, mercurial fellow, with the contrasts of former slavery and present freedom, possessed of shrewd bits of homely wisdom, fond of the banjo and the 'possum, happy, irresponsible, and good-natured.

Somewhat more substantial was the work of Sherwood Bonner (1849–1884). Miss Bonner's girlhood was spent in Holly Springs, Mississippi, where she experienced some of the most thrilling events of the war. After an unhappy marriage Miss Bonner moved to Boston in 1872 where she supported herself and infant daughter by contributing to various magazines and acting as an amanuensis to Henry Wadsworth Longfellow. Her stories were restricted largely to Southern scenes and in them she described the experiences and observations of her early life. A series of "Gran'mammy" tales dealing with the Negro, written in 1875 and 1876, won for her some recognition. In 1878 she published a novel, "Like unto Like," which has significance as one of the earliest novels of the war and its aftermath in which the theme of reconciliation is considered. Miss Bonner, in fact, covered all phases of Southern life, even, in her tales of the Tennessee mountains, anticipating Miss Murfree. Besides her use of the Negro, the plantation, and Reconstruction, she also was a pioneer in writing light, humorous tales of wartime in which the virtues of both sides are developed. Thus "A Shorn Lamb" is the story of a Confederate girl who to save her lover from capture by Federal troops cuts off her hair to furnish him a wig with which to complete his disguise as a woman. Shortly before her death in 1883, Miss Bonner published her "Dialect Tales" which the editor of *Harper's Weekly* accepted as being "peculiarly American" because they portrayed realistically the secluded lives of everyday folk.

The essence of greatness in local color fiction, however, is the complete identification of the author with the raw material he is refining. Miss Bonner did not possess such complete artistry. She seems to stand outside rather than within her subject, transcribing a life rather than living it. Nevertheless her work carried to the verge of the great writing of the eighties and prepared the way for the triumph of Southern themes in that decade.

Constance Fenimore Woolson, the only Northern author who made a positive contribution to the development of the Southern *genre,* was important as a pioneer for much the same reason. Her first Southern story, "Old Gardiston" (1876), introduced the note of pathos and exploited it more effectively than any writer before Page. "Old Gardiston" also has significance as the earliest important postwar use of an intersectional marriage as a reconciliation motif. "Rodman the Keeper" (1880), which collected Miss Woolson's Southern work, revealed the possibilities which lay in graphic and sympathetic portraiture of the overthrow of the plantation life. Yet here again, as in the case of Miss Bonner, there was missing that elusive touch which when present transforms local color realism into living romance. Page felt this to be true when he wrote that Miss Woolson failed to "find the treasure of the inner life which lies deeper than her somewhat scornful gaze penetrated," although no adjective could have been more unhappily chosen by Page than the word "scornful." [10] Miss Woolson's heart was full of love and admiration for the South, and no reader could leave her pages with other than charity for the people she described.

The background was thus prepared for the work of a great quartet of writers, George W. Cable, Joel Chandler Harris, Thomas Nelson Page, and Mary Noailles Murfree, whose activity in the eighties established the primacy of Southern themes in American literature. "Old Creole Days" (1879), "The Grandissimes" (1880) and "Madame Delphine" (1881) fixed Cable's reputation as a master in the technique of the short story and as an exquisite artist in sympathetic and sincere delineation of the intricate beauties of Creole society. "Uncle Remus" (1880) and a long succession of short stories on every theme of Southern life made Harris the greatest white interpreter of Negro character as well as a worthy successor of Longstreet and Johnston in depicting the democracy of middle Georgia. "In Ole Virginia" (1887), a collection which included "Marse Chan" (1884) and "Meh Lady" (1886), raised Page to the summit of those who painted the

[10] T. N. Page, "Literature in the South since the War," *Lippincott's,* XLVIII (1891), 740.

mellowed tradition of the plantation. "In the Tennessee Mountains" (1884) and "Where the Battle Was Fought" (1885) gave Miss Murfree renown for her vivid presentation of the strange society found in the secluded corners of the Southern Appalachians.

These writers met every canon of contemporary criticism. Seemingly they depicted with extreme fidelity the character and manners of the people whose natural lives they charmingly presented. Their use of dialect was perfect, and the technical structure of their short story form was unexcelled. Sincere in their sympathy and complete in their understanding of the material they used, they were able to find in simple surroundings the universal interest that elevated their work far beyond the provincial origins of their own careers. Their reputation thus rested upon a firm basis, but contributing greatly to added popularity was the fresh and poetic glamour which surrounded the quaint scenes they explored.

The volume of output was greatly increased by the work of lesser figures. Johnston was inspired by Northern patronage to resume his portraiture of Georgia types, becoming one of the most prolific contributors to the magazines during the eighties and nineties. A. C. Gordon and George W. Bagby were lesser reflections of Page. F. Hopkinson Smith in "Colonel Carter of Cartersville" (1891) created two classic characters of Southern fiction, the Colonel and his Negro body-servant Chad. H. S. Edwards, Virginia Frazer Boyle, Ruth McEnery Stuart, Molly Elliott Seawell, and Howard Weeden dealt in the humor and pathos of Negro life. Grace King and Kate Chopin followed Cable's lead in picturing the Creole. T. C. De Leon and George Cary Eggleston wrote with the Civil War as a background, the latter growing progressively more facile in idealizing the mutual heroism of Blue and Gray. Novels like Maurice Thompson's "Tallahassee Girl" (1881), Julia Magruder's "Across the Chasm" (1885), and Matt Crim's "Adventures of a Fair Rebel" (1890), developed the theme of social contact between Northerners and Southerners. A host of writers, whose names were rarely heard beyond local boundaries, wrote novels idealizing the Southern past, such as J. W. Moore's "Heirs of St. Kilda" (1881), F. Fontaine's "Etowah"

(1887), and Florella Meynardie's "Amy Oakly" (1879). Mrs. Burton Harrison and Mrs. Margaret J. Preston wrote stories redolent of plantation memories, while the dexterous popularizer Opie Read reached a less discriminating public with a long list of paper-back novels on conventional Southern themes. The ablest of the younger writers who began writing in the later eighties was James Lane Allen whose many short stories, novels, and descriptive articles made the "Blue Grass Region of Kentucky" a familiar possession of every American reader.

This school of writers exemplified completely the spirit of the New South which dominated Southern thought during the eighties. The war and Reconstruction provided its discipline of introspection. If the writers received scanty preparation in a formal sense, were ignorant of life in its broader aspects, and knew little of the art of criticism, they did grasp the significance of what the South had experienced. The very narrowness of opportunity in postwar Dixie stimulated them to venture into careers which would have seemed uninviting to an earlier Southern generation. Thus Page might well have pursued in ante-bellum Virginia the profession of law for which he had been trained had not contact with the tradition and the veterans of the Old Dominion's golden age made his opportunity before the bar seem insignificant in comparison. In other cases dire necessity conditioned life. The impoverished Cable turned from humble positions as an apothecary's assistant, and clerk in a cotton factor's firm, to explore the ancient lore of New Orleans, feeling that it would be "a pity to let [it] go to waste." When Harris, trudging painfully up the journalistic ladder of success, began filling columns of the *Atlanta Constitution* with Negro folklore remembered from his boyhood, he least of all men expected that Uncle Remus would soon make his name known around the world. Miss Murfree's equipment was a series of summer vacations spent in the Cumberland Mountains. She, like her colleagues, excelled only when depicting with fresh enthusiasm the intimate observations of youth. Her later works, and this was equally true of Cable, Page, and Harris, never equaled the greatness of her first success. Most of what was excellent in this Southern literature of pathos and sympathy for simple and in cases frus-

trated lives was the outpouring of young men and women putting in letters the yearnings of their own earlier and unsettled years. Success seemed to alienate them from the mainspring of their genius.

They were also typical of the new age in the love and devotion they cherished for the old. There was hardly a Negro in this fiction who could not have said with Virginia Frazer Boyle's darkey, "dey was good ole days, dose times befoah de wah!" [11] If Allen took his readers into a "green and fragrant" world of Kentucky and Page wrote of "a goodly Land in those old times," Johnston maintained that life in middle Georgia was so constituted as to breed the best traits of character, and Harris retained a living image of serenity, beauty, and nobility of "old plantation days." It was this love of subject, rather than restraint of Southern opinion, which excluded from Southern literature of the eighties all traces of grim realism. Walter Hines Page felt embarrassment from the presence of what he called Ghosts of the Southern past — the Confederate tradition, religious orthodoxy, and the fear of Negro domination. Cable, in his later and more doctrinaire moments, found the South hostile to his criticisms of the white attitude toward the Negro. But these were isolated cases. The great body of writers, and this is equally true of Cable in his fiction, seem never to have entertained a doubt as to the excellence of the region. Even the imperfections were lovingly depicted. Consequently there entered into Southern literature a rich theme of nostalgia which has never entirely disappeared and which gave to it a piquant charm in a rapidly changing world.

> I'll never hear as onst I heerd,
>   In de happy times long gone,
>   De darkeys singin' like dey sung
>   Amongst de yaller corn. [12]

And yet again it was not untypical that young men of the New South could entertain such views of the past and still embrace a whole-hearted acceptance of reconciliation. Few of

[11] "How Jerry Bought Malvinny," *Century*, XL (1880), 892.
[12] A. C. Gordon, "Home Again," in "Befo' de War" (New York, 1888), 125.

the writers could go so far as Cable in "Dr. Sevier" in asserting that the Union cause was just. But even Bagby, who believed it was "simple truth" that "there was in our Virginia
country life a beauty, a simplicity, a purity, an uprightness, a
cordial and lavish hospitality, warmth and grace which shine
in the lens of memory with a charm that passes all language
at my command," also "prayed God" that he would never
again see "the filth, the disease, the privation, the suffering,
the mutilation, and above all, the debasement of public and
private morals [which] leave to war scarcely a redeeming
feature." [13] It is a characteristic of both Page and Harris that
virtually all the characters of their fiction who, on the eve of
the Civil War, might be considered spokesmen for the author's
own point of view, were conservatives who urged moderation,
and hesitated to resort to a policy of secession.[14] Moreover
there was not an important writer of this school who did not
believe the South better off within the restored Union. So far
as the future was concerned Maurice Thompson spoke for
the group when he wrote:

> The South whose gaze is cast
> No more upon the past,
> But whose bright eyes the skies of promise sweep,
> Whose feet in paths of progress swiftly leap;
> And whose past thought, like cheerful rivers run,
> Through odorous ways to meet the morning sun.

This was one of the most important adaptations made in the
postwar South. It is what saved Southern literature from provincialism and permitted its wide acceptance in the North. So
long as slavery had been a living actuality the peculiar institution had constituted a barrier as effective in letters as in politics
and economics. No author before the war had been able to
touch on Southern themes without becoming a defender of a
system which seemed to threaten Northern interests. Against
him had been arrayed the full force of Northern hostility.
Northern writers inspired by Northern patriotism had been

[13] G. W. Bagby, "The Old Virginia Gentleman" (New York, 1910), 44,
164-165.
[14] See as typical the character of Dr. Cary in T. N. Page, "Red Rock"
(New York, 1900).

moved to exercise their skill in portraying a South of "barbarism," "cruelty," and "injustice." A civil war in literature
had been an important phase of the "irrepressible conflict."
It need hardly be suggested that the South had been conquered
by the pen as thoroughly as by the sword. Southerners who
survived the débâcle quite properly maintained that the North
had a distorted picture of the ante-bellum South, one that was
colored in every aspect by abolitionist prejudice.

Once slavery had been destroyed, and Southern writers no
longer aspired to Southern independence, the situation was re-
versed. By 1880 the North had lost its apprehension and
Northern writers ceased to have any incentive to write in a
spirit of hostility towards Dixie. A culture which in its life was
anathema to the North, could in its death be honored. This
was the richest legacy the Southern writers inherited. Without
offense to any living interest they could at last tell what they
deemed to be the truth about the land they loved.

So far as reconciliation is concerned, the important feature
of this literature is the picture of the Old South it conveyed
to Northern readers. It mattered little who the author was,
whether he had the greatness of Harris, the passionate in-
tensity of Page, or the lyrical beauty of Allen. In every case
the plantation "lived once mo', . . . an' de ole times done come
back ag'in." [15] "Uncles," "Mammies," "Colonels," gracious
ladies, fair maidens, and brave cadets crossed the pages with
smiling faces and courteous manners; and "songs floated out
upon the summer air, laden with the perfume of rose and
honeysuckle and peach blossom." [16] Even the "moonlight seemed
richer and mellower before the war." [17] What if the tradition
omitted much that was true and exaggerated the attractive
features of the departed life? It rested upon a bedrock of fact,
and distorted the actuality no more violently than had the
abolitionist attack whose unfriendly picture it was now fortunately correcting. The tradition itself became a fact, giving
to Southern youth a conception of courage, energy, and strength
upon which could be erected the foundations of a new life,

[15] Uncle Billy in T. N. Page, "Meh Lady," "In Ole Virginia" (New
York, 1889).
[16] Cf. W. M. Baskerville, "Southern Writers" (Nashville, 1896–1897), 31.
[17] Page, "Red Rock," Preface.

and to Northerners an insight into the Southern heart which made it easier to understand why erstwhile foes had been inspired to "live and die for Dixie."

Subtly and with great felicity a persuasive dogma of defense was inculcated in this literature. "All now agree," wrote a Southern observer, " — whether conservative upholders of the Old South or advanced proclaimers of a New South — that our history must be made known in all its truth and grandeur to the world." [18] The short story gave the opportunity to relate more effectively than in any other form the "story of its life, of its aspirations, its feelings, its failures, its achievements before and during and since the civil war." [19] Each of the three great issues which divided the sections — race relations, Civil War, and Reconstruction — received ample treatment. Sometimes as in Julia Magruder's "Across the Chasm" the didactic purpose was thinly veiled. But in more capable hands the reader rarely suspected the strong appeal that was being made to enlist his sympathies for the furled banner of the Confederacy.

The Negro was the focal character even as he had been in the polemic writing of the fifties. Somewhat paradoxically the two schools, so radically opposed in their sympathies, used much the same traditional types in delineating the dusky source of so much turmoil. Topsy might well have been a poem by Irwin Russell. Uncle Tom was the same devoted slave that Page depicted in such unforgettable images as Uncle Billy and Ole 'Stracted. James Lane Allen, who in his "Uncle Tom at Home" attempted to controvert the impression established by Mrs. Stowe's great novel, almost plagiarized his opponent, as the following juxtaposition will reveal:

Mrs. Stowe	Allen
The cabin of Uncle Tom was a small log building, close adjoining to "the house," as the negro *par excellence* designates his master's dwelling. In front	You will come upon some cabin set back in a small yard and half-hidden, front and side, by an almost tropical jungle of vines and multiform foliage;

[18] W. M. Baskerville, "Southern Literature since the War," *Vanderbilt Observer*, XV (1893), 209.

[19] W. M. Baskerville, "Southern Literature since the War," *Vanderbilt Observer*, 210.

it had a neat garden-patch, where, every summer, strawberries, raspberries, and a variety of fruits and vegetables, flourished under careful tending. The whole front of it was covered by a large scarlet begonia and a native multiflora rose, which, entwisting and interlacing, left scarcely a vestige of the rough logs to be seen. Here, also, in summer various brilliant annuals, such as marigolds, petunias, four-o'clocks, found an indulgent corner in which to unfold their splendors, and were the delight and pride of Aunt Chloe's heart.[20] patches of great sunflowers, never more leonine in tawny magnificence and sun-loving repose; festoons of white and purple morning glories over the windows and up to the low eaves; around the porch and above the doorway, a trellis of gourd vines swinging their long-necked, grotesque fruit; about the entrance hollyhocks and other brilliant bits of bloom, marigolds and petunias.[21]

Even the reunion of George Shelby and Uncle Tom around the latter's deathbed is based upon the same close bond of master and slave that ennobles the dying moments of Ole 'Stracted. The loyalty of slave to master is exploited in either case and the sympathy of the reader is excited by the pathos inherent in the dramatic contrasts such a relationship created. It is, of course, in the direction given to the contrasts that the great difference between Mrs. Stowe and the postwar writers appears. In the former the devotion of the slave is tragically at the mercy of the master. In the latter the impoverished and usually helpless master is normally dependent upon the loyalty of the slave. Uncle Tom was the martyr of a system, but Uncle Billy was as he himself stated the "chief 'pendance uv Meh Lady." And so in Uncle Tom the sympathy of the reader is directed to the lowly slave, while in the postwar fiction it is the overthrown gentry who are the recipients of a forgiving pity. In both cases it becomes apparent that the Negro was primarily a device by which a white philosophy of race relations was advanced.

[20] "Uncle Tom's Cabin," ch. iv, first paragraph.
[21] "Mrs. Stowe's Uncle Tom at Home in Kentucky," *Century*, XXXIV (1887), 853.

"Meh Lady" and "Uncle Remus," therefore, were primarily the answer of the Southern genius of the eighties to the Yankee genius of the fifties. Harris alone, perhaps, created in Uncle Remus a Negro character which had existence in life independent of traditional types. Yet Uncle Remus was an old man. His life had been the departed plantation and he told of days which had passed. Consequently if Harris showed unique insight into the Negro soul, he at the same time used the venerable figure of Uncle Remus to preserve and transmit the memories of antebellum days. In this respect he was as much a part of the tradition as Thomas Nelson Page.

The publication of "Uncle Remus" gave Harris immediate recognition among white readers everywhere as the greatest authority on Negro life. Consequently what Harris wrote about the colored man assumed significance beyond that of any of his contemporaries. It is important to note, therefore, that the outstanding Northern magazine of the time recognized in Uncle Remus "the best . . . study . . . of a type familiar to us all — the old plantation negro. It is a character, now [1881] almost a tradition, that has been sketched in song and story; but that will never find a more faithful or sympathetic delineator than the creator of Uncle Remus. The gentle old darkey — shrewd, yet simple-minded, devoted to the people who once owned him as a slave, yet with a certain tyrannical sense of his hold upon their affection — will live forever in these pages, a gracious relic of a time and an 'institution' whose memories for the most part are an abiding curse. Even the occasional mild little apologies for the patriarchal system which the author scatters through his work will offend no one. They lend it a pleasant old-time, 'befo' the wah' flavor; so to speak, they give the picture 'distance.' " [22]

Harris's other Negro characters have little individuality apart from the familiar types. Balaam was the faithful servant whose life was inseparable from that of his master whose weakness Balaam protected. Ananias, as his name suggests, had a common Negro failing (according to the tradition) which he craftily employed to support an impoverished Colonel and his daughter who stood helpless in the postwar upheaval. Mingo

[22] *Scribner's Monthly*, XXI (1881), 961–962.

possessed "the native gentility of the old negro" trained in slavery. Free Joe, alone, was a unique creation, the one example in all this literature that approached a sordid aspect of slavery. Yet even here it was a white man's sensibilities rather than a tortured Negro's soul that was exposed. For Free Joe was the anomaly of slavery — a free Negro in a slave community — and so embodied "that vague and mysterious danger that seemed to be forever lurking on the outskirts of slavery." [23] If Harris had a philosophy of race relations it proceeded from such opinions as the following scattered through his writings:

. . . there is nothing more notorious in history, nothing more mysterious, than the fact that civilization is not over-nice in the choice of her hand-maidens. One day it is war, another it is slavery. Every step in the advancement of the human race has a paradox of some kind as its basis.[24]

. . . self-interest combined with feelings of humanity to make it [slavery] a patriarchal institution. And such, in fact, it was. It is to the glory of the American character and name, that never before in the history of the world was human slavery marked by such mildness, such humanity, as that which characterized it in the United States.[25]

It was typical of Harris that he claimed the glory in the name of American rather than Southern character. The problem of the Negro under free conditions could best be solved in his opinion by preserving as far as possible the bonds of friendship and respect that had existed on the old plantation.

The Negroes of Thomas Nelson Page were all of the faithful, devoted type and were used primarily as accessories to heighten the effect of pathos emanating from the departed grandeur of plantation days. Yet what a galaxy Page created — Sam who serves so faithfully Marse Chan and who relates so touchingly this epic of Confederate valor; Ole 'Stracted who lives in memories of the past and Ephraim, his son, who struggles through the befuddlement of share tenancy; Uncle

[23] "Free Joe" (New York, 1887), 7–8.
[24] "At Teague Poteet's," in "Mingo and Other Sketches" (Boston, 1884), 58.
[25] "Georgia" (New York, 1896), 252–253.

Gabe boasting of his white folks; Unc' Edinburgh directing with rare finesse the intricacies of a plantation courtship; and above all the beloved Uncle Billy, the protector of Meh Lady, whose happy ending made "hit 'pear [to all his readers] like de plantation 'live once mo', and de ain' no mo' scufflin', an' de ole times done come back ag'in."

Generally speaking, the Negro of this literature was one of two standard types, — the devoted slave, happy if the scene was laid in days of slavery, the guardian of his white folks if the grimmer postwar South was the period of the story, and the confused freedman who usually was rescued from semi-ludicrous predicaments by the white people to whom he once had belonged.[26] The picture of race relations was uniformly a happy one so long as the white South was trusted to work out its own solution. Sam, the narrator in Page's "Marse Chan," epitomized the conditions under slavery as follows:

Dem wuz good ole times, marster — de bes' Sam uver see! Niggers didn' hed nothin' 'tall to do — jes' hed to 'ten' to de feedin' an' cleanin' de hawses, an' doin' what de marster tell 'em to do; an' when dey wuz sick, dey hed things sont 'em out de house, an' de same doctor come to see 'em whar 'ten' to de white folks when dey wuz po'ly, an' all. Dyar warn' no trouble nor nuthin'.

Conditions under freedom, all the authors agreed, were best when, as Allen wrote, the "superstitious, indolent, singing, dancing, impressionable creature [Negro] depends upon others [preferably the Southern whites] for enlightenment, training, and happiness."[27] In other words the kindly and affectionate relations of the races under slavery were the true basis for a proper solution of the problem of races. Here, indeed, was a startling answer to the abolitionists.

No less effectively did the writers of the eighties soften the asperities of Civil War issues into mellowed conventions which extolled the mutual valor of both Blue and Gray. Miss Mur-free's "Where the Battle Was Fought" represented the type

---

[26] A. W. Tourgee, "The South as a Field of Fiction," *Forum*, VI (1888), 409.
[27] J. L. Allen, "Blue Grass Region of Kentucky" (New York, 1900), 73.

of work which enlisted Northern sympathy for the devastation
wrought by Northern invasions. Page was best in such stories
as "The Burial of the Guns," "Meh Lady," and "Marse
Chan" where he appealed to the sentiment by picturing the
nobility of dying Confederate heroes and the sacrifices of
Southern women. Harris seemed chiefly interested, as in "Little
Compton" and "The Kidnapping of President Lincoln," in
illustrating how much common Americanism existed in both
the armies. The composite fully informed the reading public
of the extent of Southern suffering, the nobility of Southern
devotion to the "lost cause," and the basic Americanism that
underlay the Southern endeavor. The tears that fell over Marse
Chan were tears of memories long softened by passing time,
and quite unlike the tears of poignant bitterness that kept the
North and South embroiled when casualty lists caused cheeks
to blanch and hearts to faint. The pride the reader now felt in
Confederate valor was quite unlike the pride once taken in
Sherman's destructive march to the sea. It was a curious element in the emerging patriotism for Northerners to boast of
Southern heroism as an American trait.

So also were the issues of Reconstruction fully explained
in charity to the prostrate South. The work was partly accomplished by amassing incidental detail from many sources. Thus
in the short story, "At Teague Poteet's," Harris suggested
how the Radicals built up their campaign of misrepresentation
by exaggerating a fight with illicit distillers in the Georgia
mountains into an atrocity story which they labeled "a new
phase of the rebellion." However, it is chiefly in two novels,
Page's "Red Rock" and Harris's "Gabriel Tolliver," that the
complete Southern account of Reconstruction was chronicled.
Yet not a word was written which could cause offense to
Northern susceptibilities. The villains were Southern scalawags as frequently as Northern carpetbaggers. Representative Southerners were depicted never as recalcitrant but always as seeking Union, peace, and good will. In many instances
the "better type" of Northerner resident in the South assisted
the Southern white at critical moments to throw off the yoke
of oppression. This was notably true in "Red Rock" where
a Northern heroine saved from imprisonment a Ku Klux

leader whom she married. Harris concluded his indictment of Reconstruction by declaring that no "parcel of politicians" could turn the South against the restored Union.

The desire to promote good will between the sections and to achieve reconciliation was another characteristic of the Southern writers. Page declared that he had "never wittingly written a line which he did not hope might tend to bring about a better understanding between the North and the South, and finally lead to a more perfect Union." [28] Harris, with whom the desire to reconcile amounted almost to a passion, insisted that the purest and most distinctive traits in Southern life were those elements which gave it kinship to the nation.[29] A contemporary Southern critic quite aptly stated that the literature of the eighties aimed "to cement bonds of good fellowship between the sections." [30]

The reconciliation theme appeared under many guises. The writers when dealing with contentious issues were careful to use accessories which were free from any offense to the North. Their very efforts to justify the Southern record were conditioned by eagerness that the North should accept the vindication. Consequently every word in defense of Dixie was free from bitterness and tended to contribute to better understanding. More specifically the reconciliation motif became conventionalized in a plot which married a Northern hero to a Southern heroine. Thus in Harris's "Aunt Fountain's Prisoner" a Southern "Mammy" found a wounded Union officer, "captured" him, and, taking him to the home of her young mistress, nursed him back to health, thus starting a love story which resulted in the union of a Yankee and a Southern girl. The Northerner seemed to have been a noble character, and Harris could not refrain from observing that "he gave me a practical illustration of the fact that one may be a Yankee and a Southerner too, simply by being a large-hearted, whole-souled American." Harris was not subtle in his use of the reconciliation motif, but in "The Old Bascom Place" he did write one of the most popular examples of the *genre*. Here

[28] Page, Introduction to the Plantation Edition of his works.
[29] Harris, "Harris," 140–141. Note how the conception entered into such stories as "Azalia" and "The Kidnapping of President Lincoln."
[30] Baskerville, "Southern Writers," 100–101.

again the heroine symbolized all the virtues of the South, the hero those of the North, and the union, which combined the best of each, was Americanism. If in the process of courtship obstacles of misunderstanding had to be overcome, so also in the wedding of North and South contact brought reconciliation and the closing of the chasm.[31]

Harris was in no sense the discoverer of the intersectional marriage as a literary motif of reconciliation, or even its most skillful exploiter.[32] The plot appealed especially to the feminine writers, Miss Woolson employing it with notable success in "Old Gardiston," and Julia Magruder in "Across the Chasm." In fact nearly every author of the group at some time in his career used the device. But it remained for Page, supreme here as in other phases of sentimental pathos, to write the classic. "Meh Lady," told in the mellow dialect of a Negro narrator, is a story of a Southern girl who, having lost a brother in the war, is called upon to nurse a wounded Yankee back to health. Then ensued the love theme, the obstacles to overcome, and the marriage.

The simple tale of love and reconciliation unfolded with such charm and felicity of expression that it seems a sacrilege to point out that "Meh Lady" was a conscious effort of the author rather than a spontaneous expression of a heart filled with compassion. And yet it was an editor of a Northern magazine, the *Century,* who suggested the idea of the story to Page. Robert Underwood Johnson was the source, and his inspiration came from reading Lessing's "Minna von Barnhelm," in which a Prussian hero wooed a Saxon heroine in the interest of a united Germany.[33] It matters little. The alchemy was Page. "Meh Lady" was a fresh creation in which all the baser metals of sectional strife were transmuted into pure gold. A later generation may deem it insignificant but in the eighties it was one of the brightest ornaments of reconciliation.

[31] In "The Grandissimes," Cable used a theme, contributing to reconciliation, that was not copied by later writers. The novel dealt with Creole sentiment in 1804, an obvious parallel to Southern sentiment in 1865. In both cases a reluctant people were held in a union not of their choice.
[32] Even before the Civil War, W. A. Caruthers, "The Kentuckian in New York" (1834), used the plot.
[33] R. W. Johnson, "Remembered Yesterdays" (Boston, 1923), 121–122.

A group which produced "Old Creole Days," "In Ole Virginia," "Uncle Remus," and "In the Tennessee Mountains" might rest upon its laurels, content in having demonstrated that the South was not inferior to the North in native literary ability. Yet the South remained defective in one requirement for permanent literary greatness. The faculty for self-criticism was, as W. P. Trent wrote in the middle nineties, "in a very rudimentary stage, and affords no clear warrant that the next generation of Southern writers will be able to maintain the position won by the painful and ever laudable labors of their predecessors." [34] Yet even here the New South made an important contribution. Restricted as it was with the legacy of a defense reaction, the young men of the eighties laid a foundation of criticism upon which a later generation might develop.

It has never been appreciated to the extent it should that Joel Chandler Harris possessed beneath a shy exterior a deep sense of critical values. He was one of the first Southerners to frown upon the incessant clamor of his fellow Southerners for a "purely Southern literature." Even before he had won recognition as the creator of Uncle Remus he raised his voice against "controversial fiction" and the "lack of healthy criticism." [35] Repeatedly he warned the writers of Dixie of the peculiar obstacles they must overcome.[36] It was not the least achievement of this remarkable man to have recognized in 1881 that "we must get over our self-consciousness and so control our sensitiveness as to be able to regard with indifference — nay, with complacency — the impulse of criticism which prompts and spurs every literary man and woman whose work is genuine." [37]

Harris, to be sure, was in this respect little more than a single voice. The noisier Walter Hines Page in advertising "the hobgoblins of a dying civilization" received somewhat more attention. But Page lived out his life in the North, emitting an occasional sigh "for a change in his beloved South —

[34] W. P. Trent, "Tendencies of a Higher Life in the South," *Atlantic*, LXXIX (1897), 768.
[35] *Atlanta Constitution*, Nov. 30, 1879.
[36] *Ibid.*, Dec. 9, 1879.
[37] *Ibid.*, Feb. 20, 1881.

a change of almost any kind!"[38] Meanwhile young men of Harris's generation and point of view set quietly to work with the imperfect materials they found at hand and prepared in several university centers a basis of self-criticism in the South. W. M. Baskerville, born in 1850, was a pioneer in this movement. His sympathetic yet kindly discriminatory "Studies of Southern Writers" was the first important searchlight a son of Dixie focused upon the literary output of his section. Baskerville performed his chief service in teaching at Vanderbilt and Sewanee from 1881 until his death in 1899.[39] Few things gave him greater pleasure than being able to write in 1893 that "For the first time Southern intellect is in touch with the rest of the world."[40]

W. P. Trent emerged from a similar environment. In 1892 he published the most important literary biography in Southern history, a life of W. G. Simms, the prewar novelist of Charleston. Trent's "Simms" is possibly the most devastating indictment of the intellectual life of the Old South ever written by an informed scholar. Had a Northerner done the job it might readily be dismissed as of little significance outside the field of scholarship. But coming from the pen of a member of a rising generation of Southerners it became a sort of declaration of independence upon which all future literary criticism in the South might be erected.

Even now [wrote Trent] many otherwise well informed gentlemen do not understand the full meaning of that expression "Southern Chivalry," which they use so often. They know that it stands for many bright and high things, but they seem to forget its darker meaning. They forget that it means that the people of the South were leading a primitive life, — a life behind the age. They forget that it means that Southerners were conservative, slow to change, contented with the social distinctions already existing. . . . It means that Southerners lived a life which, although simple and picturesque, was nevertheless calculated to repress many of the best faculties and powers of our nature. It was a life afford-

[38] R. D. Connor, "W. H. Page," in H. W. Odum, "Southern Pioneers in Social Interpretation" (Chapel Hill, 1925), 56.
[39] J. B. Henneman, "The Late Professor Baskerville," *Sewanee Review,* VIII (1900), 26–44.
[40] *Vanderbilt Observer,* XV (1893), 209.

ing few opportunities to talents that did not lie in certain beaten grooves. It was a life gaining its intellectual nourishment, just as it did its material comforts, largely from abroad, — a life that choked all thought and investigation that did not tend to conserve existing institutions and opinions, a life that rendered originality scarcely possible except under the guise of eccentricity.[41]

Like most declarers of independence, Trent overstated his case. But it was significant that he could assert without fear of refutation that "out of the ashes of the Old South a new and better South has arisen. A disintegrated and primitive people have become united among themselves and with their former foes, and are moving forward upon the path of progress." [42] The newly born spirit of criticism created its own vehicle of expression when, in 1892, *The Sewanee Review* was founded with Trent as its editor. The *Review* had its trials and tribulations but, unlike any of its Southern predecessors, it lived, and maintained standards that won recognition far beyond the boundaries of the South it served so well.

Criticism, however, was a minor phase of the Southern literature of the eighties and the nineties. The main consideration is that the South had begun to write. Dixie was telling in its own way the story of its life, aspirations, sentiments, tragedies, and triumphs. It was a story proudly reminiscent of the past, yet perfectly attuned to the present. Its aim was to convert the Northern disbeliever. "The South," as Baskerville confessed, "is leading a new invasion against the North," [43] and our interest now turns to measure the efficiency of the pen in a field where the sword had failed.

[41] W. P. Trent, "William Gilmore Simms" (Boston, 1892), 36–37.
[42] Ibid., 289–290.
[43] *Vanderbilt Observer*, XV (1893), 210.

CHAPTER IX

THE NORTH FEELS THE POWER
OF THE PEN

EVERY progressive step taken by the New South had as a
cardinal principle the integration of Southern regionalism in the
expanding life of the nation. Nothing more strikingly illustrated this fact than the literary movement of the eighties. In
the ante-bellum period the efforts of Simms and Timrod to
foster a distinctive Southern literature had been one phase of
a sectionalism which sought complete autonomy in intellectual
matters. However, the Old South had lacked in letters even
more than in other respects the basic essentials of independence.
Potential writers and the raw materials of themes it had possessed. But Dixie had no recognized literary capital where authors congregated and publishing houses flourished. Its literary
taste had not recognized the importance of exploring domestic
themes, and it never furnished a patronage for local writers.
Without these essentials a truly sectional literature had proved
impossible of achievement. The New South was no richer than
the Old in ability to support a literature. The standards of
literary criticism which fixed the taste for local color were
Northern in origin, the publishing houses which marketed the
wares were in Northern cities, and the clientele was the Northern
reading public. The South possessed only the themes and
writers, and not until the latter surrendered all aspirations for
independence did a Southern literature really develop. Consequently it becomes obvious, as Harris stated, "that whatever in
our literature is distinctly Southern must . . . be distinctly
American." [1] The word "sectionalism" lost its prewar meaning as a force pulling the regions asunder. In letters it signi-

[1] J. C. Harris, Introduction to J. T. Clarke, "Songs of the South" (Philadelphia, 1896).

fied little more than a localism explored for traits that would
harmonize with the developing conventions of the newer nationalism. Without this adjustment there would have been no
Southern literature, and the career of Harris, for example,
would have been as much a story of frustration as had been
that of Simms.

Meanwhile the intellectual interests of the North had broad-
ened beyond the narrowness of local centers and the provincial
subserviency to European patterns. The people who had passed
through the Civil War were no longer prone to regard as insignificant the life of a country growing into greatness. A
fierce pride in American achievement generated interest in the
American scene. A fiction of local color which mirrored faithfully the elements which constituted Americanism developed in
perfect harmony to the newly awakened taste and surpassed
all other forms in popularity. True to the prevailing taste, the
great magazines of the North became vehicles of nationalism
and sought out in every corner of the country writers who
could picture the locality in which they resided. Consequently
a market was prepared for those Southern authors who had
freed themselves from such sectional traits as might prove
offensive to the national taste. In fact, as the *Atlanta Constitution* suggested, the Southern writer, because of the richness
of his field, found less difficulty in meeting the demands of the
new literature than the writers of any other section.[2]

Scribner's Monthly Magazine, which changed its name to
The Century Magazine in 1881 when the Scribner interests retired, was the chief exponent of the new nationalism, and as
such became the Mæcenas of Southern literature. The basic
creed of *Scribner's* was "a sane and earnest Americanism,"
which sought constantly "to increase the sentiment of union
throughout our diverse sisterhood of States."[3] Under the editorial direction of J. G. Holland in the seventies and R. W.
Gilder assisted by R. U. Johnson and C. C. Buell in the
eighties, the magazine pursued a consistent policy of reconciliation, holding an even balance between the irreconcilables of
both North and South.

[2] *Atlanta Constitution,* June 29, 1881.
[3] *Century,* XLI (1891), 148; XLII (1891), 950.

The first step in *Scribner's* conscious effort to promote nationalism was the exploration of American scenes by means of descriptive articles, profuse illustrations, and local color fiction. Out of this policy grew the Great South Series, reported by Edward King and illustrated by J. W. Champney, in 1873 and 1874. It was not so much a matter of *Scribner's* "opening its doors" to Southern writers as it was seeking Southerners who could write in language free from the older truculent and provincial spirit. Thus it was that Edward King, in his tour of the South, paid little heed to the writers of the Bledsoe school. But when he found the young Cable poring over the Creole legends in New Orleans he appreciated with the keen insight characteristic of the *Scribner's* staff that here was quaintness of detail and picturesque particularism perfectly attuned to the fundamental requirements of the new pride in America. Cable, through King's direction, became a contributor to *Scribner's,* and from that beginning rose steadily to fame through recognition in the North.

Scribner's thus exercised a dominant selective influence which shaped the output of Southern writers in patterns of reconciliation. There was no truckling to the contentious partisan who endeavored to keep alive the belligerence of the past. *Scribner's* was firmly Northern and even mildly Republican in its major political tenets. The Southerner who was admitted to its columns, as one of its editors stated, was "tacitly barred from any expression of the old hostility." [4] He was also "softened in spirit" by the gratitude of being sponsored by a magazine which more than any other in the United States could start an author well along the road which led to success. Lanier, Harris, Johnston, Cable, Allen, Page, Smith, Russell, Edwards, Grace King, and Ruth McEnery Stuart, were all "discoveries" of *Scribner's* and the *Century.* They owed to it such recognition as they achieved, constant encouragement, and liberal financial remuneration. Needless to say their fiction was in complete harmony with the magazine's policy of "standing against sectionalism and for the Union." Each one of them received more than one letter from Holland, Gilder, and the

[4] L. F. Tooker, "Joys and Tribulations of an Editor" (New York, 1924), 41.

assistant editors urging "the broadest patriotism," and "love for the reunited nation." Gilder, who probably more than any other American editor effectively introduced his own standards of taste and criticism into the writings of his contributors, was especially assiduous in insisting upon the setting aside of sectional strife. The great force of the *Century's* position was its unshaken preëminence as the defender of nationalism. When it manifested hospitality to Southern ideas it was insurance that those ideas were safely "Americanized." In return the Southern writers were given a perfect vehicle for carrying their message to the most important element in the reading public of the North.

That message came in time to overshadow all other aspects of the *Century,* especially in the five year period from 1884 to 1888 when the peak of Southern influence was reached. Harris, Page, and Cable were then rarely missing from any volume, and their work was supplemented by Thompson, Johnston, Allen, and Grady. The October, 1887, issue of the *Century* illustrates the point. Of the one hundred and fifty-nine pages of text, thirty-one formed a chapter in the life of Abraham Lincoln, sixteen were given to Allen's "Uncle Tom at Home in Kentucky," seven contained the concluding instalment of Harris's "Azalia," twenty-eight were devoted to Civil War reminiscences by Union and Confederate leaders, Wade Hampton among them, and two pages carried an editorial on reconciliation. Thus over half the issue dealt with aspects of Southern life and history.

The illustrations were as effective in reconciliation as the prose. The issue cited contained drawings recalling the stirring days of the war. Allen's article had illustrations idealizing race relations. One picture depicted a loyal slave rescuing his master from drowning, while another showed a white mistress nursing a sick slave. Harris's story had a picture of a Confederate and a Union soldier — both dead — lying arm in arm on a battlefield. The Confederate had given his life in bringing water to the expiring Unionist.

Lippincott's Magazine was far less influential than *Scribner's* and the *Century,* but it deserves equal rating as a pioneer in exploiting Southern themes and in encouraging the new school of Southern writers. Founded in 1868, its early numbers contained poems by Hayne, Thompson, and Lanier, articles pleading for moderation in Reconstruction, descriptions of Southern life, and some of the first Confederate reminiscences published in a Northern journal. Sherwood Bonner, Jennie Woodville, and Annie Porter were frequent contributors in the years around 1880. *Lippincott's* could not maintain the standard of quality established by the *Century*. But it did occasionally secure stories by Page, Johnston, Harris, and Allen, while in the quantity of its Southern material *Lippincott's* easily kept pace with its greater competitor.[5]

Harper's Monthly Magazine was much slower in introducing Southern themes and proved far less cordial in encouraging Southern writers. In 1865 and 1866 the House of Harper had published a number of books dealing with various phases of the war, only to find that public indifference to war themes made the ventures financially unremunerative.[6] Such an experience made for conservatism which continued to affect the editorial policy of *Harper's Monthly* long after *Scribner's* had discovered that public taste had changed. Not one article or story with the South or the Civil War as a background appeared in *Harper's Monthly* from volume forty (1869) to volume forty-eight (1874). In January 1874 *Harper's,* inspired by the success of *Scribner's* Great South series, printed a series of articles on the New South.[7] A year later Charles D. Deshler contributed his first "glimpses of Dixie," and Miss Woolson made her first essay in the Southern field. But still the *Monthly* moved slowly and Southern writers appeared infrequently. The year 1876 saw "Old Gardiston" and a sketch of

[5] The December 1891 issue of *Lippincott's* illustrates the magazine's treatment of Southern material. It contained a complete novel, "A Fair Blockade Runner," by a Confederate veteran, T. C. De Leon, who dedicated his story to a Union friend as testimony of the reconciliation of North and South. There were also articles by Sara M. Handy on "Negro Superstitions," and T. N. Page on "Southern Literature since the War."

[6] J. H. Harper, "House of Harper" (New York, 1912), 243–244. All these works were by Northerners, among them being G. W. Nichols, "Story of the Great March to the Sea" (a financial success), Draper's "History of the American Civil War" (a financial failure), and novels on war themes by Nichols and J. W. De Forest which did not sell.

[7] Edwin De Leon, "The New South," *Harper's Monthly*, XLVII (1874), 270–280, 406–422, XLIX (1874), 555–568.

Virginia in the Revolution by John Esten Cooke, and then came another stretch of silence which lasted unbroken except for an occasional contribution by Deshler until the end of the decade. The stiff Republicanism of the House of Harper during the seventies, indicated so sharply in the *Weekly,* was unquestionably a prominent factor in postponing the surrender of this great publishing house to the advancing conquest of Southern themes. Not one important Southern writer made his initial appearance to the Northern public in *Harper's Monthly.* Yet *Harper's* finally came to terms. By the mid-eighties the *Monthly* was as jammed with Southern contributions as the *Century.* Harris, Johnston, Edwards, Allen, Page, Grace King, and Ruth McEnery Stuart then found easy access, while Northerners like Charles Dudley Warner and Rebecca Harding Davis wrote series of descriptive articles on the South surcharged with the spirit of friendliness. In 1886 the editors of *Harper's Monthly* were expressing pleasure that their voyages of discovery in Southern fiction were welding the diverse interests of North and South into a closer community of national consciousness.

Even more significant was the conquest of the *Atlantic Monthly.* Sherwood Bonner scaled the ramparts of this citadel of Yankee provincialism in the mid-seventies finding a warm American welcome where she had expected an icy New England blast. The *Atlantic* "discovered" Miss Murfree and raised her to prominence. It contributed largely to the fame of Maurice Thompson and George Cary Eggleston whose "Rebel's Recollections" it published in serial form. By 1892 Southern themes had filled so many pages of the *Atlantic* that no one considered it unusual that the greatest defense and classic exposition of the creed of the Old South was sponsored by a Boston institution.[8]

New magazines founded after 1885 followed the patterns established by their older rivals. The publishing house of Charles Scribner and Sons reëntered the field in 1887 with *Scribner's Magazine* and immediately commanded some of the best work of Page and Harris. More popular in their appeal

[8] B. L. Gildersleeve, "Creed of the Old South," *Atlantic,* LXIX (1892), 75–87.

were *Cosmopolitan,* founded in 1886, *Munsey's* in 1891 and *McClure's* in 1893.[9] This trio carried the reconciliation motives and conventional Southern themes to a wider if less exacting audience than even the *Century* commanded. Inasmuch as they were all planned primarily as business enterprises with the profit motive uppermost, it is indicative of the change in public sentiment that they all proceeded on the assumption that the people wanted the Southern story as the Southern authors portrayed it, full of sympathy and pathos for the Old, surcharged with optimism for the New. Even the editors of *Youth's Companion* instructed contributors who sought access to their columns that "stories are not used . . . that would tend to revive sectional feeling between the North and South."[10]

It was through the magazines that Southern writers were rescued from isolation and brought into relation with the most influential literary figures of the North. Around each magazine clustered a group of established authors and critics who carefully scrutinized the newcomer and offered encouragement for those who were accepted. Entrance into *Harper's* meant contact with H. M. Alden, G. W. Curtis, C. D. Warner, and W. D. Howells. Acceptance by the *Atlantic* was an introduction to the important New England circle which included Lowell, Charles Eliot Norton, Thomas Wentworth Higginson, Thomas Bailey Aldrich, and Howells. The *Century* influence was far-reaching chiefly through the dominating position in New York of Gilder and his associates. It was only a natural step from entrance into the magazines to the great publishing houses of the North. D. Appleton and Company, Harper's, Scribner's, Century, Lippincott's, and Osgood (later Houghton Mifflin Company), were the firms which marketed in book form the product of the Southern school.

Joel Chandler Harris is a good illustration of how Northern editors and publishers encouraged the Southern group to write their "epitaph of a civilization." In the case of this shy

[9] *McClure's,* cited as typical, published Harris's "Comedy of War," Mackey's Confederate reminiscences, Tarbell's "Life of Lincoln," and Chamber's "The Pickets."
[10] Circular describing the type of material acceptable for publication in *Youth's Companion,* issued in 1891.

Georgian they dragged him from obscurity and placed him blushing on a pedestal of fame. Harris had grown up in poverty, was trained in the office of a plantation newspaper, and then, after service on a number of small-town Georgia newspapers, graduated to the growing city of Atlanta where he found a position on the *Constitution*. On the 18th of January 1877 Uncle Remus made his first appearance in the columns of this newspaper. For several years the stories continued in the *Constitution*. Then in 1880 Harris was surprised by a suggestion from D. Appleton and Company that the legends be collected and given permanent form in a book. Thus began a series which continued through five volumes published over a period of twenty-five years.

Immediately after the publication of the first Uncle Remus volume, Harris was besieged with letters from Northern editors asking for material. *Century* carried three of his stories in 1881 and the *Critic* two. As his fame expanded Northern newspapers clamored for interviews, the most notable one being that by Walter Hines Page in the *Boston Post* of September 28, 1881. During the next twenty years Harris contributed to the *Century, Harper's, Scribner's,* the *Atlantic, McClure's,* and *Youth's Companion*. His books were published by Appleton, Century, Scribner's, Harper's, McClure, American Book Company, and Houghton Mifflin. At one time he wrote articles for S. S. McClure, who syndicated them in such Northern newspapers as the *New York Sun, Boston Globe, Philadelphia Times, Washington Post, Chicago Inter-Ocean, St. Louis Republican,* and *San Francisco Examiner*. Through these years Harris's correspondence reveals cordial interchange with Gilder, R. U. Johnston, James Whitcomb Riley, Mark Twain, Charles A. Dana, H. M. Alden, W. D. Howells, Brander Matthews, and E. W. Burlingame.[11]

Cable and Thomas Nelson Page duplicated Harris's experience. Page especially proved a success in reading his dialect stories to Northern audiences on the lyceum circuit of Major J. B. Pond. Bayard Taylor was a close friend of Sidney Lanier, giving the struggling Southern poet constant advice, marketing much of his poetry, and securing for him the op-

[11] Harris, "Harris," *passim.*

portunity of writing the "Centennial Cantata." Sherwood
Bonner was the protégé of Longfellow. Miss Murfree was a
ward of the *Atlantic,* receiving from Thomas Bailey Aldrich
especially valued advice and encouragement. Holmes, Taylor,
and Whittier were the main props upon which Paul Hamilton
Hayne relied in the dark years of Reconstruction. Even
Timrod's poetry was placed in permanent form as the result
of Hayne's intercession with New England writers who
Hayne recognized were the sole means through which the
South could find adequate publication. Whitman was typical
of the Northern men of letters when he wrote, "I compre-
hended all [Southerners who] came in my way, . . . and
slighted none. . . . It has given me the most fervent views
of the true *ensemble* and extent of the States." Through such
exchanges "men forgot the asperities of politics and warmed
to each other" as friends. Hayne, gratified by Whittier's appreciation of Timrod, was eager that "henceforth all jealousies,
all unworthy prejudices may be annihilated between North
and South," and stretched "forth warm hands of cordiality
and love towards you . . . feeling sure that I shall meet with
the electric touch of sympathy." He was not disappointed. The
Quaker and erstwhile abolitionist was happy that "the past is
dead," and "ardently desired to see the two sections of the
Union united in peace and harmony.[12]

While the older generation of Northern writers — men like
Taylor, Holmes, Whittier, and Lowell, who had fought through
the crises of antislavery agitation and the Civil War — learned
the lesson of forgiveness and cordially endorsed the new spirit
in the South, certain of the younger writers endeavored to
share in the triumph of the Southern school by ventures of
their own in the "undiscovered country." For the most part
these Northern imitators were second-rate hacks without especial insight or capacity for expression. They exploited with-

[12] J. Albree, "Whittier Correspondence" (Salem, 1911), 175–176, 187, 200,
203, 218, 221–222; R. Page, "Thomas Nelson Page" (New York, 1923),
125; L. L. C. Bikle, "George W. Cable" (New York, 1928); R. Gilder (ed.),
"Letters of Richard Watson Gilder" (Boston, 1916); J. T. Morse, "Life
and Letters of Oliver Wendell Holmes" (Boston, 1896), I, 312–313; M. H.
Taylor and H. E. Scudder, "Life and Letters of Bayard Taylor" (Boston,
1884); G. C. Knight, "James Lane Allen" (Chapel Hill, 1935); W. Whitman, "Complete Prose Works" (Boston, 1898), 72.

out adorning or improving the conventional types and themes. If there was nothing that was new and little that was felicitous in their output, they nevertheless served the purpose of effecting further the shift from hostile to sympathetic portraiture of the South.

The transition from a critical attitude to a complete espousal of the tradition of a South of heroism and beauty is well illustrated by contrasting two facile narrators of popular tales, J. W. De Forest and Charles King, both veterans of the Union army. It is difficult for a later generation to recognize De Forest as an important writer, yet contemporary critics, including Howells, rated him highly and considered his "vigorous realism" and "blunt direction" important, if rare, elements in American letters.[13] De Forest first used the war as a background in "Miss Ravenel's Conversion from Secession to Loyalty" (1867). The novel was not unkind to the South in detail, but it was altogether a triumph of Yankee virtue over Rebel frailty. The conversion of the lovely Miss Ravenel was accomplished by means of her devotion to a Union hero and it resulted in too much of an "unconditional surrender" of South to North to be of much aid in reconciliation. In his short stories De Forest portrayed both the virtues and the vices of the South.[14] But instead of handling the vices with a soft and tender touch, as the later writers were to do, De Forest approached them with a direct criticism that knew no compromise. A second novel, "Kate Beaumont" (1871), an account of family feuds among the gentry of South Carolina, was again a mixture of praise and blame, but certain of the traditional concepts, especially the Southern heroine and the plantation, emerged in stronger outline. De Forest's third and last novel of the South, "The Bloody Chasm" (1881) was the author's most direct effort to write uncritically a novel of reconciliation. It seems unnecessary to add that the chasm in the story was bridged by means of a love theme which united characters representative of the two sections.

[13] W. D. Howells, "Heroines of Fiction" (New York, 1901), II, 152–163; *Century*, XXIII (1882), 627; *Harper's Bazaar*, XXXV (1901), 538.
[14] "A Gentleman of the Old School," *Atlantic* (May 1868); "Parole d'Honneur," *Harper's* (August 1868); "The Colored Member," *Galaxy* (March 1872); "Independent Ku Klux," *ibid.* (April 1872).

While De Forest began writing in the cold and gray morning of Southern themes and permitted the warmth of the ascending sun to enter slowly into his work, Charles King gloried in the splendor of the full noon. King was a prolific novelist of military adventure, writing more than twoscore books with the Civil War or Indian fighting on the plains as his background. "Kitty's Conquest" (1884), "A War Time Wooing" (1888), and "Between the Lines" (1888) will suffice to indicate the nature of his work. Miss Kitty was a pretty little arch-rebel with such a hatred of Yankees that she must be brought into conflict with a young lieutenant of the United States army whom she marries on the last page. The ingredients used in the making of this lively tale are the contrasts of the risks of war and the pleasures of love, with the deeper implication that Kitty and her lieutenant symbolize the destiny of North and South. Again in "A War Time Wooing," Northerners and Southerners fraternize and intermarry. King was a believer in the Harris dogma of the Americanism of both armies, and he endeavored constantly to show both Blue and Gray acting with bravery, integrity, and devotion to cause. "Between the Lines" was written in this spirit. Such an account as the charge of Hampton's legion was a classic tribute to Southern valor. The reader of King's novels never quite knew on which side of the chasm his sympathies lay until the end when it appeared there was no longer a chasm. It had been closed by the alchemy of sentiment — such alchemy, for example, as permits an author, in the closing scene of "Between the Lines," to make a Southern kiss upon a Northern saber scar seem adequate reparation for all past wrongs.

The current of sentiment swelled into a flood that engulfed the nation's readers. There was hardly a writer in the North who did not venture his literary craft into the waters of Southern themes. With all the critical restraints broken down, with the conventional plots and characters firmly established, it was a simple matter to follow in the popular trend. The ease with which the thing could be accomplished was illustrated by Maud Howe (Elliott) who accompanied her celebrated mother, Julia Ward Howe, to the New Orleans Exposition of 1885, and then embodied in a novel, "Atlanta in the South" (1886), the "unfailing kindness and hospitality" of her half-year residence in Dixie. The book is a repository of conventionalized ideas and situations, including the basic plot of a New England girl's romance with a Southern youth, and yet the story was not uninteresting. It is eloquent of the revolution in sentiment to find the daughter of the woman who wrote the "Battle Hymn of the Republic" asserting that the Negroes were happier and better off under slavery than freedom, although Miss Howe continued to show that emancipation in removing an incubus of responsibility from the white man's shoulders was a progressive step. Her own remedy for sectional misunderstanding was plenty of marriages between the "too-cold intellectual" Northerners and the "emotional, overhot" Southerners. The result would be (not, let us hope, lukewarm but) balanced Americanism.

It was all sweet and simple. Another virtue was that the story never seemed to cloy the popular taste. A certain S. T. Robinson, in "The Shadow of the War" (1884), moved, with a novelist's omnipotence, a Massachusetts manufacturer, his wife, and his beautiful daughter into the deep South with their assortment of preconceptions. The result, after the normal number of pages had intervened, was something in the way of a New South, for the New Englander was operating a busy plant in his new home, the wife had learned to appreciate the inner charm of Southern society, and the daughter was married to a native youth. Another obscure scribbler, James S. Rogers, unblushingly dedicated his tender romance, "Our Regiment" (1884), of Civil War lovers to the G. A. R. in the hope that it might be dramatized for purposes of Post celebrations — as it was. To end this treatment of the commonplace one further illustration may be offered. In John Habberton's "Brueton's Bayou" (1886) the author apparently felt that one intersectional marriage for each novel did not suffice to insure the permanent reunion of the States. Consequently a second romance between Southern hero and Northern heroine is interwoven around that of Northern hero and Southern heroine. And Habberton was not unique. There were others who even progressed into larger numbers.

It was not merely the lesser known Northern writers who

thus exploited the popular Southern themes. Frank R. Stockton, as facile a story teller as the North contained, portrayed the Negro with a skill scarcely inferior to that of Thomas Nelson Page. Stockton's Negroes were the "old time darkeys," genial and loyal, living in memory of the past. Uncle Elijah, in "The Cloverfields' Carriage" (1886), was as worthy a representative of the type as Uncle Billy or Ole 'Stracted. Stockton further explored the plantation and Negro character in the short story, "Seven Devils" (1888), and the novel, "The Late Mrs. Null" (1886). Sarah Orne Jewett contrasted the memories of prewar grandeur with the actualities of postwar ruin in "The Mistress of Sydenham Plantation" (1888). Apparently her sympathy resided in the Negro retainer who uttered the sentiment, "I done like dem ole times de best. . . . Dere was good 'bout dem times." There was the sweetness of sadness in Miss Jewett's "A War Debt" (1895) in which war memories were softly woven into a reconciled present. Thomas Bailey Aldrich was another prominent writer of the North who, in "My Cousin the Colonel" (1891), used a conventional Southern type; and Bret Harte in "Colonel Starbottle" (1891) and "Sally Dows" (1892) did likewise.

The themes seemed to grow more popular with usage. There was no appreciable falling off in quantity as the eighties passed into the nineties. An examination of several examples in the late nineties reveal that the Northern imitators were still writing in conformity to the patterns established by the Southern school. Thus Robert Chambers told, in "The Pickets" (*McClure's,* October 1896), a story of wartime fraternizing very much in the spirit of Joel Chandler Harris. *Harper's,* January 1897, published a story "Between the Lines," on the familiar reconciliation theme of divided love. A few months later another Northerner, Harriet Prescott Spofford, contributed a story of pathos, "A Guardian Angel," in which a Negro mammy protected the well-being of her impoverished mistress. W. E. Barton in the same year published his novel, "A Hero in Homespun," based upon Civil War events, in which again the reader is instructed that "the same kind heart beats under gray that beats under blue, and we are one in spirit today." Joseph A. Altshler's "The Last Rebel" (1897) was another variation on the theme of a Northerner winning the hand of a Southern colonel's daughter.

The efforts of Northern writers to duplicate the successes of Harris, Page, and Cable produced no masterpiece in the realm of fiction. In the theater, however, Northerners working with Southern material had unquestioned supremacy. Yet no Civil War drama achieved real success until the middle eighties. By that time Northern sentiment had shifted to a full acceptance of the idealized picture of the South presented by the writers. Popular drama followed the dominant trend. The dramatists incorporated without restraint the conventionalized plots and characters of fiction. Every contentious issue between North and South was softened. Offensive words like "rebel" were carefully deleted. The tradition of mutual valor of Blue and Gray, the love theme of reconciliation, the tug of divided loyalties in individual consciences, and the glorious climax of reunion were unexcelled opportunities for dramatic construction especially in a day of vigorous, red-blooded acting. So also the wealth of character was gold in the playwright's hand. Civil War drama ruled the stage from the appearance in 1886 of William Gillette's "Held by the Enemy," the first great success, until the end of the century. In that period were staged Bronson Howard's "Shenandoah" (1889), David Belasco's "The Girl I Left Behind Me" (1893) and "The Heart of Maryland," Gillette's "Secret Service" (1896), James A. Herne's "Griffith Davenport" (1899), and Clyde Fitch's "Barbara Frietchie" (1899). In all these outstanding plays there was as much love and more tears for the Gray as for the Blue.

There is no gainsaying the popularity of the Civil War dramas. They were the greatest "hits" of the time, and no American play except "Uncle Tom's Cabin" has ever aroused the popular enthusiasm caused by "Shenandoah" which brought the thrill of battle to the very stage and in the end made certain the future safety of the nation by uniting five (no less!) pairs of lovers whose loyalties had been divided by the war. There were many contemporary observations to the effect that the playwrights were contributing to better understanding, Henry Watterson advancing the opinion that the play "Alabama" "had done more to reconcile the two sections of this country than

his editorials had done in twenty years." [15] Actually it would
have been more accurate to say that Northern opinion had
been conquered by the sweep of sentiment in favor of the South
before the great popularity of reconciliation drama gave further evidence of the fact.

But belligerency in literature did not die without a final
struggle. Abolitionists like Anne E. Dickinson ("What Answer?"), and discredited carpetbaggers like A. T. Morgan
("Yazoo"), endeavored to keep alive the conflict over issues
time was ruthlessly discarding. But of the group only one deserved and gained a wide publicity for his views. Judge Albion
W. Tourgee was a legion in himself. Few writers of the late
seventies could equal the quality of his fiction and none could
excel the vigor of his style. At a time when the Southern
states were removing the last vestiges of Reconstruction and
Northern opinion was acquiescing in the work, this returned
and honorable carpetbagger fought the new opportunism by
renewed emphasis on the old issues of moral reform and justice to the Negro. Within the decade from 1874 to 1883 he
published a series of five novels and one treatise which embodied his complete argument on sectional and race relations:
—"Toinette" (later renamed "A Royal Gentleman"), "A
Fool's Errand," "The Invisible Empire," "Bricks without
Straw," "John Eax and Mamelon," and "Hot Plowshares."
Of these "A Fool's Errand" was both the ablest and most
powerful. It still stands as a strong defense of the conduct of
one group of actors in a painful quarrel. But the fact remains
that Tourgee's work came at the latest possible date when
such writing could be successful. The eighties was not a decade
in which belligerency could survive and even Tourgee went
down to defeat.

No one realized it better than Tourgee. He was among the
first to appreciate the completeness of the conquest of the
Southern pen. "Not only is the epoch of the war the favorite
field of American fiction today," he wrote in 1888, "but the
Confederate soldier is the popular hero. Our literature has become not only Southern in type but distinctly Confederate in

[15] A. H. Quinn, "History of the American Drama from the Civil War to
the Present Day" (New York, 1927), I, 245.

sympathy." [16] There was some justification for this observation
when it could be supported by the fact that, during the year
Tourgee wrote, nearly two thirds of the stories furnished to
the newspapers by syndicates were what the trade described as
"Southern stories."

For better or for worse Page, Harris, Allen, and their associates of the South, with the aid of Northern editors, critics,
magazines, publishing houses, and theaters, had driven completely from the Northern mind the unfriendly picture of the
South implanted there in the days of strife. In place of the discarded image they had fixed a far more friendly conception of
a land basically American and loyal to the best traditions of
the nation, where men and women had lived noble lives and
had made heroic sacrifices to great ideals, where Negroes
loved "de white folks," where magnolias and roses blossomed
over hospitable homes that sheltered lovely maids and brave
cadets, where romance of the past still lived, a land where, in
short, the nostalgic Northerner could escape the wear and tear
of expanding industry and growing cities and dwell in a Dixie
of the storybooks which had become the Arcady of American
tradition.

Even though this image did not completely eradicate the
picture of another South which still lynched its Negroes and
under-educated its whites, the cumulative effect of the literature of Southern themes was to soften the tension of sectional
relations and produce a popular attitude of complacency to
Southern problems. Not untypical in this respect is the picture
of an eminent New England clergyman, Thomas Wentworth
Higginson, — who as a youth had led a jail delivery of a recaptured fugitive slave, and who in the Civil War had commanded a regiment of Negro troops, — sitting in his study
thirty years after the war had ended with a copy of "Marse
Chan" on his lap, shedding tears over the death of a slave-
owner.[17]

[16] "The South as a Field for Fiction," *Forum*, VI (1888), 405.
[17] The incident was related to me by the late Edward Channing. Much the
same type of story was told with other men shedding the tears, notably
Dr. Joseph Parker. Page, "Page," 92–93.

CHAPTER X

THE VETERAN MIND

THE spirit of good will which permeated every aspect of American life during the eighties received its deepest and sincerest expression from the aging veterans who once had borne the heat of battle. North and South, the soldiers professed to be the friends of peace. "You could not stand up day after day in those indecisive contests where overwhelming victory was impossible because neither side would run as they ought when beaten," averred Oliver Wendell Holmes, Jr., in 1884, "without getting at least something of the same brotherhood for the enemy that the north pole of a magnet has for the south — each working in an opposite sense to the other, but each unable to get along without the other." [1] Consequently when the war ended it was the soldiers who first forgave.

It would be difficult to find an opinion more widely asserted than this. So often did it appear in the postwar oratory of veterans that one is inclined to believe that if all America had been on the firing line there would have been no estrangement after Appomattox. Yet when an investigation of the activities of the formal organizations of veterans is made, important qualifications necessarily appear.

The organization properly claiming to be most representative of the Union veteran was the Grand Army of the Republic.[2] This society, founded in the first winter of peace, weathered

[1] As quoted in the *Boston Advertiser*, May 31, 1884.
[2] My account of the G. A. R. is based upon the *Proceedings of the National Encampments* (1866–1881) ; *Journals of the Annual Sessions* (1882–1900) ; similar volumes of proceedings of departmental encampments; official newspapers, as the *National Tribune* (Washington), *Home and Country* (New York), the *American Tribune* (Indianapolis), the *Grand Army Gazette* (New York), and the *Western Veteran* (Topeka) ; and the weekly G. A. R. column in the *New York Tribune*.

the early storms of hostility and indifference until it assumed a prominent place in national life. With a membership of thirty thousand in 1878, indicating to this date a slow, uphill fight, the G. A. R. grew consistently and rapidly throughout the next decade until the peak of four hundred and nine thousand was reached in 1890. Thereafter death worked faster than new members could be added and the membership gradually declined until it fell to slightly more than a quarter million at the century's close. It may be said that the society was most vigorous in the eighties, whereas in the nineties advancing age and the steady encroachment of death upon its thinning ranks produced in the minds of the younger generation the personified image that will remain in history as representing the Grand Army of the Republic — a bent and gray-haired figure uniformed in blue, assembling on village lawn or city square to recall a former age of heroic deeds.

The Grand Army soon arrogated to itself the special prerogative of maintaining inviolate the tradition of national patriotism. At its first encampment it resolved to stand guard over "those great principles" for which its members had fought "during the late war against traitors." [3] As a necessary corollary there must be a "just condemnation of that fell spirit of rebellion, which would have destroyed not only the country, but rooted liberty itself out of the land." [4] It was natural for men who had organized a society whose motive was the preservation of war ideals to presume that "those who wore one uniform and fought under one flag, fought for their country and were right, while those who wore the other uniform and fought under the other banner, fought against their country and were wrong, and no sentimental nor commercial efforts to efface these radical differences should be encouraged by any true patriot." [5] The G. A. R. never retreated from this position.

In practice this attitude resulted in a jealous surveillance of all that appertained to the war, and an adherence to what the veterans considered to be the true account of the causes, aims, and conduct of the struggle. Committees scrutinized school

[3] Proceedings, First Encampment, 8.
[4] Ibid., Fourth Encampment, 37.
[5] Journal, Thirtieth Encampment, 58.

textbooks, protested against "false emphasis," bemoaned the absence of words like treason and rebellion, and berated Northern publishers who issued separate texts for Southern sale.[6] Outside the organization a man might reflect upon the possibility of divided right and wrong. Within he was committed to belief in a rigid creed which permitted no variation. Such a situation gave opportunity for mistaken zealots to dress in the garb of patriotism crank theories of history, devotion to the flag and loyalty, and pass them off as representative of the men who had fought for the Union. Most of the rekindling of old animosities may be traced to the essentially false position of maintaining an uncompromising attitude toward the truth.

The members of the G. A. R. professed no desire to keep alive or to engender the ill feeling of wartimes. They repeatedly defended themselves against the accusations that their memorial services perpetuated a spirit of animosity toward their former foes. However, they deemed it unreasonable that they should be asked "to forget the sacred cause for which their silent comrades died, and cease to glory in its vindication and triumph." To them the war had been no "unhappy feud" for which an apology was due. Rather was it an heroic contest in which brave men stood together resisting an effort to obliterate "the fairest form of government that man ever devised." Never could they acknowledge that they were wrong. Never could they cease to condemn the cause for which their enemy had bravely struggled. Nor could they allow the memory to "sink into indifference and oblivion." Justice and gratitude demanded "that we at least should claim for dead comrades the places to which they are rightfully entitled among the heroes and martyrs of liberty."

And yet while thus insisting upon maintaining a distinction between "those who died to preserve the Union and those who sought to destroy it," the Grand Army readily admitted the bravery and sincerity of its opponent in the field. The fraternal contacts between the sections that were becoming common in the late seventies found a response in the proceedings of the

---

[6] *Ibid., Twenty-second Encampment,* 210–217; *Twenty-eighth Encampment,* 250; *Thirty-first Encampment,* 238. See also B. L. Pierce, "Public Opinion and the Teaching of History" (New York), 164–170.

national encampment. In 1882 the society met for the first time
"among people whose sympathies and influences were largely
with the rebellious States during our war for the Union." Baltimore received with marked cordiality ten thousand veterans
of the Union army, as well as the President of the United
States, members of his cabinet, the Speaker of the House of
Representatives, the General of the United States Army, and
others prominent in the national government. The G. A. R.
invited Southern soldiers to march with them in their procession, and when the veterans in Gray responded the occasion
was hailed as "one of the happy feats of peace which count
among renowned victories." As a consequence of the "genuine
hospitality" shown the G. A. R., the encampment prepared an
address to the city of Baltimore testifying to the "restored
feeling of brotherly love between the people of the South and
the people of the North," engraved it on a tablet made of
metal from Union and Confederate cannon, and presented it
amid further scenes of peacemaking.[7]

Thirteen years later the G. A. R. encamped a second time
on the borderland of the South. In the interim persistent
efforts to secure a meeting for the lower South had failed, but
the project had revealed a growing spirit of friendship within
the ranks of the G. A. R. toward the South and on the part
of Southerners toward the G. A. R. At Pittsburgh, in 1894, a
"Confederate delegation" from Louisville, led by the eloquent
spellbinder, "Marse Henry" Watterson of the *Louisville
Courier Journal,* appeared before the national encampment of
the G. A. R. and urgently invited the "boys in blue" to "come
South" so that their "countrymen who dwell on what was
once the nether side of the line, but whose hearts beat in ready
response to your hearts," might greet them "with arms wide
open." Responding to the fervent persuasion of the Kentuckian's hyperbole, the encampment voted to meet the next year
in Louisville, "not because it is the finest city in the Union,
but because in that invitation, coming from representative men
who stood for the Lost Cause, we see, as we never have seen
before, the dawn of that day when every feeling of animosity

---

[7] *Journal, Sixteenth Encampment; ibid., Seventeenth Encampment.* For
a photographic reproduction of the tablet see *Harper's Weekly,* July 7, 1883.

upon the part of either section shall be lost and forever lost in that patriotic glow for one common country for which we are ready to die if necessary." [8]

The Louisville encampment illustrated the ease with which the now aged veterans assumed the rôle of friends. The celebrations followed the usual round of parades, speeches, banquets, and tribute-paying over the dead of both armies.[9] Again the country had a striking object lesson of the healing influence which war memories were exerting.

So in the end the G. A. R., while sheltering its share of cranks, had no place for irreconcilables. No portion of its program was accepted more eagerly or received more space in the newspapers than, as its commander in chief declared in 1897, the work of strengthening "in those good people [of the South] their devotion to the land we all so dearly love, — to help blot out the resentments of the past." [10] One wonders why the resentments which had been blotted out on so many previous occasions still needed attention. But the clichés of popular oratory are long enduring and are not to be taken too literally. More important is the consideration that certain sentiments have become conventionalized so that their repetition is expected on every occasion. The fact that even the Grand Army had fallen into the habit of extending friendly overtures to the men they had fought in war is indicative perhaps of the fact that "time has softened our griefs, healed our sorrows, and obliterated sectionalism." [11] It is in this light that one should interpret the remarks of President McKinley addressed to the G. A. R. at Buffalo in 1897 that "the army of Grant and the army of Lee are together . . . one now in faith, in hope, in fraternity, in purpose, and in an invincible patriotism." [12] It was something at least that an American president

[8] *Journal, Twenty-eighth Encampment.*
[9] *Ibid., Twenty-ninth Encampment.*
[10] *Journal, Thirty-first Encampment.*
[11] *Ibid.*
[12] *Public Opinion,* Sept. 2, 1897. It might be noted that lesser organizations of Union Veterans reënacted the story of the G. A. R. See as typical the meeting of the Army of the Potomac with the Robert E. Lee Camp of Confederate Veterans (*Reports of the Army of the Potomac for 1885*), and the encampments of the Army of the Cumberland at Chattanooga and Chickamauga (*Annual Reports of the Army of the Cumberland, 1881, 1889, 1892*).

could make such a statement and have it wildly applauded by an organization of Union veterans.

In the South the development of veteran organizations proceeded at a slower pace than in the North. The lateness of their origin is partially accounted for by the hostility confronting "rebel societies." It may also be explained by the tendency noted everywhere of the Southern veteran to withdraw from the public gaze and preoccupy himself with the arduous task of reconstituting his damaged estate. The first societies were local and restricted in membership. Unlike the North where national federation came early and showed the way for smaller groupings, the scattered efforts of the former Confederates to organize were not concentrated in one body until 1889. Then was formed the United Confederate Veterans and a distinct impetus given to the activity of the men who wore the Gray.[13]

The problem of the Southern veteran was one of adjustment. He retained the memory of a manly fight for principle. He revered the martyrhood of comrades slain in battle and recognized the duty devolving on himself to protect them from aspersion. He experienced a warm glow of affection for the banner furled forever in defeat and for associations it recalled. He could not repudiate and assume a false humility towards a past he gloried in. Rather he resented bitterly the epithets of rebellion and treason when applied to his conduct. He demanded a "true" history of the struggle which would justify his motives and explain how men could honestly espouse a cause too often execrated by the misunderstanding world outside. But while the past was thus to receive its due, the present and the future also had their claims. He was back within the Union, and daily the widening activities and interests of life urged the conviction that it was well the cherished cause of Southern independence had gone down in defeat. With a sensitive regard to the past, therefore, the ex-Confederate proceeded to rationalize the inconsistencies of his position until he arrived at a solution which enabled him to salute "Old Glory" while retaining his devotion for "the Southern Cross."

[13] *Proceedings of the Convention for the Organization of the United Confederate Veterans; Minutes of the United Confederate Veterans,* I, 1889–1897. The official organ of the U. C. V. was the *Confederate Veteran,* the first issue of which appeared in 1893.

All the essentials of the solution may be found in a masterful address delivered in Richmond, Virginia, in 1896 before the sixth reunion of the United Confederate Veterans by the general agent of the Peabody Education Fund, J. L. M. Curry, a former Confederate well known and respected both South and North.[14] Curry undertook to explain "why Americans, pure and simple, without prefix of condition," could come together in an association the membership of which was based upon an earlier effort to disrupt the American Union. This would constitute dishonesty had there not been reconciliation. But advocating peace and friendship the assembly of Confederate veterans had "no such purpose as recital of wrongs endured, or indulgence in vain pride, or egotistic laudation." They met not "in malice or in mischief, in disaffection, or in rebellion, nor to keep alive sectional hates, nor to awaken revenge for defeat, nor to kindle disloyalty to the Union." They came together "in common love for those who bore the conquered banner." Curry then proceeded to demonstrate that this "recognition of the glorious deeds of our comrades is perfectly consistent with loyalty to the flag and devotion to the Constitution and the resulting Union." He was supported in this sentiment by the official report of the assembly which declared that the Confederate veteran "returned to the Union as an equal, and he remained in the Union as a friend. With no humble apologies, no unmanly servility, no petty spite, no sullen treachery, he is a cheerful, frank citizen of the United States, accepting the present, trusting the future, and proud of the past." [15]

The Southerners were on the defensive even when assembling for such a purpose. Defeated and discredited, they were confronted by efforts on the part of bigots in the North "to paint the Lost Cause in darkest colors, to sully it with crimes more horrible than matricide, to overwhelm its supporters with the odium and infamy of traitors." Even when the Northern critic essayed to be fair and to forgive the past, he frequently was

[14] *Address Delivered before the Association of Confederate Veterans* (pamphlet, Richmond, 1896).
[15] *Minutes, Sixth Reunion.*

unable to appreciate why the supporters of "rebellion" should
be honored in ways similar to those observed for the upholders
of the "right." Consequently the Confederate societies assumed the rôle of vindicating themselves and their deceased
comrades in much the same manner as the G. A. R. had constituted itself the guardian of the fruits of victory. The men
who had followed Lee and Jackson felt no duty more imperative than "to see to it that our children do not grow up with
false notions of their fathers, and with disgraceful apologies
for their conduct."

The vindication usually was based upon a careful distinction between "constitutional resistance" and "treason." Thus
Curry defined the war as one "of ideas, in which each army
signalized its consecration to principles, as each understood
them." This led him into a long exposition on slavery, nullification, and secession, in which he established the mutual
responsibility of the two sections in regard to slavery, the
readiness of the North to use the doctrine of nullification when
coinciding with its interests, and the existence in 1860 of
secession as a reserved right of the states. He admitted that a
different interpretation had arisen in the North, but he insisted that the South adhered to its view with as much legality
and honesty as did the North. When the "inevitable" conflict arose between the two attitudes, principle and courage
engaged on either side. The conclusion, once the orator had
satisfactorily vindicated every one, was easy. The war, or, to
employ language often used, "the bloody arbitrament of the
sword," had entirely changed everything. The right of secession was abandoned and slavery abolished. The Confederate
survivors were making good "their asseverations of loyalty to
the Republic by observing in strictest fidelity the letter and
spirit of the Constitution."

It is obvious that such historical analysis might lead to endless wrangling especially when contrasted to the G. A. R.'s
views on the same subjects. But ordinarily the mass of veterans on each side accepted an easy camaraderie while the cranks
fought along in endless wrangling over details that had become insignificant with the passage of time. The meetings of

the Confederate Survivors' Association of Augusta, Georgia, illustrate the flow of Confederate sentiment as expressed in veteran organizations.[16] The annual meetings reveal a surprising lack of vindictiveness or bitterness, although such an episode as Sherman's march was never mentioned except in terms of denunciation. Speakers extolled the virtues of the defeated and emphasized the duty of preserving the noble traditions of the Lost Cause. Resolutions insisted that the "martyred heroes of Dixie" had not been rebels, but "lovers of liberty, combatants for constitutional rights, and . . . benefactors of their race." Much attention was devoted to recollections of the battlefield which led at times to a distrust of the utilitarianism of the New South and a fear that its growing commercial spirit would tend to belittle the achievements of the war generation. Lastly, the veterans of Augusta recognized the desirability, if not the accomplished fact, of reconciliation in terms the sincerity of which seems beyond dispute.

Often the aging veteran of the South was made to feel as though the spirit of the changing life around him had little sympathy for the ideals and characteristics of former years — years he typified. The indifference with which the young shove aside the old, the patronage shown to outworn things by preoccupied youth, must ever bring sadness to the veteran. When the normal change is accentuated by the overthrow of all for which the old has contended, the experience may well prove unbearable. It is not unnatural, therefore, to find the Southern veteran seeking emotional relief in sentimentalizing the "Conquered Banner," and in passionate outbursts of popular enthusiasm when opportunity permitted. Two such demonstrations deserve comment — one at Montgomery, Alabama, in 1886, and the other at Richmond four years later.

Unfriendly critics in the North might complain that the ovation given to Jefferson Davis when laying the foundation of a monument to the Confederate dead of Alabama bespoke an attachment to the past on the part of Southerners which precluded any true regard for the restored Union. Certainly "Dixie

[16] *Reports of the Annual Meetings of the Confederate Survivors' Association of Augusta, Georgia* (pamphlets, Augusta, 1879–1892).

reigned" amid scenes of wildest excitement. For three days
Montgomery revelled in an extravagance of act and utterance
characteristic of a people lost in sentiment. Retrospection harked
back to the day twenty-five years earlier when Davis had
stood on the same spot in the Capitol grounds to take the oath
of office as president of the newly born Confederacy. Now aged
and unforgiven by the government that had overthrown the
fondest aspirations of himself and of his people, he stood again
the central figure commemorating the Lost Cause. Over his
head floated the American flag. Before him stood citizens of
a restored Union. They cheered him fondly as "the highest
type of Southern manhood." The sympathy with which they
attended his eulogy and defense of the past testified to the
sincerity and permanence of their devotion for what he represented. Yet through it all no discordant note was struck and
no one complained of the fate that had overtaken the Confederacy after four brief years of checkered life. If memory
of the past was a treasured legacy, the Union of the present
was also a reality in the Southern mind. It was this fact which
permitted a local newspaper to exclaim without inconsistency,
"We honor the furled under the unfurled flag," and another
to hail the event as one "without parallel in history." [17]

Such events, however, were not unparalleled. On May 29,
1890, Mercie's equestrian statue of Lee was unveiled in Richmond. The mighty tribute paid the Confederate general was
worthy of his greatness and testified eloquently of the love in
which his memory was held. As prominently as at Montgomery
there was evident an undercurrent of satisfaction that the cause
had been lost. Military companies bore both flags, that of the
Confederacy in affection, that of the Union in loyalty. If this
constituted a paradox it might be explained, as one observer
noted, "by the fact that the former no longer meant disunion.
It stood for past trials and heroism in adversity looked back

[17] Newspaper comment of this event is collected in *Public Opinion*,
May 8, 1886, and Rowland, "Davis," IX, 419–439. The *New York World*
noted the prominence of Yankees in the celebration. An Ohio veteran wearing his G. A. R. badge supplied the American flags which decorated the
line of march and hung draped around the platform from which Davis spoke
his defense of the South. A Northerner was also in charge of the electric
illuminations, while a Bostonian was the proprietor of the hotel at which
Davis stayed.

upon from the standpoint of changed views and unforeseen prosperity."[18]

The adjustment thus made lost in time the awkwardness of self-conscious rationalization which first characterized its appearance. The process was emotionalized as the humiliation of defeat passed away and the memory of the men in Gray mellowed into a conception of American valor and manhood which could be appreciated North as well as South and thus no longer cause division. The middle nineties which witnessed the G. A. R. love-feast at Louisville and the dedication of Confederate monuments in Chicago and New York, also found the spirit of fraternity triumphing within the ranks of the United Confederate Veterans.[19] The Houston reunion of 1895 gave evidence of reconciliation. The permanent committee on history reported that "the love of a common country [was] now invoking a spirit of truth, concession and fairness in reviewing the causes which led to the war, and in discussing the conduct of the war and its results."[20] With his regard for the past thus satisfied, the Confederate veteran readily accepted his calling as an American, under the same flag and with the same destiny as his former enemy in Blue.[21]

Far more than the activities of organized groups of veterans, the publication of books of recollections testified to the mellowing of war memories and the softening of unreconciled emotions. It is of course possible to find any sentiment sought for in the great mass of reminiscences set on paper during the eighties and nineties. But no reservation need be made to the generalization that the great majority of veterans, who in these later years wrote their memoirs, shared the same spirit that prompted George Cary Eggleston, "A Rebel's Recollection" (1875), and John S. Wise, "The End of an Era" (1899), to avoid all recrimination and to promote friendly

[18] *Harper's Weekly*, June 14, 1890. See also *Public Opinion*, June 7, 1890, and E. Owen, "The Confederate Veterans' Camp of New York," *National Magazine*, XVII (1892), 455–467.

[19] For the dedication at Chicago see the *Confederate Veteran*, III (1895), 176–179. For that at New York see *ibid.*, V (1897), 177.

[20] *Ibid.*, III (1895), 163–170. Quotations on page 166.

[21] See as typical H. L. Flash's poem "Memories of Blue and Gray," read at the second anniversary reunion of the Confederate Veterans' Association of Los Angeles, Sept. 25, 1897. H. L. Flash, "Poems" (New York, 1906).

feelings between the foemen of former years. Richard Watson Gilder was typical when he maintained

> . . . never in all the world
> Was braver army 'gainst a braver hurled,
> To both the victory, all unawares,
> Beyond all dreams of losing or of winning.[22]

North and South the soldiers seemed to have outlived their prejudices and were now endeavoring to demonstrate "how American soldiers pay willing tribute to each other's prowess." [23]

When the *Century Magazine* undertook in November 1884 a three years' task of presenting articles on the Civil War by surviving Federal and Confederate leaders, the publishing of reminiscences entered upon its most significant phase.[24] The editors sought frankly to promote the sentiment of national unity by encouraging papers which eschewed all resentment, prejudice, and bitterness. They wanted "sincere contributions" that "celebrated the skill and valor of both sides," and "cultivated the feeling of mutual respect which cemented the restored Union." Gilder set the pitch. "This is the time for the unveiling of all hearts. If the North can see the heart of the South, and the South the North's, they will love each other as never before! This is truth and not sentimentalism." [25]

John Hay believed that the country had fallen into a period of "blubbering sentiment." [26] Actually the sustained enthusiasm for war memoirs suggested that it had taken the nation just twenty years to reach the stage where tragedy could be idealized as a noble and inspiring tradition. The veterans had forgotten their nightmares. They thrilled to the experience of

[22] R. W. Gilder, "The Great Remembrance," in "Poems of Richard Watson Gilder" (Boston, 1908), 197. The poem was written in 1893.
[23] G. F. Williams, "Lights and Shadows of Army Life," *Century*, XXVIII (1884), 810.
[24] The articles appeared in each issue from Nov. 1884 to Nov. 1887. They were then collected and published in four volumes under the title of "The Battles and Leaders of the Civil War" (New York, 1887). Grant, Sherman, McClellan, J. E. Johnston, Beauregard, and Longstreet were among the contributors. See also R. U. Johnson, "Remembered Yesterdays" (New York, 1923), 124–131, and L. F. Tooker, "Joys and Tribulations of an Editor" (New York, 1924), 180–188.
[25] Gilder, "Letters," 130–131.
[26] J. R. Thayer, "Life and Letters of John Hay" (Boston, 1915), II, 32.

finding a new generation grown up around them eager to hear the story of the age of heroism. The Century War Series was a sensational success. Its message penetrated deep into the nation's heart. Not one of its varied, vivid, thrilling pages told of a war where men went mad with hatred, starved in prison camps, and invoked God's aid in damnation of the enemy. The history that the veterans told was of a war in which valor countered valor, and each side devotedly served the right. The blood that was shed was baptismal blood, consecrating the birth of a new and greater nation.

Meanwhile one by one the "lofty actors" of the great drama were leaving the stage and becoming memories. Grant, Lee, Davis, Lincoln — what would posterity do with them? What traditions cluster around their names? We take our heroes and bend them to our wishes. The aging generation still had use of their leaders after death. Before the century closed Lincoln and Lee, Davis and Grant, were idealizations, and the idealizations apostles of fraternity.

Grant was still a soldier when in 1868 he phrased a nation's yearning in his memorable "Let us have peace." The campaign for that elusive good, however, proved more difficult than the military problems of the war. From this point of view, his presidency was a failure, the magnanimity of Appomattox giving way to the excesses of Reconstruction. But in retirement the sturdy qualities of the soldier reappeared. There was something about Grant which suggested indifference to petty quarrels, the bigness of a man who once having fought deplores the indulgence of continued strife. His life closed as did his "Memoirs" with a fervent prayer for good feeling between the sections. Gradually succumbing to an incurable disease his tranquil and manly fortitude at Mount McGregor won the sympathy of the nation. Throughout his suffering he gave evidence of a hearty and unreserved friendliness toward those who had fought against the Union. The magnanimity of his last words revealed a spirit which went far in composing lingering differences.[27]

[27] "Personal Memoirs of U. S. Grant" (New York, 1885), II, 553–554; H. Garland, "Ulysses S. Grant" (New York, 1920), 478–481, 521; *Century*, XXXI (1885), 125–126; *Harper's Weekly*, Feb. 21, 1885.

He would not have been displeased, therefore, had he been able to witness the union of the sections around his outworn body. The entire country felt the bereavement of his loss. Distinguished Confederate generals wearing gray sashes served as pallbearers with leading officers of the Union army. The spectacle was striking and sincere. One who was too young to know firsthand the story of the war has left his impressions of the scene in a leading New York hotel the night before the public funeral:

The corridors were thronged with well known veterans of both armies, but what one chiefly noted in the great gathering was that while Union men met Union men like old friends, and Confederates met Confederates in the same manner, Union men and Confederates greeted one another like long-lost brothers. I lingered about for hours. . . . [When] I went home, it was with a feeling of pride I shall never forget. I had just witnessed a great sight — the kindly, open hearted meeting of men who had fought bitterly against one another.[28]

It was no "sentimental effusion," therefore, but demonstrated sincerity which led representative men to interpret "the memorable pageant at the tomb of the great soldier" as the "virtual conclusion of sectional animosity in America."[29]

If the North welcomed the idea of Confederate pallbearers the South showed an equal willingness to bring tribute to her conqueror. The generous victor of Appomattox was remembered, his faults forgiven. One writer who may be taken as representative recalled Grant as the savior of the Union in which capacity the South was now as grateful for his work as was the North. The manifestation of sympathy on the part of Southerners, it was generally observed, was spontaneous evidence of their loyalty, if not of their emotional attachment, to the government under which they lived.[30]

[28] Tooker, "Joys and Tribulations of an Editor," 46.
[29] *Harper's Weekly,* Aug. 15, 1885; *Boston Advertiser,* Aug. 10, 1885; *Century,* XXX (1885), 965; *Nation,* Aug. 13, 1885.
[30] *Harper's Weekly,* Aug. 1 and 8, 1885, quotes from a number of Southern newspapers. Most Southerners who wrote memoirs had distinctly favorable impressions of Grant. See Taylor, "Destruction and Reconstruction," 149, 242; Gordon, "Reminiscences," 460–464; Clay, "Belle of the Fifties," 316; and C. E. Merrick, "Old Times in Dixie Land" (New York, 1901), 134–135.

A stately marble mausoleum now occupies a majestic site overlooking the Hudson. On its southern wall are inscribed the words by which its honored inmate is best remembered, LET US HAVE PEACE. Grant's wish was realized in his death. He entered the traditions of his country as a pacificator.

Far more than to Grant, it is owing to the great warrior who has come to typify the chivalry of the South that the Civil War has left no lasting division between the sections. Lee's character was free of malice, patient, and motivated by an unselfish regard for principle. The South saw in him personified all that it cherished most. The North learned in time to claim him with pride as an American. Then the Southerner found no further need for justification. His advocate was Lee.

Lee's example after Appomattox has been variously appraised.[31] To some it has seemed that he performed his greatest service in leading his countrymen to an acceptance of the situation forced upon them.[32] "The questions which for years were in dispute," he wrote in August 1865, "having been decided against us, it is the part of wisdom to acquiesce in the result, and of candor to recognize the fact. The interests of the State [Virginia] are therefore the same as those of the United States. Its prosperity will rise or fall with the welfare of the country. The duty of its citizens, then, appears to me too plain to admit of doubt. All should unite in honest efforts to obliterate the effects of war, and to restore the blessings of peace." [33] Invariably recommending this course to his former officers and men who came to him for advice, he himself turned his back on all contention and devoted the remaining years of his life to the training of Virginia's youth. "I have a self-imposed task which I must accomplish," he wrote in assuming the presidency of Washington College. "I have led the young men of the South in battle; I have seen many of them die in the field; I shall devote my remaining energies to training young

[31] D. S. Freeman, "Robert E. Lee" (New York, 1935), IV, chs. 12–28, is the definitive account.
[32] Field, "Bright Skies and Dark Shadows," 313–314; Wise, "End of an Era," 344; C. F. Adams, "Lee at Appomattox" (Boston, 1902), 1–30.
[33] J. W. Jones, "Life and Letters of Robert Edward Lee" (New York, 1906), 387.

men to do their duty in life." [34] Few scenes are more inspiring than that of the hero of the Confederacy, the pathos of the Lost Cause centering in him, stilling by his example "the angry tempest that the war had left behind." [35]

The full significance of Lee's later years was not at first apparent. When he died in 1870 the unreconciled sections found in the occasion another opportunity to quarrel. The North still bracketed him with Benedict Arnold.[36] The South denied that he had one aspiration in common with America, claiming instead that he was of the South exclusively, a "martyr, of whom America was not worthy." [37] Before many years had passed, however, Lee the Confederate was to become Lee the American, and the South rather than resenting remembered with satisfaction that Lee had advised the policy of painful upbuilding and of embarking upon the new national life which was bringing peace and the promise of prosperity.

It was well for the South that Lee could be represented as the "very incarnation of the Confederate cause." That cause had been portrayed in the North as an iniquitous attempt to destroy a worthy form of government in order to perpetuate and extend the institution of slavery. What could better efface this impression and establish in its place one of the South fighting "for the right as it saw the right" than the picture of Lee, torn between two loyalties, deciding after an agonizing conflict to follow that which the traditions of birth and upbringing told him to be correct? "As an American citizen," he had written early in 1861, "I take great pride in my country, her prosperity and institutions, and would defend any State if her rights were invaded. But I can anticipate no greater calamity for the country than a dissolution of the Union. It would be an accumulation of all the evils we complain of, and I am willing to sacrifice anything but honor for its preservation." [38] The Union in his mind rested voluntarily upon the sovereign

[34] R. E. Lee, Jr., "Recollections and Letters of General Robert E. Lee" (New York, 1904), 376.
[35] Field, *op. cit.*, 313.
[36] See as typical Thurlow Weed's letter of Oct. 23, 1870, in T. W. Barnes, "Memoir of Thurlow Weed" (Boston, 1884), 467–470; *Harper's Weekly*, Oct. 29, 1870; and *Nation*, Oct. 20, 1870.
[37] See Lamar's letter in Mayes, "Lamar," 658.
[38] Jones, "Life and Letters of Lee," 121.

rights of individual states. It could not be maintained by swords and bayonets. When force was resorted to in an attempt to settle the issues between the sections the Union seemed to him dissolved. "Trusting in Almighty God, [and] an approving conscience," he took his stand with his neighbors in defense of his state — the state of which his father had exclaimed in another day of divided loyalties, "Virginia is my country. Her I will obey, however lamentable the fate to which it may subject me."

Whether or not Lee properly analyzed the crisis is beside the point. The world saw a man faced with the necessity of breaking with a past made memorable by his own people, of following Virginia out of a Union it had taken the lead to establish. The Northern public could appreciate such a picture. Standing within the precincts of Washington and Lee University, delivering the address commemorating the centennial of Lee's birth, Charles Francis Adams expressed dramatically an opinion which had become general in the North. Having recalled the fact that for four years he had stood in arms against the Southern leader, Adams asserted that after long study and mature reflection he would have done exactly as Lee had done under similar circumstances. "It may have been treason," he continued, for Lee to take the position he did; "the man who took it, . . . sacrificing as he sacrificed, may have been technically a renegade to his flag, — but he awaits sentence at the bar of history in very respectable company. Associated with him are, for instance, William of Orange, known as the Silent, John Hampden, the original *Pater Patriae*, Oliver Cromwell, the Protector of the English Commonwealth, Sir Harry Vane, once a governor of Massachusetts, and George Washington, a Virginian of note." [39]

Geography, then, the accident of a man's birth, and not the difference between virtue and moral turpitude, becomes under this new dispensation the factor that had divided equally patriotic Americans into Federals and Confederates. How simply the conclusion follows: "Every man in the eleven States seceding from the Union had, in 1861, whether he would or

[39] C. F. Adams, "Lee's Centennial," in "Studies Military and Diplomatic" (New York, 1911), 305.

no, to decide for himself whether to adhere to his State or to his Nation: and I finally assert that, whichever way he decided, if only he decided honestly, putting self-interest behind him, he decided right." [40]

Not every one would have gone so far as Adams. The "rightness" of one's cause and the converse "wrongness" of one's opponent are hard for a partisan to surrender. But ordinary people find no difficulty in living together harmoniously when the defeated generally "accept the situation," when the victors recognize the courage and devotion to principle of the vanquished, and the two together join in celebrating "as a priceless heritage the memory of the mighty men and glorious deeds that the iron days brought forth." [41] Lee led his people in the first, made possible the development of the second in the North, and of the third was himself one preëminently honored and respected by both sections within a generation of his death. When in 1901 he took his place, therefore, in the American Hall of Fame in New York City, it was not only as a man of war, or as a defender of liberty in the Southern sense, but as a great reconciler whom the nation properly remembered with pride.

The years that brought honor and respect to Lee were ones of continued strife for the man who had presided over the Confederacy. Jefferson Davis ended his active rôle on the stage of national life in 1868 with his release from imprisonment in Fortress Monroe. From then until his death in 1889 the broken statesman lived in retirement watching one by one nearly every other prominent leader of the war precede him to the grave. It would have been well for his peace of mind had he achieved that dignified reserve which is content to leave to the arbitrament of a later generation judgment of the controversies in which he had engaged. But the ghosts of past disputes were real to Davis. They projected their disturbing shades into his retirement and robbed his later years of peace. The North heaped unrestrained vilification upon him. The South rose in his defense and, without loving him as Lee was loved, was equally indiscriminate in its praise.

[40] *Ibid.*, 296.
[41] Letter of Theodore Roosevelt, *Sewanee Review*, XV (1907), 174–176.

A man so situated could not avoid occasional indulgence of self-pity. Nor could Davis ever free himself from the haunting sense of obligation that the cause which once meant all to him still needed justification. But the South — his people — was moving steadily along the road of a reunited nation. He followed slowly in the wake. His "Rise and Fall of the Confederate States," published in 1881, ended with the recognition that the war had shown the right of secession to be impracticable. His later speeches softened in tone and suggested the reality of accomplished facts. In his last address he stood looking into the faces of young men and spoke briefly as follows:

The past is dead; let it bury its dead, its hopes, and its aspirations; before you lies the future, a future of golden promise, a future of expanding national glory, before which all the world shall stand amazed. Let me beseech you to lay aside all rancor, all bitter sectional feeling, and to make your places in the ranks of those who will bring about a consummation devoutly to be wished — a reunited country.[42]

A year later Jefferson Davis was dead.

An epoch ended with his death. He alone seemed to represent a past that could not be assimilated to the present. Others received amnesty. Others participated with growing satisfaction in the expanding life of the New South. Davis remained apart, an object of contention until his death. In the nineties there emerged an interpretation of the man which promised a common ground upon which the sections might stand in viewing his life. Davis was then pictured as a statesman who remained steadfast to what he conceived to be the true reading of the Constitution. But Davis never fitted graciously or completely into the pattern of reconciliation. The North in time ceased to revile him but it did not learn to admire him.

Lincoln presented a more complicated problem. So far as the North was concerned it is clear that his memory became an influence for peace. The heritage of his example transcended the pettiness of strife, recalling to an erring country the greatness of forbearance. The mildness of his policy

42 Rowland, "Davis," X, 48.

toward the prostrate South and his hesitancy to attribute guilt were remembered after the assassin's bullet left to less capable hands and more vindictive wills the awesome responsibility of Reconstruction. By the time of the Hayes administration an uneasy suspicion existed in the North that in some way a grievous and shameful mistake had been committed in handling the Southern problem. The ordinary man, unaware of the complexity of historical forces, reached out for a simple solution which would at the same time ease his conscience. Then arose the consoling thought that if Lincoln had been spared the tragedy would have been avoided. The might-have-been of history fascinated. Had Lincoln lived — the North would have been magnanimous!

In a more vital sense the idealization of Lincoln worked for fraternity. The elevation of his character meant also the elevation of the virtues which he represented. If the North sensed in him its most exemplary American it meant that the North must define Americanism not in terms of Radical philosophy but in terms of Lincoln's life. A broader and more tolerant attitude resulted.

Yet no Southerner ever took the pride in Lincoln that Northerners took in Lee. The picture of the Black Republican who unleashed the hounds of war did not altogether fade from memory although writers like J. S. Wise, Mrs. Pryor, and Mrs. Avary filled the pages of their reminiscences with anecdotes of Lincoln's charity and moderation. Joel Chandler Harris and Henry Grady paid tributes to the Northern leader that indicated that they at least found no awkwardness in harmonizing love for the South with an appreciation of Lincoln's greatness, while Watterson went further than any contemporary, North or South, in eulogizing Lincoln as a God-inspired leader.[43] Nevertheless Lincoln, like Davis, remained essentially the hero of a section. The Southern heart never yielded to the sentiment that caused the North to bow in worship of its wartime leader.

Throughout the eighties the routine of daily life brought together individual veterans in contacts which furthered the

[43] Address in Chicago, Feb. 12, 1895, H. W. Watterson, "Compromises of Life," 137–180.

work of reconciliation. Little more than the nature and scope of these meetings can be illustrated. Usually they were dramatic coincidences possible only in the aftermath of a Civil War which had divided families and disrupted friendships of long standing. One need but leaf through a volume of reminiscences or read an address delivered to veterans in the closing decades of the century to find examples of these "individual reunions of Blue and Gray." [44] General Gordon reported them assiduously. His best story, that of the succor he administered to the wounded Union general, Francis C. Barlow, on the field of Gettysburg, and their later friendship in times of peace, was typical of many like experiences which Gordon interpreted as the "truest indices of the American soldier's character." [45] General O. O. Howard, while superintendent of West Point, witnessed a scene in which "enemies became friends." Two fathers met in his office, one from New York, the other from Georgia. Each was bringing a son to the Academy to enter as a cadet. In the conversation that ensued it developed that both had been wounded at Malvern Hill, falling on the same part of the battlefield, one in Blue, the other in Gray. The men parted the closest of friends.[46] Such episodes might be multiplied. A traveler recording "glimpses of Dixie" for *Harper's* noted how easily Union veterans traveling in the South exchanged reminiscences and how often in relating their stock of anecdotes they found common ground for friendship.[47]

The spirit of good will received a more striking exemplification in the fraternizing of men in Blue and Gray. Reunions of the veterans of a particular locality or section, or of an army unit, had not been uncommon in the seventies. With increasing age and retirement from active life, it was only nat-

[44] See as typical C. F. Manderson, "The Twin Seven-Shooters" (New York, 1902); N. P. Hallowell, *Memorial Day Address* (pamphlet, Boston, 1896), 3–8; J. S. Wise, "End of an Era" (Boston, 1899), 300–301, 449–453; J. B. Foraker, "Notes of a Busy Life" (Cincinnati, 1916), I, 30–31; and Pryor, "My Day," 214–215.
[45] J. B. Gordon, "Reminiscences of the Civil War" (New York, 1903), 105–119, 222, 287, 408.
[46] O. O. Howard, "Enemies Who Became Friends," *Boston Globe,* May 21, 1892.
[47] C. D. Deshler, "Glimpses of Dixie," *Harper's Monthly,* LI (1875), 667–671.

ural that the war generation should live more than ever in the memories of past experiences.[48] Reunions became a common occurrence, and of these there developed a type hitherto unknown in history. The veterans of both armies met in mutual celebration, giving a convincing object lesson of the truth that those who fought most honorably in war are the first to forgive in peace.

It might be said that the participation of the Virginia and South Carolina companies in the Bunker Hill celebration of 1875 was the first public demonstration of fraternizing between the former enemies. That, however, was occasioned by an event not of the Civil War, and it was not until 1881 that veterans of both armies met for the sole reason of rejoicing that they were no longer foes. Then quickly the practice spread, culminating in two great spectacles, one commemorating the twenty-five anniversary of the battle of Gettysburg, the other the dedication of the national military park at Chickamauga and Chattanooga in 1895.

In many ways the visit of New York and Boston troops in New Orleans during the Mardi Gras festival of 1881 resembled that of the Southern troops in Boston six years earlier. The olive branch passed back and forth. "We of the South" the invitation to the Union veterans read, "are anxious to show to you of the North that the war is over. . . . Come and visit us that we may show you how sincere we are." Where all were united in a purpose so apparent it is unnecessary to emphasize the interchange of courtesies that marked the visit. The popular enthusiasm, already at a high pitch during the holiday period, exaggerated the relative importance of the episode as "one of the most auspicious circumstances" since 1865. The Northern troops entered into the festivities with hilarity. They spoke glowing words of friendship, and touchingly decorated the graves of the Confederate dead. Papers

[48] The statement of General M. M. Trumbull, in 1890, is typical: "For me the war is an omnipresent reality. . . . At the bivouac of memory around the old camp-fire we sit and smoke our pipes together once again. I listen to their boisterous laughter and their merry jests. Again I hear them singing, 'Glory Allelulia,' 'Rally round the Flag,' and I know they are not dead." M. M. Trumbull, "Decoration Day Thoughts," *New England Magazine*, II (1890), 381.

as widely separated as the *Philadelphia Record,* the *New York Mercury,* the *Cincinnati Commercial,* and the *New Orleans Democrat* saw fit to hail this holiday excursion as an important factor in effecting good will between the sections. *Harper's Weekly* went to the extreme of a full page cartoon in which "Louisiana" and "New York" are personified in Gray and Blue. They shake hands before an approving Uncle Sam, while "Columbia" proudly writes on a map of the United States, "No North! No South! But the Union!" [49]

The importance of such an emotional outburst might easily be misread. Alone it signified but little. But the Mardi Gras reunion was not an isolated phenomenon. It was the forerunner of a movement that steadily gathered momentum until it attained a climax of national interest. A contemporary observer enumerating the reunions that occurred between 1881 and 1887 was able to list twenty-four "more prominent formal" ones.[50] To these may be added "informal" meetings such as the visit of Connecticut troops headed by Governor Bigelow to Charleston, South Carolina, an episode which influenced the poet Hayne to write, "strife lies dead 'twixt Gray and Blue," [51] and the not infrequent return of captured battle flags.[52] Gettysburg alone saw three reunions on its classic battlefield before the greater one of 1888. Men in Gray a second time marched through the streets of Boston as the John A. Andrew post of the G. A. R. played host to the Robert E. Lee camp, Richmond, of Confederate veterans. An "Ex-Federal and Ex-Confederate Association" made its appearance in Kentucky, while in another border state, Missouri, the reunion of Confederates was participated in by Federals. Fredericksburg, Antietam, and Kenesaw Mountain were noteworthy instances of meetings on battlefields.[53]

It is apparent, therefore, that the country was familiar with

[49] *Harper's Weekly,* March 19, 1881. The New Orleans episode is fully described in J. F. Cowan, "A New Invasion of the South" (New York, 1881).

[50] G. L. Kilmer, "A Note of Peace," *Century,* XXXVI (1888), 440–442.

[51] P. H. Hayne, "Union of Blue and Gray," *Harper's Weekly,* Nov. 12, 1881.

[52] *Harper's Weekly,* July 14, 1883; Sept. 24 and Oct. 1, 1887.

[53] *Nation,* June 23, 1887; *Boston Advertiser,* June 17–20, 1887; *Harper's Weekly,* July 9, Sept. 10, Oct. 1, 1887.

"Blue and Gray reunions" before the twenty-fifth anniversary
of the battle of Gettysburg gave opportunity for a spectacle on
a larger scale. The naturalness with which the Society of the
Army of the Potomac extended an invitation to the survivors
of the Army of Northern Virginia is illustrative of the spirit
of the times. Political and utilitarian interest had not been absent from many of the earlier gestures of reconciliation. The
Gettysburg celebration arose spontaneously from a desire
"that the survivors of both armies may on that occasion record
in friendship and fraternity the sentiments of good will, loyalty, and patriotism which now unite us all in sincere devotion
to our beloved country." [54]

In that consists its significance. The number of Confederates
attending the reunion was not large. But they came with the
approval of their section and were led by men capable of
speaking responsibly for those left behind. They were met
cordially, and mixed with the far larger number of Unionists
on terms of easy good-fellowship which none at the time
doubted was sincere. Not for a moment of the three-day encampment was the central theme lost sight of. Northern or
Southern, all spoke the same language of pride in a common
Americanism. Speakers representing both sides vied with
each other in extolling the gallantry of the opposing forces
which gave to North and South an equal share in the glories
of Gettysburg. Mutually they paid tribute to the other's sincerity and bravery in waging war. Together they hailed the
beneficent solution of all disputed issues and welcomed the
new day of peace and union. If there was a tendency to overlook or underestimate the remnants of passion still persisting,
one truth was obvious, as Curtis emphasized in his oration:
"The line across the Union drawn by the flaming sword of
hostile social and industrial institutions, and irreconcilable
theories of the nature and powers of the government itself"
had disappeared forever.[55]

The casualness with which the accomplished fact of recon-

[54] *Proceedings of the Society of the Army of the Potomac, Eighteenth
Reunion*, 9.
[55] *Proceedings . . . , Nineteenth Reunion, passim; Harper's Weekly*,
July 7 and 14, 1888; Curtis, "Orations," III, 61–83; Gilder, "Poems," 163;
Century, XXXVI (1888), 791–792.

ciliation is taken nowadays should not obscure the remarkable nature of this scene at Gettysburg. Twenty-five years after a sanguinary battle survivors of the opposing armies met again in amity to celebrate the outcome. The South had had much at issue in 1863. Its defeat involved the greatest suffering and humiliation. Yet not one of the Southern soldiers listening to General Sickles in 1888 would have dissented when he said "To-day there are no victors, no vanquished. As Americans we may all claim a common share . . . in the new America born on this battlefield." It was this feature of the Gettysburg reunion which made it seem to contemporaries "one of the most remarkable incidents in history," and gave to it great significance as an object lesson to those who still stirred among the dying embers of an ancient feud.

The dedication of the Chickamauga and Chattanooga National Military Park, September 18–20, 1895, was the occasion for the people of the Mississippi Valley to witness a like event which attracted even greater interest and certainly a larger representation from the two sections.[56] The dedication was provided for by act of Congress. Delegations from both Houses of that body accompanied by the Vice-President of the United States were in attendance. Twenty-four states were officially represented, in fourteen cases by the governor and his staff. The Societies of the Army of the Cumberland (Federal), the Army of Northern Virginia (Confederate), the Army of the Potomac (Union), and the Army of the Tennessee (Confederate) held reunions in conjunction. The Grand Army of the Republic and the United Confederate Veterans were represented by their presidents. Conservative estimates placed forty thousand veterans in the park on the day of its dedication, while the lesser meetings, usually reunions of the societies, regularly filled the large tent which had been erected for the occasion and had a seating capacity of ten thousand.

The opening day was devoted to the dedication of state monuments on various parts of the Chickamauga battlefield. The sentiment everywhere expressed was pride in the fact

[56] Fully described in *The Dedication of the Chickamauga and Chattanooga National Military Park, 54 Cong., 1 Sess., Senate Report, No. 637.*

that after thirty-two years the survivors of the two armies
could meet again on the field of conflict "under one flag, all
lovers of one country" to "perform an act of unusual significance." In the evening the Society of the Army of the Cumberland held its annual reunion in the tent at Chattanooga and
invited the Confederates to meet with them. A fair number of
men in Gray attended and heard their spokesman, Hilary A.
Herbert, declare that the present loyalty to the Union on the
part of those "who once fought so bitterly against it, is the
crowning glory of the heroes in Blue." The sections shared
alike in the dedication exercises of the Nineteenth, the orators
being chosen from Illinois and Georgia. That evening the two
Societies of the Army of the Tennessee and the Army of the
Cumberland held a common reunion. The concluding day was
marked by the dedication of the Chattanooga portion of the
field, and a reunion of the Societies of the Army of Northern
Virginia and the Army of the Potomac.

Some twenty-three years before this scene at Chickamauga,
in the heat of the Reconstruction period, Charles Sumner,
remembering the policy of republican Rome where warfare
between citizens was not officially recorded, had risen in the
United States Senate to propose:

Whereas the national unity and good-will among fellow-citizens
can be assured only through oblivion of past differences, and it
is contrary to the usages of civilized nations to perpetuate the
memory of civil war; therefore, be it enacted, etc., that the names
of battles with fellow-citizens shall not be continued in the Army
Register, or placed on the regimental colors of the United States.

He was not then alone in fearing that the preservation of war
memories would perpetuate war passions, and those who believed as he did recognized in his action a sincere effort to
restore harmony between the embittered sections. But, hatred
or no, the trials and sacrifices of war had become too much
a part of the nation's being thus lightly to be erased. In the
long night of sordid contention through which the North and
South passed before true peace was realized the people clung
to the ennobling memory of four years' heroic effort, until in
time, at Gettysburg and at Chickamauga, they welcomed the

mellowed recollection of their quarrel as a bond of union, where once they feared it might divide. No blame to Sumner that he could not foresee the rôle that soldiers were destined to play in reconciliation. Something remarkable in history had occurred.

CHAPTER XI

THE PASSING OF THE SECTIONAL ISSUE IN POLITICS 1880–1898

DESPITE the potency of the new forces that were transforming American life the activity of the major political parties remained rigidly fixed in patterns established by the bitter controversies of the Civil War and Reconstruction. No political leader of the era seemed aware of the new horizons, the new activities, and the new emotions that were affecting the people in everyday pursuits. No party platform grasped or intelligently phrased the issues arising from the development of a new and far more complex economic organization of society. No statesman capitalized upon the spirit of the new nationalism to bring its surging power into harmony with the aspirations of a people seeking a richer life. The dead issues of a passing era remained to nullify the significance politics might have for a living age.

The major parties were stalemated, with ancient watchwords inappropriate to modern issues and fossilized alignments unresponsive to new demands. In election after election the average man voted out of habit and without much thought for candidates who had little vision and less constructive ability. Cheap men with low standards of public conduct reached high office to corrupt government and divorce it from positive achievement. Given such a situation, political activity was a factor detrimental to the nationalizing process, even as it operated to retard every other progressive movement of the day.

The strife-filled years previous to 1880 had given to each of the major parties a traditional allegiance. Roughly speaking, the Solid South, the working classes and immigrant groups of the eastern cities, and a large proportion of debtor farmers in the West were Democratic. New England, the propertied groups, especially the investors and tariff-protected manufacturers, and the more prosperous farmers were Republican. Actually the two parties were nicely poised with neither in full command of the national government. Control of Congress fluctuated between narrow margins and no President from Hayes to McKinley enjoyed more than four continuous years in office. Groups of discontented reformers and new voters held the balance of power, and each recurrent election saw them make a "choice of evils" between an errant Republicanism and a still discredited Democracy. The evenness of party strength contributed to the lack of consistent achievement. It also produced a bitter scramble for votes in which the habitual arguments of the past were not allowed to die.

Conditioning all political activity was the fact that the parties had been shaped in the era of sectional controversy. The only issue that made division between Democrats and Republicans intelligent was the North-South rivalry. On the issues of tariff, control of corporations, railroad regulation, finance, civil service reform, honesty in politics, and labor organization, the divisions were intra-party rather than inter-party. Consequently all living issues were straddled or ignored, while easy retreat into the past was resorted to whenever and wherever the party chieftains felt it would succeed.

Not untypical of the apprehensions deeply rooted by a generation of partisan campaigning were the many ordinary people who went to the polls in November 1884 in the North believing that the election of Cleveland would mean the re-enslavement of the Negro and in the South convinced that a victory for Blaine would cause the recrudescence of Reconstruction evils. The case of Albert J. Beveridge, of Indiana, was the common experience of his generation. "I was born," he wrote, "when the Civil War was reaching its red climax; and my father and brothers were all officers in the Union Army. From earliest infancy I was taught that 'Uncle Tom's Cabin' and the speeches of Wendell Phillips, Sumner, and others like them, were the real truth." [1] The youthful Theodore Roosevelt

[1] Beveridge to W. C. Ford, March 2, 1926, quoted in C. G. Bowers, "Beveridge and the Progressive Era" (Cambridge, 1932), 575.

entered upon his political career believing that the annexation of Texas, the Mexican War, the repeal of the Missouri Compromise, the Dred Scott decision, and the Civil War itself were treasonable conspiracies of an aggressive and arrogant slavocracy. Counterparts of these Northern views are readily found in the South, where service in the Confederate army was almost an indispensable prerequisite of political success, where few political orations omitted a reference to the nightmares of Reconstruction, and where Jefferson Davis's "The Rise and Fall of the Confederate Government" taught as partisan a creed in regard to the past as did the Yankee Henry Wilson's "The Rise and Fall of the Slave Power."

Nevertheless the early eighties gave ample evidence that the nation was growing weary of the sectional issue in politics. President Garfield took occasion in his inaugural address to phrase platitudes about a reunited nation and "countrymen, who do not now differ in our judgment concerning the controversies of past generations." His assassination a few months later gave politicians a chance to join with the nation at large in a sincere demonstration of common patriotism.[2] President Arthur's first annual message to Congress in December 1881 made no reference of any sort to the South, a fact which caused many commentators to observe that this had not occurred before in any presidential message for over a quarter of a century. *Harper's Weekly* entered upon the Congressional campaigns of 1882 asserting that "there is no longer a bloody shirt in politics" and the elections of that year did take place in an atmosphere of moderation which indicated that the observation was more than wishful thinking.[3]

It was not the partisan politician, however, who hailed these auguries of a new day of sectional peace, but moderates and reformers who sought to discard the "bloody shirt" so that "henceforth the people can turn away from old issues and direct their attention to those questions of civil service and revenue reform . . . that have too long been kept in the background."[4] R. W. Gilder opened the columns of the *Century* to

[2] *Supra*, 141–142.
[3] *Harper's Weekly*, March 18, 1882.
[4] W. M. Barrows, in a paper on "The New South" read before the

editorials and articles on "the difficult and delicate questions, such as the questions of the tariff, of the domination of corporations, of the secret and corrupt government of our municipalities by irresponsible 'bosses.' " [5] In the South Joel Chandler Harris hoped for a national Democratic victory in 1884 so that the North could be shown "that the new generation of the South is really and thoroughly devoted to the Union and to the vast interests of the American republic." [6] Shrewdly capitalizing upon the growing chorus of protests against the persistence of old issues in politics, General E. S. Bragg, in seconding the nomination of Grover Cleveland before the National Democratic Convention of 1884, demanded that "our old war horses be retired with honor. Let the record of their achievements be recorded and pointed at with pride and pleasure; but our people say give us new life, give us new blood, give us something that has come to manhood and position since the war, that we may hear no more about what took place before and during the war." [7]

The proponents of the new political order sang an anthem of sectional harmony rich in dulcet tones. Recent history was resurveyed to prove the thesis that the Solid South and injustice to the Negro were inescapable concomitants of a harsh policy of Northern coercion and distrust. The departure from the policy since 1877 had, according to men like Gilder, Carl Schurz, G. W. Curtis, and E. L. Godkin, resulted in the development of law and order in the South, greater security and increasing participation in politics for the Negro, and a "gratifying drift" toward broader and more liberal divisions of opinion. A final interment of the "bloody shirt" would mean the disintegration of the Solid South and the permanent elimination of the Southern question from party contests. [8]

National Convention of the Home Missionary Society at Saratoga, N. Y., June, 1884.

[5] Gilder to James Bryce, May 8, 1883, "Letters of R. W. Gilder," 116.

[6] Harris to R. U. Johnson, Sept. 28, 1884, Johnson, "Remembered Yesterdays," 383.

[7] "Proceedings of the Democratic National Convention of 1884," 176.

[8] See as typical, Schurz, "Party Schisms and Future Problems," North American Review, CXXXIV (1882), 431–435; Nation, May 25, 1882, and Sept. 18, 1884; and editorial, "The Political Situation," Atlantic Monthly, LXIX (1882), 393–398.

The intellectuals who thus so plausibly prophesied a pleasing future for Southern politics expected to receive an especially cordial response from the newer generation of voters who had come of age since Lee had surrendered at Appomattox and Lincoln had gone to a martyr's grave. It seemed utterly impossible to Thomas Wentworth Higginson in 1884 that "the formidable element of youth" could be marshaled beneath the banners of the Civil War.[9] Had Higginson opened his *Boston Daily Advertiser* for October 21, 1884, he might have read a speech delivered by a twenty-six-year-old tyro in politics named Theodore Roosevelt, soundly berating the South and the Democratic party for attempting "to rule the Union with loaded dice." And out in Indiana the youthful Beveridge was winning his spurs by imitating the "bloody shirt" oratory of his elders.[10] Nevertheless the eighties did witness a definite transition in the personnel of party leadership. An older cycle merged with a new. The traditional arguments could never again have the reality they once possessed. Wendell Phillips was among those who lamented that voters who had been in their cradles when the war broke out could never know the full infamy of the South and consequently would not respond to the fundamental issues of right and wrong.[11]

In 1884 a baby born when the Confederacy reached its highest tide at Gettysburg could vote for President without memory of slavery or the Civil War. In 1888 nearly two-fifths of the voting population was under thirty years of age. In the same year not more than one-fourth of the electorate was old enough to have cast a vote in 1860. No one remained in the Senate who was there when Preston Brooks made his assault on Sumner. Of the representatives who held office when Lincoln was elected, John Sherman, now in the Senate, L. C. Q. Lamar, now a Supreme Court Justice, and Allen G. Thurman, still in the House, were the sole survivors active in national affairs. When the President of the Confederacy died in 1889 he had been preceded to the grave by his Vice-President, twelve out of the sixteen men he had appointed to Cabinet positions, and thirty-

[9] T. W. Higginson, "Young Men's Party," reprint from the *New York Evening Post*, Oct. 4, 1884.

[10] Bowers, "Beveridge," 22–31.

[11] *North American Review*, XCIX (1878), 99.

seven of the forty-nine signers of the Confederate Constitution. A new generation had arrived and the old issues were expiring with the men who had given them the breath of life.[12]

Momentarily it seemed as though even the most convinced partisan would surrender the frayed garment of the "bloody shirt." James G. Blaine in his letter accepting the Republican nomination for the presidency in 1884 made a gesture of friendship to the South. He gave his approval to the growing confidence and mutual esteem existing between the sections and deplored any suggestion of fighting the campaign upon issues which grew out of the memories of the past. The honeyed words died upon his lips, however, when it was early demonstrated that the South would remain solidly Democratic. The plumed knight again donned his shining armor to attack treason, defend the Negro, and rally a united North against the enemies of the Republic.

The traditionalist in politics saw no reason why in 1884 an attack on conventional lines should not again prove successful. Democratic rule was still unpalatable to purists like Godkin who repeatedly lectured the South for its "misguided alliance" with the "corrupt and unintelligent" elements of the North. The belief that a national Democratic administration would disturb business, debase the currency, deprive the Negro of his rights, pay the rebel debt, pension the Confederate veteran, and bring general disaster had been painstakingly elaborated by years of Republican campaigning. A large proportion of the good people of the North entertained a vague conviction that the only normal condition for the country was to have a Republican in the White House. This attitude was perfectly, if somewhat blatantly, expressed by Eugene Feld:

> These quondam rebels come to-day
>   In penitential form
> And hypocritically say
>   The country needs "Reform!"
> Out on reformers such as these;

[12] For various comment on this phenomenon, see E. P. Clark, "The New Political Generation," *Century*, XXXVI (1888), 851–854; *Nation*, Sept. 10, 1885, and Sept. 22, 1887; *Harper's Weekly*, Feb. 20, 1886; Schurz, "The New South," 21–22; and McClure, "The South," 60–62.

By Freedom's sacred powers,
We'll run the country as we please;
We saved it and it's ours.

The Southern question, however, received comparatively little attention in the campaign.[13] It certainly exercised no decisive influence on the outcome. The dominant issue was probity in public office. Here Blaine was vulnerable. A powerful group of independent Republicans considered him "tainted," bolted the ticket, and supported the Democratic candidate, Grover Cleveland, whose stubborn fight for honest government in New York State had endeared him to the reforming element. The "bloody shirt" was only one of the devices (and insignificant, indeed, when compared to the use made of whispers against Cleveland's private life) by which the alarmed managers of the Republican party attempted to stop the tide which resulted in Cleveland's election.

Blaine attributed his defeat in large measure to a Solid South which rested upon the fraudulent disfranchisement of the Negro. Murat Halstead, the gifted journalist, developed the idea, and warned the country that the conduct of the South was a menace of reviving sectionalism.[14] So began a new crusade. The Republican press with the *New York Tribune* in the van vigorously condemned "the new rebellion against the establishment of manhood suffrage." Even such a conservative-minded gentleman as W. M. Evarts added his apprehensive voice to the clamor. Orthodox Republican dogma maintained that the Democrats had gained power by suppressing the Constitution and desecrating the "sacred ballot" in the Southern states.[15] The corollary seemed inescapable. The Republicans when returned to office would force the South to give the Negro free and open access to the polls.

On the other hand, those who had supported Cleveland widely proclaimed that his election marked an epoch in re-

[13] H. C. Thomas, "The Return of the Democratic Party to Power in 1884" (New York, 1919), is an excellent analysis of the campaign. See also Schlesinger, "Rise of the City," 396–401; and A. Nevins, "Grover Cleveland" (New York, 1932), 145–188.

[14] M. Halstead, "Revival of Sectionalism," *North American Review*, CXL (1885), 237–250.

[15] See as typical C. M. Clay, "Race and the Solid South," *North American Review*, XCLII (1886), 134–138.

conciliation. Southern newspapers were unanimous in expressing the opinion that the return of the Democratic party to power "swept away all sectional distinctions," "brought the South back into the Union," and "gave it the opportunity of impressing itself upon the national policy." [16] Moderate Northern journals like the *New York Times* and the *Evening Post* informed their readers that the era of political sham had come definitely to an end. Never again, in their opinion, would the voters of the North be frightened by the hobgoblins of "bloody shirt" oratory. Travelers in the South reported "unclouded peace and trust" between the sections.[17] The theme of a nation reunited in spirit as well as in name reverberated through all the comment of Democrats and Independent Republicans exulting in their triumph. "There never has been such a rupture," exclaimed Henry Ward Beecher, "never such a conflict, never such a victory, never such a reconstruction, . . . never such a reconciliation and gladness between good men on both sides as come to us today." [18]

Actually the truth lay somewhere between Republican sullenness and Democratic exuberance. The Solid South was to reappear as a bugbear used to keep the Republican party united. Cleveland was to face angry attacks of Civil War veterans and to have his patriotism assailed. The deep-rooted and far-reaching conviction that the Republican party was more American than the Democratic and normally should be in power was not destroyed. Yet the friends of reconciliation could point to a number of factors which unquestionably moved the balance in their favor.

It was indeed a progressive step to have men like Godkin, Schurz, and Curtis, with the large group of Independents they represented, support an honest Democrat rather than continue the irresponsible rule of stalwart Republicanism. It at least gave variety to the picture to see Thomas Nast use the same savage technique of caricature against Blaine that he had once

[16] Files of the *Atlanta Constitution,* the *Charleston News and Courier,* and the *Louisville Courier-Journal* for Nov. 1884. See also H. W. Watterson, "The Reunited Union," *North American Review,* CXL (1885), 22–29.

[17] McClure, "The South," 53–54; Schurz, "New South," 31.

[18] H. W. Beecher, "Retrospect and Prospect," an address delivered Nov. 27, 1884, reprinted in Beecher, "Patriotic Addresses," 835.

employed against Greeley.[19] It was significant that veteran Republicans like Lyman Trumbull and former abolitionists like J. M. Forbes and Thomas W. Higginson would leave a party they had helped to found, accept the Democratic ticket as honest and patriotic, and declare that a Republican, Blaine, constituted the real menace to the nation's future.[20] Most significant of all, the election of Cleveland restored to office a party that had been discredited for a generation and gave to millions of Americans the opportunity of dispelling the aspersions on their loyalty.

The vacuity of national politics in this era is perfectly demonstrated in the fact that, except in the matter of honest administration where Cleveland proved an able and sturdy champion, the restoration of the Democrats made no appreciable change in any national policy. At every other stage in our history when a new party or an old party long out of power won the presidency far-reaching reversals of policy ensued. The election of Jefferson in 1800 was spoken of as a "revolution." Jackson's victory in 1828 resulted in dynamic alterations which indicated that the apprehensions of his conservative opponents were not without a basis of fact. Lincoln's election in 1860 changed the course of American history. Wilson in 1913 and F. D. Roosevelt in 1933 came to the presidency with programs of radical reform. But in spite of all the extremes of partisan invective, the prophecies for good and evil, and the fears of Confederate domination, Cleveland's administration proved not unlike those of Hayes and Arthur. The new President was an eastern conservative. He threatened no established interest and promised only honest and vigorous administration. He was a perfect choice to dissipate the superstition that the Democratic party with its Southern wing would or could disturb the existing order. His tenure of office demonstrated convincingly the hollowness of the pretensions that the sectional issue had any significance in the political life of the nation.

Efforts were made at the outset to assure the country that the new administration meant no interruption in the regular course of government. The *Atlanta Constitution* affirmed that

[19] *Harper's Weekly*, July-November, 1884.
[20] Trumbull to Tilden, June 7, 1884, "Tilden Letters," II, 642; Forbes, "Recollections and Letters," 208.

"the negro will find his best friend in the Southern Democrat."
Nast pictured Grover Cleveland bringing the white Southerner
and the Negro together in a cordial handclasp.[21] Schurz cor-
roborated the opinion that the freedom and rights of the
black man "do not depend upon the predominance of any
political party, but are safe under the one as well as the other." [22]
McClure and Curtis reassured the "sensitive capitalist" and
Northern business man and promised "a priceless blessing
in the absolute and stable faith [Cleveland's election] . . .
has established between the material interests of the two
sections of the country." [23] Cleveland himself devoted an important section of his inaugural to allaying fears that his
course of action would disturb the *status quo* of sectional relations.

The influence of the South in national affairs was not much
greater under Cleveland than it had been under Hayes and
Arthur. A tremendous gain in morale did result from the feeling that a "friendly" administration sat in Washington and
that the older proscriptions had been removed. Southerners
valued the sense of security that came from the knowledge
that no federal measure of force would be enacted to interfere
with their election practices. They expressed gratification over
the appointment of two ex-Confederates, Lamar of Mississippi
and Garland of Arkansas, to cabinet positions. But while the
New York Tribune grumbled over the honor given to these
"Rebel Brigadiers," most Northerners recognized the men as
conservatively inclined and completely loyal to the restored
Union.[24] Cleveland's point of view was distinctly Northern in
focus. He at no time "thought as a Southerner," and he relied
chiefly upon eastern friends for advice.

There were times when even Republicans seemed ready to
admit that the Southern issue was dead and that a new era
of good feeling had arrived. John Sherman stated in 1886 that
the South must be let alone to work out its own salvation and
confessed that much that he and his party had attempted in the
past was based upon the false principle of meddling in local

[21] *Harper's Weekly*, Nov. 22, 1884.
[22] Schurz, "The New South," 31.
[23] McClure, "The South," 53–54; *Harper's Weekly*, Nov. 15, 1884.
[24] *Harper's Weekly*, March 14, 1885.

affairs.[25] Most curious of all, perhaps, was a speech made in Faneuil Hall by Henry Cabot Lodge before a reunion of Blue and Gray veterans. Because of Lodge's later prominence as a "Force Bill" statesman it is well to put the rising young politician fully on record.

We respect and honor the gallantry of the brave men who fought against us, and who gave their lives and shed their blood in defense of what they believed to be right. We rejoice that the famous general [Lee] . . . was one of the greatest soldiers of modern times because he, too, was an American. We have no bitter memories to revive, no reproaches to utter. Reconciliation is not to be sought, because it exists already. . . . Your presence here . . . breathes the spirit of concord, and unites with so many other voices in the irrevocable message of union and goodwill. Mere sentiment some may say. But it is sentiment, true sentiment, that has moved the world. Sentiment fought the war and sentiment has reunited us.[26]

Until Cleveland sent his message to Congress in December 1887 asking for a reduction in the tariff, there was no real issue upon which he as a Democrat could divide with the Republicans. Primarily for this reason the attacks made upon him were for the most part sham affairs which sought to bring his "patriotism" into question.[27] Cleveland's sense of economy and honesty in government influenced him to scrutinize with greater care than any of his predecessors the increasing demands of Union veterans for pension awards. In all he vetoed more than two hundred individual pension bills and in February 1887 he refused his signature to a general dependent pension bill. These vetoes gave his opponents the opportunity of representing the President as inimical to the Union veterans. A vociferous campaign of abuse ensued in which the "old soldier" was pressed into service as a pawn in the game of politics.[28]

[25] Speech at Washington cited in Sherman, "Recollections," II, 949–953.
[26] *Boston Daily Advertiser,* June 18, 1887. The speech is reprinted in Lodge, "Speeches and Addresses, 1884–1909," 25–30.
[27] For example, the attack upon Lamar's appointment to the Supreme Court, Mayes, "Lamar," 523–538.
[28] Press comment of all shades of opinion on this topic is given in great detail in *Public Opinion,* II, III and IV (1886–1887), *passim.*

New fuel was added to the controversy by a blunder on the part of one of Cleveland's underlings. The War Department had in its possession a number of captured Union flags which had been recovered on the fall of the Confederacy and Confederate flags taken in battle by Union troops. The practice for some years had been to return the Union flags upon proper request to organizations within the Northern states. The Adjutant-General, R. C. Drum, thought the time had at last arrived when it would be a propitious and gracious act to return all the flags, Union and Confederate, to the states for preservation. The Secretary of War and President Cleveland approved the suggestion and letters offering the flags were dispatched to the governors.[29]

A veritable storm of protest broke about the person of the unsuspecting Cleveland. The Republican press denounced the "monumental treason" of a "sneaking doughface." [30] Resolutions poured in from Grand Army of the Republic posts throughout the North. General Fairchild, Commander of the G. A. R., was quoted as exclaiming "May God palsy the hand that wrote that order! May God palsy the brain that conceived it! May God palsy the tongue that dictated it!" [31] The St. Louis Republican considered the excitement "a strange anachronism in the bustling, prosperous, peaceful life of the present. For an instant it seemed that time had turned backward for a quarter of a century and that the passions which precipitated the carnage of civil war were still in their first heat and glow. Then it passes, and we see that it is not a development of the life of the present, but only old men's memories." [32] Whether Cleveland would have persevered in his intention is a matter for speculation. It was discovered that the flags could not be returned without an act of Congress and Cleveland revoked the order. Years later in the administration of Theodore Roosevelt a Republican Congress made the restoration which a Democratic President was prevented from performing.

Not "old men's memories" but current politics instigated the

[29] Fiftieth Congress, First Session, House Executive Document Number 163; Richardson, "Messages and Papers of the Presidents," VIII, 578–579.
[30] Public Opinion, III (1887), 229–234.
[31] New York World and New York Tribune, June 16 and 17, 1887.
[32] St. Louis Republican, June 18, 1887.

excitement. Issues were hard to find and Republican chieftains were desperately in need of ammunition. John Sherman perfectly exemplified the absurdity of their antics. This veteran of many partisan campaigns, now Senator of Ohio, aspired to the presidential nomination in 1888 and was vigorously attempting to impress his somewhat cold personality upon the rank and file of the party. In March 1887 the Senator spoke at Nashville, Tennessee, where he adroitly made gestures of peace and expressed confidence that the South could handle its own "local" problem of the Negro. June 1, 1887, however, found him addressing the Illinois State Legislature in Springfield. On this occasion he divided the American people into Republicans and Confederates and dismissed the Democrats as the left wing of the Confederate army. He dwelt upon the atrocities inflicted upon the Negro in the South and promised his audience that he would use his power in Congress to secure a fair count of the Republican vote in the Southern states. This reversal of opinion seemed not at all inconsistent to Sherman. In his own words he explained, "At Nashville it was expected that I would make a conciliatory speech, tending to harmony between the sections, while at Springfield I could only make a partisan speech, on lines well defined between the two great parties." [33]

Sherman next attempted to "spruce up" the voters of his own state where Governor Foraker was waging a battle for reelection. At Wilmington he assailed the "tenderfeet . . . who would banish the word 'rebel' from our vocabulary, who would not denounce crimes against our fellow-citizens, [and] who thought that . . . we must surrender our captured flags to the rebels who bore them." [34] A "bloody shirt" campaign was Foraker's idea of what the people wanted. Foraker in some ways resembled Blaine, brilliant in personality, eloquent, extremely partisan, "popular," according to ex-President Hayes, "with the hurrah boys," but distrusted by the sober and conservative element of the Republican party. He had gained national attention in the battle flag episode by a comic-opera defense of the

[33] Sherman, "Recollections," 984–986; *Harper's Weekly,* April 9, and June 11, 1884; *Century,* XXXIV (1887), 310; *Public Opinion,* III (1887), 193–195.
[34] Sherman, "Recollections," 999.

Confederate flags in the State House at Columbus. He concluded from this experience that the people desired "to hear Cleveland flayed, and they expected me to do it. . . . They wanted hot stuff and got plenty of it." His judgment was apparently correct inasmuch as he won the election.[35]

Sherman failed to gain the nomination he coveted, but his activity and the success of Foraker in Ohio gave prominence to the suppression of the Negro vote in the South and suggested its use as a major topic in the presidential campaign of 1888.[36] Murat Halstead, of the *Cincinnati Commercial-Gazette,* and other Republican editors had much to say to the effect that the Democratic party owed its control of the presidency and the lower house of Congress to the nullification of the Constitution.[37] Benjamin Harrison, who was to secure the Republican nomination for the presidency, made it the theme of an important political speech in Detroit on Washington's Birthday.[38] There was no doubt or denial (Watterson frankly admitted it) of the fact that Negroes were not permitted to vote in the South.[39] The only query was whether the Republican party would follow up its agitation by proposing a remedy. Would the party dare espouse a measure to use Federal force for the purpose of re-imposing Negro suffrage on the South?

The prospect was not an appealing one to those Republicans who remembered the tragedies and embarrassments of the Recontruction era. There were many who had wearied of the Negro problem and the endless sectional controversies it involved, and who suggested that the wisest statesmanship would be to leave the settlement to non-political agencies.[40] The *New York Times* wisely advised the Republican managers to forego the perils of fighting another campaign on the issue of the Solid South. The great party, it cautioned, was in danger of "steadily wasting away as the Whig party did when it in-

[35] J. B. Foraker, "Notes of a Busy Life" (Cincinnati, 1916), I, 240–242, 277–283, 422.
[36] *Harper's Weekly,* Dec. 10, 1887.
[37] *Public Opinion,* VII and VIII (1887, 1888), *passim,* gives copious extracts from the press.
[38] B. Harrison, "Speeches of Benjamin Harrison, 1888–1892" (New York, 1892), 12–13.
[39] *Harper's Weekly,* April 14, 1888.
[40] See the editorial comment in the *Philadelphia Inquirer,* as quoted in *Public Opinion,* II (1887), 214–215.

sisted on voting on dead issues and ignoring living ones." [41] Yet where could the party find an issue? The country was prosperous. Cleveland's record in administration was invulnerable. No one dared to touch the currency question. No one believed the Southern issue kept as many votes within the party as it drove out. Hence, as the year 1887 drew to a close, great pessimism prevailed among the Republican leaders. Cleveland's reëlection the next year seemed a certainty. [42]

From this unhappy dilemma Cleveland himself inadvertently rescued his opponents. His annual message to Congress in December 1887 broke all precedents in that it was devoted to a single topic, the urgent need of tariff reduction. Here was unexpected ground upon which to fight a decisive battle. A bill embodying Cleveland's views passed the Democratic House but met with defeat in the Senate. The great debate passed into the presidential campaign and the country witnessed the unusual spectacle of the two major parties actually dividing on a living issue. The Republicans accepted with elation Cleveland's challenge to fight the battle on the tariff, rallied their strength, and fought a vigorous campaign. [43] The sectional issue dropped into the background until it almost completely faded from the picture. [44] When the votes were counted in November and Harrison emerged the victor, the Republican party had at last elected a President without the aid of the "bloody shirt."

Cleveland's tenure of office had removed many Northern apprehensions by revealing the unsubstantial basis upon which they rested. It was now the turn of the South to wait in dread expectation of what the restoration of Republican rule would mean. Southern politicians, preaching the necessity of sectional solidarity, had during the campaign immoderately portrayed the dangers of Republican victory. They prophesied the re-opening of all "the burning issues of negro supremacy," and predicted evils worse than Reconstruction. [45] Now that the Republicans had gained the victory the South did not know

[41] *New York Times*, Aug. 28, 1887.
[42] Nevins, "Cleveland," 367.
[43] Nevins, "Cleveland," 367–442.
[44] *Harper's Weekly*, Oct. 13, 1888.
[45] See as typical the *New Orleans Picayune*, Oct. 23, 1888.

whether it faced merely a hobgoblin of its own creation or a dread dragon of destruction. But most Southerners joined with the editor of the *Atlanta Constitution* in viewing the future with "deep foreboding," and clinging in the crisis to "the integrity and supremacy of the Democratic party in the South." [46]

The Republican Congress elected in November 1888 did not assemble for its first session until December 1889. The thirteen months' interval gave ample opportunity for press, pulpit and rostrum to discuss in detail proposals for remedying the Southern problem. The Republican argument moved with simple logic from premise to conclusion. Stripped of the subterfuges by which the South disguised its action, the actual situation in the Southern states was that Negro citizens were deprived of the right to vote because of their race and previous condition of servitude. This violated the spirit if not the letter of the Fourteenth and Fifteenth Amendments to the Constitution. The practice of disfranchising colored voters strengthened the Democratic party in the House of Representatives and the electoral college. The evil therefore became national rather than local in scope. Congress must safeguard the integrity of federal elections by enacting a measure which gave federal supervision in every polling booth in the country where national representatives and presidential electors were being chosen. [47]

Independents and moderates united with professional Democrats in presenting the opposite point of view. Washington Gladden expressed an opinion widely entertained when he challenged the assumption that sound government could ever be based upon the suffrage of men so ignorant as the Southern Negro. Godkin in the *Nation* and Curtis in *Harper's Weekly* hammered on the idea that the primary requirement in promoting the welfare of the black man was to take him as an issue out of politics. Most of the social agencies working in the

---

[46] *Atlanta Constitution*, Nov. 7, 1888.

[47] Various expressions of this argument are found in President Harrison's first annual message to Congress, Richardson, "Messages," IX, 57–58; *Public Opinion*, VIII (1889), *passim;* Hoar, "Autobiography," II, 150–165; T. B. Reed, "Federal Control of Elections," *North American Review*, CL (1890), 671–680; and A. T. Rice, "The Next National Reform," *North American Review*, CXLVIII (1889), 82–85.

field of race relations looked with disfavor upon a measure that would engender further controversy. Bitter words were uttered by the more partisan-minded, challenging the integrity of Republican motives and assailing the men who prolonged sectional strife for party profit. A great deal was said about Northern investments and business relations in the South being placed in jeopardy and it seems true that business classes did protest against a policy that promised to create an uncertain future. Southerners grew bolder as they felt Northern opinion rallying to their defense and bluntly asserted that under one device or another the South was determined to rule its own local affairs.[48]

The Republican party was in no sense united in its stand on the issue. The party managers faced a busy Congressional session in which perplexing and intricate legislative problems in regard to the tariff, silver coinage, and trust regulation had to be solved. Little time could be afforded for what was after all a matter of secondary importance, especially when it threatened to impede the progress of other legislation. Nevertheless the party had talked a great deal, if somewhat nebulously, about safeguarding the rights of their Negro wards. An element within the party, notably Senator Hoar of Massachusetts, sincerely wished to discharge the obligation. But the majority of Republicans supported the measure because they felt it vaguely incumbent upon them to do something. Their hearts were never more than half in the business and when the opportunity came to drop the affair they did so with far more enthusiasm than they had shown when they picked it up.

The remedy which the Republicans finally formulated was a bill introduced into Congress by Henry Cabot Lodge early in 1890. The measure, styled a Federal election bill, was surprisingly moderate in tone. It was expertly drawn to meet the test of constitutionality and to appear both national in scope and non-partisan in application. It provided that Federal supervisors representing both parties were to be appointed in any

[48] W. Gladden, "Safeguards of the Suffrage," *Century*, XXXI (1889), 621–622; *Harper's Weekly*, Nov. 1888–Dec. 1889, *passim*; *Public Opinion*, VI and VII (1889), *passim*; E. L. Godkin, "The Republican Party and the Negro," *Forum*, VII (1889), 246–257; and files of the *Louisville Courier-Journal*, the *Charleston News and Courier*, and the *Atlanta Constitution*.

election district where five hundred voters petitioned the Federal authorities. The supervisors had power to pass on the qualifications of challenged voters in elections involving the choice of Congressmen and presidential electors. They had authority to receive ballots which were refused by local officials and to place them in the ballot box. The bill moved slowly through the House where it passed on July 2, 1890. In the Senate it slowly expired from inanition and neglect. Republican members interested in the smooth progress of the tariff bill acted to postpone consideration of the Lodge bill. Senator Hoar who fathered the measure in the upper house seemed hesitant to face a final vote. Public distaste for the bill became increasingly apparent. In January 1891 eight Republican senators from the West, bargaining for Southern support on a pending silver measure, united with the Democratic opposition in voting a final defeat of the bill.[49]

Several explanations for the defeat were given. Hoar blamed the opposition of Northern business men, on which point Lodge agreed, and the antagonism of "self-styled reformers" who preferred "purity" to equality in politics. Senator Cameron, of Pennsylvania, preferred to see the measure die than cause interruption to the flow of Northern capital into the South. The *New York Tribune* attributed responsibility to the silver alliance of West and South. Actually the measure was killed by the hostility of Northern public opinion. James Bryce who rarely erred in his judgments of the United States noted that the prevailing sentiment interpreted the Lodge bill to be "an attempt to overcome nature by law."[50] The public showed its bias by accepting as its own the derisive appellation "Force Bill" which had been affixed to the bill by partisan Democrats. The *Philadelphia Inquirer* (Republican) canvassed Republican opinion and flatly asserted that most of the party's leaders and rank

[49] *Congressional Record,* 51 Cong. 1 sess., *passim;* G. F. Hoar, "The Fate of the Election Bill," *Forum,* XI (1891), 127–136; Hoar, "Autobiography," II, 150–165; *Harper's Weekly,* Feb. 1890–Jan. 1891, *passim; Public Opinion,* VIII, IX and X (1890–91), *passim;* files of the *New York World* and the *New York Tribune.* Especially informative is a series of articles by Lodge, T. V. Powderly, R. Smalls and A. W. Shaffer in the *North American Review,* CLI (189), 257–273, 593–609.
[50] J. Bryce, "Thoughts on the Negro Problem," *North American Review,* CLIII (1891), 654.

and file privately hoped for the bill's defeat.[51] The moderately Republican *St. Louis Globe-Democrat* summed up the matter by affirming, "We can better afford to tolerate the evil than to attack it in the form of arbitrary Federal interference in local affairs." [52]

During the controversy a group of Southern Congressmen published a book with the significant title, "Why the Solid South?" [53] The authors reviewed state by state the history of the Reconstruction era, depicting its tragedies and affixing responsibility for the Solid South on the blundering statesmanship of the Republican party. The book was obviously propaganda intended to establish the thesis that the Lodge bill was a return to the errors of the past. But it made a profound impression in the North. The first detailed representation of the Southern view of Reconstruction to reach a wide audience, the book can be said even to have affected later historiography. "Why the Solid South?" was an important step in the process of historical revision by which judgments were altered and understanding between the sections promoted.

The defeat of the Lodge bill marked the final passage of the sectional issue in its Civil War guise from politics. The Republican party tacitly accepted the fact of white supremacy in the South. It never again hoisted the "bloody shirt" to its masthead. Hoar sadly admitted that the issue drove more voters out of the party than it retained. A strongly partisan Republican Congress had made its final surrender in obedience to the clearly expressed sentiment of the nation. The last threat to what Southerners cherished most — control of their domestic affairs — was permanently destroyed. All unwittingly the young representative from Massachusetts who had so wanted to thunder like the Republicans of the heroic age had cleared the political stage for peace.

The decade of the nineties gave a new fixation to American politics. The tremendous development of national wealth and power brought about one of those recurrent periods in our history when social and economic maladjustments demanded re-

[51] *Philadelphia Inquirer*, Jan. 27, 1891.
[52] *St. Louis Globe-Democrat*, Aug. 23, 1890.
[53] H. A. Herbert and others, "Why the Solid South?" (Baltimore, 1890).

adjustment. Prosperity and depression, tariff and silver coinage, agrarian unrest and labor turmoil, foreign markets and world diplomacy — such issues of the new day did not conform to the old North-South alignment of political forces. There was not on any of these issues a definable "Southern opinion" that could be applied to the section as a whole without infinite qualification and exception. The South remained solid as a legacy of the past and Southerners continued to wear the label of Democrats. But in the practical matter of voting for what they wanted in Congress their representatives divided on economic lines and sought support in union with kindred interests in the East and West where and when a bargain could be effected. The words of President McKinley in his inaugural message of March 4, 1897, were based on unassailable fact. "The North and the South no longer divide on the old lines, but upon principles and policies; and in this fact surely every lover of the country can find cause for true felicitation."

CHAPTER XII

THE NEGRO PROBLEM ALWAYS YE
HAVE WITH YOU

No question connected with the South rested more heavily and, it must be said, more wearily upon the American mind during the eighties than the problem of the Negro. For half a century the black man had been a symbol of strife between the sections. The chasm dug by the intemperance of the abolition attack against slavery and the Reconstruction crusade to give equality of status to the freedman had fortunately closed. But a line of demarcation still divided the nation. On one side lived a people faced with the menace of Negro domination, on the other a people committed by their intervention in the past to securing justice for the inferior race. Final reconciliation waited upon an adjustment that would quiet the apprehensions of the South and still the conscience of the North.

Southern whites had fought stolidly and unyieldingly for control over a problem they insisted was domestic in nature. They continued to resist without compromise any suggestion of outside pressure. Their minds were strong in the conviction that orderly society could exist only when the Negro was rigidly disciplined. The people of the North after 1877 were for the most part in substantial agreement that the Negro was not prepared for equality and that the South should be allowed to deal with the problem in its own way, "Henceforth," as one Northern journal observed, "the nation as a nation, will have nothing more to do with him [the Negro]." [1] The South had won its major point. No longer would the black man figure as

[1] *Nation,* April 5, 1877.

"a ward of the nation" to be singled out for special guardianship or peculiar treatment.

The discipline the South elaborated in the years following Reconstruction rested frankly upon the premise of the Negro's inferiority. Much was said about the South acting defensively to erect bulwarks against the threat of Negro domination. But actually the South moved aggressively to reduce the Negro's status to something comparable to serfdom. The intention openly averred was to give an inferior people an inferior rôle and to efface them as positive factors in the section's life. To this end the new discipline excluded the colored man from politics by disfranchising him, rendered him economically impotent by making him a peon, and isolated him socially by an extensive practice of segregation. The net result was to deprive the Negro of more privileges than was necessary to keep him from becoming a menace and to make the South a "white man's country."

The methods of suppressing the Negro vote softened after the whites gained control of the machinery of state and local government, but they continued to be a mixture of fraud, trickery, intimidation and violence. Polling places were set up at points remote from colored communities. Ferries between the black districts and the voting booths went "out of repair" on election day. Grim-visaged white men carrying arms sauntered through the streets or stood near the polling booths. In districts where the blacks greatly outnumbered the whites, election officials permitted members of the superior race to "stuff the ballot box," and manipulated the count without fear of censure. Fantastic gerrymanders were devised to nullify Negro strength. The payment of poll taxes, striking at the Negro's poverty and carelessness in preserving receipts, was made a requirement for voting. Some states confused the ignorant by enacting multiple ballot box laws which required the voter to place correctly his votes for various candidates in eight or more separate boxes. The bolder members of the colored race met threats of violence and, in a diminishing number of instances, physical punishment. When the black man succeeded in passing through this maze of restrictions and cast his vote there was no assurance that it would be counted. Highly centralized election codes vested arbitrary powers in the election boards, and these powers were used to complete the elimination of the Negro vote.[2]

These practices testified eloquently to the resourcefulness of the Southern whites, but they could not be considered as an adequate or permanent solution. So long as the South persisted by extra-legal and illegal methods to nullify the spirit of the Fifteenth amendment of the Federal constitution and to violate the letter of their own state constitutions framed in the Reconstruction era, there remained a potential danger of a Federal "force bill" or a refusal on the part of Congress to seat a congressman elected from a Southern district where the abuses seemed more than ordinarily flagrant. Furthermore the practices worked to the disadvantage of certain elements of the Southern whites. Fraud could not be used against the Negro without demoralizing the whole structure of politics. Walter Hines Page pointed to instances where a group in power used its control of the election machinery to "count out" white opponents who had polled a majority vote. The illiterate and impoverished white man frequently found himself enmeshed in the restrictions that had been framed to embarrass the Negro. But most serious was the fact that, so long as the constitutional provisions for universal suffrage remained unchanged, division among the whites might result in a recrudescence of Negro voting. When Benjamin F. Tillman led the dirt farmers of South Carolina in a common man's movement against the conservatives who had ruled the state since 1877 he found his opponents voting the Negroes of the Black Belt against him.[3] The rise of Populism in the nineties accentuated the evil. Wherever the whites divided as Democrats and Populists, the rival factions courted the colored vote and some of the turbulence of Reconstruction came back again.[4]

Obviously the time had arrived for the constitutional disfranchisement of the Negro. The negative language of the

[2] The best monograph on Negro suffrage is P. Lewinson's, "Race, Class, and Party" (London, 1932).
[3] F. B. Simkins, "The Tillman Movement in South Carolina" (Durham, N. C., 1926).
[4] R. D. W. Connor and C. Poe, "The Life and Speeches of Charles Brantley Aycock" (Garden City, 1916), 64–72.

Fifteenth amendment [5] was easily surmounted. But it was not so easy to frame a measure without at the same time disfranchising the illiterate white. The Mississippi Constitutional Convention of 1890 found the solution in a cleverly devised literacy test. No person was permitted to vote who was unable to read any section of the national constitution when submitted to him, or to interpret its meaning when read to him. Significant discretionary powers permitted the registration officers to discriminate in accepting illiterate whites and rejecting illiterate blacks. South Carolina followed in 1895 with a literacy test based upon that of Mississippi. Louisiana in 1898 introduced a variant in the "grandfather clause" whereby any person was exempt from the literacy test who had voted before January 1, 1867, or who was the son or grandson of a person who had enjoyed that right. By this device her registration lists were purged of colored voters but included all classes of whites. Other variants in the form of literacy tests or educational requirements flatly designed to discriminate against the Negro were adopted in North Carolina in 1900 and Virginia in 1902. Before the twentieth century was a decade old the constitutional disfranchisement of the Negro was a fact throughout the South.

Southerners universally hailed this as an achievement of constructive statesmanship for which no apology was necessary. The Negro was branded as an alien whose ignorance, poverty, and racial inferiority were wholly incompatible with logical and orderly processes of government.[6] No difference of opinion separated Southern leaders on this point. A champion of the dirt farmers, Tillman, led the disfranchisement in South Carolina. A conservative, Aycock, waged his most significant campaign on the issue of "white supremacy" and dominated the North Carolina movement to eliminate the Negro from politics. Vardaman, of Mississippi, might express the sectional attitude with greater violence and less regard for consequences than Carter Glass, of Virginia, but it was the latter who asserted

[5] "The right of citizens of the United States to vote shall not be denied or abridged by the United States or by any State on account of race, color, or previous condition of servitude."
[6] Cf. H. W. Grady's speech at Augusta, Ga., Nov. 1887, quoted in Harris, "Grady, 126; and C. H. Otken, "The Ills of the South" (New York, 1894), 8.

on the floor of the Virginia Constitutional Convention, "Discriminate! Why that is precisely what we propose; that, exactly, is what this convention was elected for — to discriminate to the very extremity of permissible action under the limitations of the Federal Constitution, with a view to the elimination of every negro voter who can be gotten rid of legally, without materially impairing the numerical strength of the white electorate." Thoughtful Southerners found consolation in the fact that the unworkable principle of universal suffrage had been frankly discarded and looked forward to an era of peace when political battles would not be fought in terms of race antagonism.

The conditions which placed the Negro in economic peonage have been discussed in an earlier chapter.[7] It was a prevalent notion among Southerners that the colored man was shiftless, prone to idleness, and unstable as a worker. But the fact remains that he continued to do most of the rough labor of the section. Sixty per cent. of the race were farmers, and of these the vast majority were tenants on the land of white men. Thirty per cent. found employment in domestic and menial service. Others worked as unskilled laborers in mining, industry and transportation. A diminishing proportion earned a livelihood as skilled artisans while some, especially in the cities, entered the middle class occupations of tradesmen, ministers, lawyers and doctors.

The dominant race universally believed that "darkies should work for white folks." But the lowly estate of the black man resulted from his poverty, ignorance, lack of opportunity and the evils of tenancy rather than from any conscious program of the white classes. Everywhere the Negro's right to work was recognized and his permanence in the South accepted. The spread of trade unions excluded him from certain occupations he formerly had held, but with this exception the Negro at work met with little race antagonism. Nevertheless he stood on the lowest rungs of the economic ladder with little chance to mount higher. The control of industry and agriculture rested firmly in the hands of white employers. This phase of the new discipline received little contemporary attention. But its significance was great in giving stability to the structure of Southern society.

[7] *Supra*, 145–148.

The social segregation of the Negro, on the other hand, pro-
voked almost as much discussion as the process of disfranchisement. Here the South had to move positively against the earlier
program of social equality and racial association advocated and
applied by the politicians and missionaries of the Reconstruction
era. State legislatures, upon the expulsion of the Carpetbaggers,
stringently prohibited interracial marriages. The educational
system was revised to make obligatory separate schools and
colleges. Separation extended into the churches where mixed
congregations became a thing of the past. The South received
encouragement in its stand on segregation when the Supreme
Court in 1883 virtually nullified the restrictive features of the
Civil Rights Act of 1875. "Jim Crow" cars became universal
on Southern railways. Negroes were barred from admittance
to hotels, inns, restaurants, and amusement places which catered
to white people. Street cars had separate sections reserved for
whites and blacks. Local ordinances and customs supplemented
these general features of segregation, and everywhere throughout the South a color line separated the races.

Segregation did not proceed from or necessarily imply race
antagonism. It was in harmony with a basic Southern assumption that "there is an instinct, ineradicable and positive, that will
keep the races apart." [8] It recognized the biracial character of
Southern society and greatly lessened the opportunities for
friction. Yet it must be obvious that it did little to separate the
races where the Negro came into contact with the white man as
a menial. It affected mostly the black man's aspirations for
equality. As such it further accomplished the oft stated purpose
of making the South a land where the white man dominated.

The South paid heavily for its new discipline. The subordina-
tion of all other political issues to the one great principle of
Negro disfranchisement suspended the natural development and
operation of a two-party system. Democratic solidarity remained
after the colored man was safely eliminated as a factor in
politics. In fact its necessity was preached as a creed to which
all respectable Southerners must subscribe. In places this descended to the mean device of "nigger baiting" by which the
lower type of politicians perpetuated their hold on office. Inas-

[8] Harris, "Grady," 289.

much as the one issue that justified party solidarity had been settled, there remained little inducement for the ordinary citizen to participate in politics or even to vote. Politics in the South became a game for professionals, and in every state where constitutional disfranchisement occurred the number of white votes diminished in alarming proportions. The social segregation of the races added burdens equally as onerous. The meagre resources of the South proved insufficient to provide adequately for the double system of schools made necessary by the color line. Most costly of all the consequences of segregation was its retarding influence on new proposals for social and economic reform. The South could ill afford to espouse measures for progressive change until those measures had been conservatively adjusted to the biracial nature of its population. The fact that thoughtful Southerners fully appreciated the price they were paying is proof, perhaps, that the new discipline grew out of necessity and was not a reflection of an inhumane spirit.

The Negro, likewise, paid a heavy price. Disfranchisement, ruthlessly extended even into the upper classes of the race, closed to him the practical school by which democracies have trained their citizens. Economic peonage was a dreary routine of work and debt which tended to discourage ambition and enterprise and to encourage a shiftless adaptation to a bare subsistence standard of living. Segregation with its countless distinctions beat endlessly against the black man's pride and self-respect. Early in life the Negro child learned the hazards of the color line. It was the lot of every Negro to accept, as most of his race did, the badge of inferiority or to carry hidden within his inner soul an impotent yet agonizing spark of rebellion against the fateful injustice of his position.

Yet the discipline possessed advantages which far outweighed its evils. The South lived no longer in the fear of "Negro domination." The centrifugal force engendered by the doctrinaire theories of Reconstruction was definitely blocked. The new order gave a sense of security, a feeling of permanence and stability, upon which the basis of a better understanding between the races could be soundly erected. The clearly expressed superiority of the white race carried with it implications of responsibility. Throughout the South forward-looking men began advocating improved opportunities and better training for the Negro. Best of all, the discipline prevented the Negro from slipping into semi-barbarism, gave him a job and a permanent place in Southern life, and permitted a slow but definite progress for the race as a whole.

Men who like Wendell Phillips were goaded by an impatient lust to make immediately all things new viewed with pessimistic eyes the snail-like progress of the Negro. But those who based their judgment upon a more realistic conception of the actual conditions in the South took a more cheerful attitude. One careful observer reported in 1891 that the Negro not only was advancing as rapidly as any fair-minded person could expect but was also building his progress upon sound principles. He had discarded the foggy notions of Reconstruction. He no longer sought salvation in politics and legislative measures. Education he recognized as the means of redemption and he was making immense sacrifices to secure it. In spite of limited opportunities and oppressive handicaps colored men were buying farms, building homes, accumulating property, establishing themselves in trade, entering the professions, and in the cities forming centers of a cultural life. Above all it could be noted that these people, only recently emerged from slavery, were silently and steadily "developing a sense of self-respect, new capacity for self-support, and a pride in their race, which more than anything else secure for them the respect and fraternal feeling of their white neighbors." [9]

All this presupposed acquiescence in the discipline on the part of the Negro. White reporters averred that the Negro cared little for the loss of suffrage, accepted the notion that "white folks should boss," and preferred to have separate schools, churches, societies and amusements.[10] These opinions correctly mirrored the easy and even indolent adaptation of the mass of the Negroes. But the ordinary colored man left no record of his

[9] S. J. Barrows, "What the Southern Negro Is Doing for Himself," *Atlantic Monthly*, LVII (1891), 805–815.
[10] A. G. Haygood, "The South and the School Problem," *Harper's Monthly*, LXXIX (1889), 226–231; E. Kirke, "How Shall the Negro Be Educated?" *North American Review*, CXLII (1886), 422–426; E. G. Murphy, "Problems of the Present South" (New York, 1904), 34–35; J. Bryce, "Thoughts on the Negro Problem," *North American Review*, CLIII (1891), 649.

feelings, and it is impossible even to offer a guess as to what
was in his heart. Frederick Douglass raised an occasional note
of protest from the North.[11] But Douglass's leadership belonged to a passing era. The man who dominated the new period
was one who had been trained in the Hampton program of industrial education.

Booker T. Washington pointed the way along the only road
by which the aspiring Negro of the eighties could escape the
apathy and stagnation which characterized the vast majority
of the race. Tuskegee Institute and its offshoots taught the
dignity of work and endeavored to instill in students miserably
poor in preparation the moral stamina and craft skill which
would fit them for useful lives as farmers and mechanics.
Washington deplored the mistaken folly that demanded political
privileges for a race as yet unable to discharge them creditably.
He urged his people to begin at the bottom, to learn how to
read and write, to acquire farms and skills in all the trades. "It
is through the dairy farm, the truck garden, the trades, and
commercial life," he maintained, "that the negro is to find his
way to the enjoyment of all his rights." [12] Rather than protest
against the wrongs suffered by his race, he counseled patience
and the gradual remedy of economic advancement. "Nothing
else so soon brings about right relations between the two races
in the South," he wrote, "as the industrial progress of the negro.
Friction between the races will pass away in proportion as the
black man, by reason of his skill, intelligence, and character, can
produce something that the white man wants." [13] At the Atlanta
exposition of 1895 he summed up his philosophy in a speech
which received wide acclaim and which included the much
quoted: "The opportunity to earn a dollar in a factory just now
is worth infinitely more than the opportunity to spend a dollar
in an opera-house." [14]

[11] F. Douglass, "The Color Line," *North American Review*, CXXXII
(1881), 567–577.
[12] B. T. Washington, "The Awakening of the Negro," *Atlantic Monthly*,
LXXVIII (1896), 326.
[13] *Ibid.*
[14] B. T. Washington, "Up from Slavery" (New York, 1901), 218–225,
See also Washington, "The Story of the Negro" (New York, 1909), II,
passim. For the opinions of Washington's mentor, see S. C. Armstrong,
"The Future of the Negro," *North American Review*, CXXXIX (1884),
95–96.

Critics of Washington, notably the younger and brilliant W. E. B. Du Bois, argued that Washington compromised too much with the *status quo,* that the wrongs and sufferings of the colored man should be kept before the public, and that the emphasis on industrial education worked to the disadvantage of the broader cultural training necessary to produce leaders for the race. But so long as Washington lived his leadership remained unshaken. His attitude pleased the white South and contributed to the lowering of the prejudice against Negro training.[15] He was accepted in the North as the great interpreter of the Southern Negro. Northern philanthropy for the most part followed the outlines of his program. Accordingly he exercised a major influence in promoting a better mutual understanding between the North and South on the Negro question.

While the South shaped its new discipline and the Negro adjusted his life to the new conditions, Northern opinion was subjected to a flood of propaganda which sought to describe and to debate the Negro's place in American society. Congressmen discussed the issues in the national legislature, newspapers sent special reporters on tours of investigation, publicists wrote books, periodicals undertook series of articles on all sides of the question, scholars prepared what purported to be impartial and learned monographs, business men contributed their opinions, and clergymen preached sermons.[16]

The Southern point of view was forcibly presented. One line of approach was taken by Thomas Nelson Page and Basil L.

[15] J. L. M. Curry, "Report of the Commissioner of Education for 1894–1895," II, 1373.

[16] Contemporary books dealing with various aspects of this debate are: F. Bancroft, "The Negro in Politics" (New York, 1885); P. A. Bruce, "The Plantation Negro as a Freeman" (New York, 1889); G. W. Cable, "The Silent South" (New York, 1885), and "The Negro Question" (New York, 1888); W. H. Crogman, "Talks for the Times" (Atlanta, Ga., 1896); H. M. Field, "Bright Skies and Dark Shadows" (New York, 1890); T. T. Fortune, "Black and White" (New York, 1884); A. G. Haygood, "Our Brother in Black" (New York, 1881); T. N. Page, "The Old South" (New York, 1892); and A. W. Tourgée, "An Appeal to Caesar" (New York, 1884). Periodical articles appeared in great number. In one decade the *North American Review*, CXXXV–CXLIII (1877–1886), published more than two-score articles on the Negro. Godkin's editorials continued to make the *Nation* valuable. The *Forum*, newly founded in 1886, sought provocative articles. The *Century*, *Atlantic*, *Harper's Monthly*, and *Lippincott's* all contain material of importance.

Gildersleeve, the distinguished classicist. They pictured the beauties of race relationships and the mutual understanding that had existed under slavery, noted how extraneous forces had broken the entente during Reconstruction, and suggested that the reëstablishment of a discipline over the Negro would restore a spirit of friendship between whites and blacks. Henry Grady and Henry Watterson vigorously defended the disfranchisement of the Negro and attempted to explain how a Solid South was a matter of imperative necessity and constituted no menace to any national interest. P. A. Bruce was foremost among those whose scholarly approach won recognition. His "The Plantation Negro As a Freeman," published in 1889, was a careful delineation of the Negro's mental, moral and physical traits with the pessimistic conclusion that he was unfit for self-government, needed direction, and should confine himself to the lower occupations. Atticus G. Haygood explained to the North the need for separate schools, stressed the importance of patience and pleaded for Northern aid and coöperation. The Southern argument was effectively summarized by Page: "We have educated him [the Negro]; we have aided him; we have sustained him in all directions. We are ready to continue our aid; but we will not be dominated by him. When we shall be, it is our settled conviction that we shall deserve the degradation into which we shall have sunk." [17]

The close of the century gave Southerners two additional arguments. For a long time assertions had been made to the effect that in spite of their pretensions Northerners possessed as much race antipathy toward the colored man as did Southerners. It remained for a Negro historian and sociologist, W. E. B. Du Bois, to produce conclusive documentation of the fact. Du Bois's "The Philadelphia Negro, A Social Study," published in 1899, revealed a problem in the North not unlike that in the South, one that was handled in much the same way, and one that was equally as far from solution. The moral, if one needed to be drawn, was, as expressed in the *Nation*, "patience and sympathy toward the South whose difficulties have been far greater than those of the North." [18] The acquisition of the

[17] T. N. Page, "Old South," 344.
[18] *Nation*, Oct. 26, 1899.

Philippine Islands under Republican auspices taught another lesson in consistency. The party refused to grant equality of rights to a "backward people" in the new possession. Could it continue the pretense of championing the right of a "backward people" at home to participate on equal terms in the affairs of government?

One important Southern voice was raised in protest against the treatment of the Negro. George Washington Cable refused to recognize a system built on discrimination, exclusion and subjugation. He charged his fellow-Southerners with deliberate and persistent evasion of the laws enacted to protect the freedmen. He charged them with cherishing and perpetuating prejudices born in slavery and building a false creed on the fiction of instinctive and ineradicable differences between the races. Cable wrote effectively and at length. He received a courteous hearing in the North but his influence was negligible. Even his unpopularity and voluntary exile from the South caused little comment. The drift of Northern opinion was distinctly set in channels other than Cable wished to direct it. Thomas Nast caught the essence of this fact in a cartoon captioned "A Dead Issue," in which the South is pictured as too busy at work to find time for mistreating Negroes, much to the chagrin of Northern doctrinaires who reluctantly see the Negro issue die.[19]

Among Northerners the attack on the Southern position was limited to politicians like Foraker and Blaine, die-hards like Judge Tourgée and General Sherman, and partisan editors like Murat Halstead and Whitelaw Reid. The ordinary citizen left no record of his views, but newspapers commented on his growing unconcern with the welfare of the Negro, an opinion which finds corroboration in the inefficacy of the "bloody shirt" in politics. Northern reporters of Southern conditions after the middle eighties followed the pattern of McClure, J. B. Harrison, and Schurz and sympathetically portrayed the Southern attitude. Meanwhile the intellectuals who controlled the Northern periodicals were exceedingly understanding. This was especially true of Gilder, in the *Century,* and Godkin, in the *Nation,* both of whom waged consistent campaigns to explain the conditions which made necessary in the South a discipline

[19] *Harper's Weekly,* Aug. 29, 1885.

over the colored man. "The fact is, and the sooner the fact is recognized the sooner we shall be rid of many dangerous illusions," wrote Gilder in a typical passage, "that the negroes constitute a peasantry wholly untrained in, and ignorant of, those ideas of constitutional liberty and progress which are the birthright of every white voter; that they are gregarious and emotional rather than intelligent, and are easily led in any direction by white men of energy and determination." [20] The obvious conclusion is the one made by Godkin, "I do not see, in short, how the negro is ever to be worked into a system of government for which you and I would have much respect." [21]

It seems even more remarkable that the men in the North most interested in the welfare of the Negro should accept so largely the Southern defense. Thomas Wentworth Higginson, who will be remembered as an ardent abolitionist and an officer of Negro troops, revisited the South in 1878 and reported that he found the Negroes industrious, prospering, and progressive, and noted a conspicuous absence of any strained relations between the races.[22] Six years later Higginson paid a glowing tribute to the South. "I know nothing more manly in this generation than the manner the Southern whites since the war have addressed themselves to the problem of educating the blacks." [23]

What was true of Higginson was true of A. D. Mayo whose great educational work in the South was a bright feature of sectional coöperation in the field of humanitarian endeavor. He too believed that the Negro was far below the standard of meriting full citizenship. He was as fulsome as Page in praising the personal attachment of Southerners to the colored folk and as meticulous as Harris in defending the necessity of white leadership. His conclusion was that "the logic of the new Southern life is all on the side of the final elevation of the Negro." [24]

[20] Editorial, *Century*, XXIII (1883), 945–946.
[21] Ogden, "Godkin," II, 114.
[22] T. W. Higginson, "Some War Scenes Revisited," *Atlantic Monthly*, XLII (1878), 1–9.
[23] T. W. Higginson, "Young Men's Party" (pamphlet, New York, 1884).
[24] A. D. Mayo, "The Negro-American Citizen in the New American Life" (pamphlet, Lake Mohonk, N. Y., 1890).

Workers who canvassed the North for funds to aid the Negro in the South also spread a conciliatory message. Industrial training was the fancy of the day and the prestige of Tuskegee further popularized the tendency to ask for funds in terms of an acquiescing philosophy. In any case Northerners heard the voice of philanthropy saying that the blacks must be for some time servants, farm laborers, and mechanics, that they should be trained to do skillful work and thus be made good citizens, that they needed to be taught less about books and more about life and daily duties, that they must begin at the bottom and slowly move upward.

From the prolonged discussion of the Negro problem certain conventional attitudes gradually emerged to become fixed and basic formulæ in the American credo. It might be informative to list a number of these attitudes, associating with each the names of several Northerners who expressed it in print.

1. The mass of Negroes are unfit for the suffrage. — R. W. Gilder, A. D. Mayo, and the Englishman James Bryce.

2. The only hope for good government in the South rests upon the assured political supremacy of the white race. — Edward Atkinson, E. L. Godkin, Carl Schurz, Charles Eliot Norton, C. D. Warner.

3. The Negroes are the American peasantry. — N. S. Shaler, J. B. Harrison, H. M. Field.

4. One race or the other must rule; the true interests of both races require that the control should be in the hands of the whites. — Hugh McCulloch, A. K. McClure, G. F. Hoar.

5. If there be a race problem, time and education can alone supply its solution. — R. C. Winthrop, A. W. Tourgée, C. F. Adams.

6. Northerners when confronted with the race problem at home show the same prejudices Southerners do. In fact, the attitude of the Anglo-Saxons toward the Negro the world over is essentially the same. — E. L. Godkin, S. C. Armstrong, J. G. Holland, T. W. Higginson, H. M. Field.

7. The Negro is better off in Southern hands. — A. D. Mayo, T. W. Higginson, R. W. Gilder.

8. The history of the Negro in Africa and America "leads to the belief that he will remain inferior in race stamina and race achievement." — A. B. Hart.

Few Northerners could be found at the close of the century who did not subscribe to the greater part of this credo. A tremendous reversal of opinion had materialized. The unchanging elements of the race problem had become apparent to most observers and the old impatient yearning for an immediate and thorough solution had passed away. Once a people admits the fact that a major problem is basically insoluble they have taken the first step in learning how to live with it. The conflicting elements of the race problem had dropped into a working adjustment which was accepted and rationalized as a settlement. Imperfect as it was, it permitted a degree of peace between North and South hitherto unknown, gave to the South the stability of race relations necessary to reconcile her to the reunited nation, and gave to the Negro a chance to live and to take the first steps of progress.

CHAPTER XIII

THE NEW PATRIOTISM

THIRTY years after Appomattox there remained no fundamental conflict between the aspirations of North and South. The people of the United States constituted at last a nation integrated in interests and united in sentiment. In spite of differences in past traditions and continuing regional divergences the structure of society North and South rested upon approximately the same foundations. The controlling influences which shaped national destiny operated in one section as freely as in the other. The interlocking of economic dependence had completed its mastery over particularistic trends. Programs of social and economic progress found definition in terms to which Southerners as well as Northerners subscribed. The memories of the past were woven in a web of national sentiment which selected from bygone feuds those deeds of mutual valor which permitted pride in present achievement and future promise. The remarkable changes that had taken place within the short span of a single generation had created a national solidarity hitherto unknown in American life. The reunited nation was a fact.

Testimony of the extent to which the South responded to the dynamic currents of national life was found in its participation in the educational revival of the closing decades of the century. The country rededicated itself to faith in education as the agency for molding the complex forces of modern life. New energy and greater wealth poured into a movement which accomplished improvement in every part of the educational system from the primary school to the university. Progress in the South was much slower than in the North. Poverty, sparsity of population, and the costliness of a biracial system made for inadequate schools and undereducated people. Nevertheless, not since the days when Thomas Jefferson made public education a cardinal principle of Americanism had Southern leaders in and out of politics demanded so insistently the attainment of the "American ideal" of universal education. Furthermore, while much remained to be accomplished, the foundations for future success had been laid. When the century closed Southern education no longer constituted an entity with basic ideals and comprehensive programs peculiar to itself. The South was part of the national educational system.

Common faith and common objectives made possible common understanding and common endeavor between the sections. The fight for better schools in the Southern states was a typical American epic which paralleled the experience of communities in the East and West. Northerners, knowing full well the nature of the battle, could easily understand and participate in the Southern movement.

So much Northern energy, time, thought and money entered into the effort to improve Southern education that the movement is properly described as a "narrative of coöperation between Northern and Southern leaders." On many occasions men from all parts of the country sat down together in conferences for a full and frank discussion of educational problems. The *Atlanta Constitution* asserted in 1889 that "more money has been spent by Northern men for collegiate education for negroes in Atlanta alone than any six Southern states have given to collegiate education for white boys. The Northern Methodist Church alone is spending more money in the South for higher education than all the Southern States combined give to their colleges." Possibly the *Constitution* exaggerated. But Northern philanthropy, notably the Congregational and Northern Methodist churches, and the John F. Slater Fund, founded in 1882, still carried the major load of Negro education. Even Southern white colleges, as Vanderbilt, Tulane, and Emory testified, rested heavily upon Northern financial support. The two most active workers in the field of Southern education were J. L. M. Curry, a Southerner who served as general agent of the Peabody Education Fund, and A. D. Mayo, a Northerner who in 1880 entered a long and valuable "ministry of education in the South." The identical nature of their work suggests that harmony of thought and action which existed between the sections on the subject of education.

The "narrative of coöperation" reached its natural culmination in a series of annual conferences for education in the South which began in 1898 at Capon Springs, West Virginia. Outstanding leaders from both sections participated in these meetings where problems were fully discussed and plans formulated. The conferences led to the organization of the Southern Educational Board in 1901 and the General Education Board in 1902, agencies which in the succeeding years were to achieve much in the South. The men who participated in this work — R. C. Ogden, G. F. Peabody, Albert Shaw, D. C. Gilman, R. I. McIver, E. A. Alderman, W. H. Page, J. D. Rockefeller, Jr., and others — exemplified the new patriotism which brought about "an interweaving of minds and intermingling of hearts." [1]

In a much deeper sense the economic interests of the South could not be separated from those of the country at large. In the background of national life many prosaic influences operated to weld together the vast territories and regional varieties of the United States. The romantic souls who still insisted that Northerners and Southerners constituted two peoples with more points of difference than resemblance were prone to overlook such commonplace factors as the absence of tariff barriers, the uniformity of business methods and business ethics, the ease of transportation and communication, the standardization of advertising, the easy flow of credit and the wide expanse of investments, the uniformity of currency and of weights and measures, the free movement of salesmen with only one language to speak and similarity of taste to satisfy, and the prevalent acceptance in all sections of the business man's objectives as desirable. Nevertheless these phenomena were the most potent influences of the day. They combined to effect a nationalizing of business which embraced the South as completely as the North and West. [2]

[1] See Schlesinger, "Rise of the City," 160–201, for an account of the national revival in education. On the South see Knight, "Public Education in the South," 415–435, and Murphy, "Problems of the Present South," 205–250. The many speeches, articles, and reports of Curry and Mayo are invaluable. The periodical literature continues to be useful.

[2] Cf. I. M. Tarbell, "The Nationalizing of Business" (New York, 1936).

Every phase of Southern industry testified to the interlocking dependence of economic activity. If the Louisiana
sugar farmers raised a crop worth millions annually, the
money was paid out as rapidly as received and percolated into
every state of the Union — into Kentucky and Missouri for
mules, into Pennsylvania for oil and coal, into Iowa and
Kansas for oats, corn and hay, into Minnesota and the Dakotas
for wheat, into Illinois for meat, into Wisconsin for butter,
milk and cheese, into Ohio and Illinois for wagons, carriages,
and agricultural implements, into Massachusetts for shoes, and
into New York and Pennsylvania for clothing.[3] The eight
billions of dollars which the South received in payment for her
cotton crop in the years from 1865 to 1900 explained in part
her rapid recuperation. But it also had a direct bearing on
the growth of financial centers in New York and Philadelphia,
and kept many a New England mill and Mid-Western farm
busily engaged in manufacturing goods and raising food which
the South consumed.[4] Even the localizing of cotton manufactures in the Piedmont created connecting links as significant
as the more publicized rivalry of the sections. The flow of New
England capital into the South after 1890 did not mean the
destruction of the industry in the older section. It meant a
further specialization in which mills under the same ownership would turn out in the South products unlike those in the
North. Thus Augusta might be considered a complement of
New Bedford and Charlotte of Lowell. As one observer
noted, "Pennsylvania declines in cotton but, if the competi-
tion of North Carolina silences its spindles, the soft yarns of
that state supply its hosiery looms." [5] Or again, "The sheetings
and print cloths of the South are consumed in Northern homes
and Southern yarns are woven on Pennsylvania looms and
made into hosiery on New York and Pennsylvania frames." [6]
A new occupation appeared, that of middleman between the
sections, and more than one Yankee and Southerner found

[3] W. C. Stubbs, in "The South in the Building of the Nation," VI, 85–86.
[4] Edmonds, "South's Redemption," 26–28; Hoke Smith, "Disastrous
Effects of the Force Bill," Forum, XIII (1892), 692.
[5] V. S. Clark, in "The South in the Building of the Nation," VI, 302–
303.
[6] Eleventh Census (1890), "Manufactures," part III, 172.

profitable employment sitting on the boards of cotton mills North and South.[7]

Other industries likewise demonstrated that complexity and diversification resulted in a closer relation with the other portions of the country. The story of iron and steel in the Birmingham-Chattanooga district changed into a narrative of ever greater combination leading to final inclusion in the vast corporations that had their headquarters in Pittsburgh.[8] The trend in tobacco manufactures was toward concentration of ownership and the creation of one of the country's greatest trusts, with the South's wealthiest individual, James Buchanan Duke, playing the dominant rôle.[9] Everywhere throughout the South the influence of expanding markets and broader contacts was in evidence. The railroad net expanded while major consolidations produced a few great systems which gave stability and permanence to the Southern transportation system.[10] The activity of the banking house of J. P. Morgan indicated the absorption of the South in national economy as did the spread of chain stores whose red front architecture told the American he was as much at home in Mobile and Dallas as in Sacramento, Des Moines and Hartford.

The South remained basically agricultural, and agriculture was seriously depressed throughout the nineties. Nevertheless the ills of the South in this respect were the ills of the nation at large. Falling prices, maladjustment in production, defective farm credit, and increasing tenancy were in a sense problems that brought together farmers of all sections of the country in a community of interest.[11] Furthermore important progressive steps were taken in agricultural education, and most of these were made in harmony with Northern influences. Equally significant was the spread of Southern farm journals and the interchange of editorial opinion with the journals of the Mid-West.[12]

[7] Various biographical sketches in Lamb's "Textiles."
[8] Armes, "Coal and Iron in Alabama," *passim.*
[9] Boyd, "Story of Durham," 95, 129.
[10] Bruce, "New South," 286; U. B. Phillips, in "The South in the Building of the Nation," VI, 311.
[11] J. D. Hicks, "The Populist Revolt" (Minneapolis, 1931).
[12] *Cf.* the comment of R. H. Edmonds, "Facts about the South" (Baltimore, 1894), 29–30.

An important new feature in the agricultural situation was the development of truck farming for Northern markets. Changes in the nation's dietary habits, the extension of transportation facilities, the invention of the refrigerator car, and a longer growing season combined to give the South a lucrative industry which united it more intimately with the North. The trucking district extended along the coast from the eastern shore of Maryland and Virginia through the Carolinas into Florida and thence along the Gulf of Mexico into Texas. Baltimore, Norfolk, Wilmington, Charleston, Savannah, Mobile and Galveston were among the cities which profited as shipping centers of this produce. Various districts specialized in green vegetables, potatoes, onions, peanuts, strawberries, peaches, citrus fruits and melons. The South by 1900 had become "the market garden of the North," and another economic bond had been established between the sections.[13]

Apart from the movement of business men, intersectional migration remained chiefly a matter of travel southward for health and recreation. The winter resorts of the South Atlantic region increased steadily in popularity. Florida developed so rapidly that the large number of rich and middle-class visitors who annually sought pleasure and relaxation in its semi-tropical climate profoundly changed its social, political and economic life. On the other hand, the continued efforts of railroad companies and state and local agencies to attract settlers to the agricultural areas of the South met with slight success.[14] The census of 1900 did show a larger percentage of newcomers than that of 1890, but the figures were insignificant when compared both with the immigrants who settled in the North and West and with the number of Southerners who were lured to the metropolitan centers of the Northeast and Mid-West.[15] Nevertheless it can be said that the Northerners who made their living in the South as business men and college professors exercised an influence greater than their numbers while Southerners found no door closed to them in the

[13] Bruce, "New South," 63–77.
[14] W. L. Fleming, "Immigration to the Southern States," *Political Science Quarterly*, XX (1905), 276–297. See as typical Illinois Central Railroad, "Homeseekers' Guide for 1895."
[15] Twelfth Census (1900), "Population," I, cxxvi–cxxviii.

North. Yankees in the South for the most part conformed
with the prevailing attitude of the community. But in the North
it was an asset for the Southerner to treat his origin with
pride. To be of the South was, to say the least, a social asset
which few Southerners resident in the North failed to appreciate.

An examination of the South in 1898 would still reveal
a predominantly agricultural people living in a relatively
sparsely settled country. Vast proportions of the population
lived in poverty and isolation. Every index of wealth and
culture revealed the Southern states below the average of the
Union. Progress in the main had been in other fields than
agriculture. The advancing South stood in stark contrast to
the South of social wastage and unchanging ways. No traveler
could miss the conflicting patterns. On one page he would note
the town "with mills and shops and paved streets and electric
lights," "well-maintained schools," "men who have wider range
of activities and women who have more clothes," "the spread
of well-being," and "the quickening of the intellectual life."
On the next page a dismal picture would appear of unkempt
farms on which "the general structure of life is the same —
a dull succession of the seasons where agriculture is practised in
old-fashioned ways, where weary housewives show resignation
rather than contentment and where ignorance has become satisfied with itself." [16]

The rural South was far from being progressive and it was
here that poverty and isolation erected barriers against the
currents of national life. The problem was not one of living
antagonisms to the Union. Not bitterness but loneliness caused
memories of the old to linger and prevented the infusion of
the new. Ministers of the old gospel could present to such people
liberalism as a Yankee menace. Politicians of the dominant
party could treat them as citizens of a section. Men and
women who represented the old order of things could "incul-
cate social and political principles alien to American ideals." [17]
Nevertheless the reactionary influences were spent impulses

[16] W. H. Page, "The Rebuilding of Old Commonwealths" (New York,
1902), 109, 110, 116.
[17] W. P. Trent, "Dominant Forces in Southern Life," *Atlantic Monthly*,
LXXIX (1897), 50-51; Page, *op. cit.*, 134-142.

fighting a losing battle with the constructive forces of industry and education. The rich potentialities of Southern life could be realized only if the section adjusted itself to modern ways.[18] The rejuvenation of North Carolina, once "a valley of humiliation between two mountains of conceit," the careers within the South of Curry, Tompkins, Aycock and Harris, and the achievements on the national stage of Duke, Woodrow Wilson and W. H. Page, testified to the fact that wealth and leadership came to the communities and individuals that were in harmony with the major trends of national life.[19]

Men and women of irreconcilable temper survived in both the North and South. Once they had found in the divergent interests of the sections fertile ground for advancing their programs of suspicion and distrust. But the new age gave little encouragement to their outworn attitude. The Southern states no longer had any common object to pursue aggressively against the interests of the nation. The North could in no realistic sense picture the South as a menace to its life. The irreconcilables were rendered insignificant. The only outlets for their venom were the relatively harmless activities of insulting the heroes of the other section, founding historical societies on narrow bases, and vexing the writers of history textbooks. Even the hatred of the opposing section no longer implied hatred of the Union. The tradition of past antagonism could not retard in either section the development of common pride in a common country.

Nevertheless the loyalty which both professed to the reunited nation was marked by a fundamental difference in attitude. Northerners were prone to think of their section as being more characteristically American than any other part of the Union. Southerners thought of Dixie as a unit within a larger unit. Yet even this attitude was not antagonistic to the new nationalism. The patriotism of locality is as firm a base upon which to build a broad love for the nation as the Northern

---

[18] Cf. H. W. Odum, "An American Epoch" (New York, 1930), 327, and Bruce, "New South," 421–435.

[19] Cf. C. H. Poe, "The Rebound of the Upland South," World's Work, XIV, (1907), 8961–8978; Curry, "Address in Charleston, S. C., May 12, 1889"; Alderman, "Memorial Address on the Life of J. L. M. Curry"; and Hendrick, "Training of an American."

tendency to extol the greater at the expense of the lesser. In fact, one of Dixie's major contributions to the new patriotism was its insistence that a valid nationalism could be premised only upon respect for and conservation of properly integrated variations in regional culture. This in a sense had been the Southern cause in the Civil War. Its survival was a tribute to Southern success in resisting an exclusively Northern formulation of Americanism.[20]

The varied threads of reconciliation had woven their garment of reunion when the outbreak of the war with Spain advertised the fact that the people of the United States were a nation. Protestations of loyalty on the part of Confederate veterans had commonly been accompanied by assertions that, if the war cloud again hovered above the country, the former boys in gray would rally as proudly in defense of the Stars and Stripes as did the wearers of the blue. The Spanish-American war demonstrated their sincerity and in doing so completed the revolution in sentiment through which the generation had passed. For a time all people within the country felt the electrifying thrill of a common purpose. When it subsided a sense of nationality had been rediscovered, based upon consciousness of national strength and unity.

The South at once responded to the national excitement which followed the sinking of the *Maine*. The first active movement of the regular army was the mobilization of troops in Southern centers. Two of the four major-generals appointed from civil life were veterans of the Confederate army, Fitzhugh Lee and "Fighting Joe" Wheeler. This was recognition of a fact that Southerners proudly proclaimed, that "upon any battlefield of the war Confederate veterans and their sons will be seen upholding the national honor and guarding the country's safety with all the steadiness and resolution that characterized them in the early sixties." [21] When the blood of the two sections was shed in common it was only natural for the country to feel that, as the Confederate Survivors' Association declared in their Charleston meeting of 1899,

[20] *Cf.* on this point B. B. Kendrick and A. M. Arnett, "The South Looks at Its Past" (Chapel Hill, 1935), and H. W. Odum, "Southern Regions" (Chapel Hill, 1936).
[21] *Richmond Times,* as quoted in *Public Opinion,* XXIV (1898), 326.

"These dead, at least, belong to us all." [22] The unofficial laureates of the American countryside again felt their muse inspired. From their voluminous production, which filled the magazines and newspapers of the time, one can gain sure insight into the popular frame of mind. The theme is unvaried. The foes of bygone days were friends. President McKinley made the final gesture when at Atlanta in 1898 he affirmed the care of Confederate graves to be a national duty. [23]

The youngest boy who could have carried arms at Gettysburg was a man of fifty when the century closed while those who remembered "Bloody Kansas" were in their sixties. By far the greater portion of the generation which had listened with awe while the guns boomed in Virginia and the ships of war steamed on the Mississippi slept in silent graves in which the issues for which they had contended were buried with them. The old had given way to the new. Around the lingering survivors pressed eager youth. Slowly the bent figures of the past took their leave. Behind them stretched in mellow retrospect a record of heroic war and greater peace. No discontent accompanied their departure. Reconciled themselves, they left a heritage of complete adjustment to the conditions which the war had brought.

Greater than sacrifice on the field was this victory of peace. How different it would have been had the generation of the war died unreconciled and bequeathed to children the antipathies of their lives! Then would the task of reunion have been complicated beyond the hope of solution, for nothing is more ineradicable than hatreds that are inherited. Americans registered one of their noblest achievements when within a single generation true peace had come to those who had been at war.

[22] *Confederate Veteran*, V (1899), 246.
[23] See, as typical of Southern opinion, the remarks of S. D. Lee, in "Confederate Military History," 360–368.

THE END

INDEX

Deshler, Charles D., work of, 224, 225
Dickinson, Anne E., abolitionist, 234
Douglas, Stephen, 72
Douglass, Frederick, raises note of protest, 291
Downing, Fannie, her "Dixie," 40
Draper, John W., his history of the war, 56, 57
Drum, R. C., 274
Du Bois, W. E. B., and Negro problem, 292, 293
Duke, James Buchanan, tobacco manufacturer, 302, 305
Durham, growth of, 184
Dwight, Theodore, 180

EARLY, JUBAL A., fraternizing with Blaine, 106
Edmonds, Richard H., booster of Southern industry, 171; his "South's Redemption," 190, 191
Edmunds, Senator, and amnesty bill, 125
Education, Southern, 162–166; of the Negro, 166, 167; revival of, 298–300
Edwards, H. S., work of, 204, 222, 225
Eggleston, Edward, writing of, 201
Eggleston, George Cary, 161; work of, 204, 225, 246
Eliot, President, of Harvard, receives Southerners, 136
Elliott, Maud Howe, quoted, 22
Emerson, Ralph Waldo, quoted, 11, 12
English, Thomas Dunn, his dialect poems, 201
Evarts, W. M., 269

FAIRCHILD, GEN., 274
Farnsworth, Representative, supports amnesty bill, 124
Farragut, Admiral, 165
Ferry, Senator, supports amnesty bill, 124
Fessenden, W. P., 87, 88

Field, Eugene, Republicanism of, 268, 269
Field, H. M., on the Negro, 296
Finch, Francis Miles, his "Blue and the Gray," 118, 119
Fish, Hamilton, 165
Fisk University, founded, 166, 167
Fitch, Clyde, 233
Florida, its development as winter resort, 303
Fontaine, F., work of, 204
Foraker, Gov., 275, 276; attacks South, 294
Forbes, J. M., accepts Democratic ticket, 271
Forrest, Gen. N. B., 86, 120
Forsyth, John, editor of Register, 186
Frick, H. C., 180

GARFIELD, JAMES A., 78, 265; indicts Sherman, 88; an ardent Republican, 108; and campaign of 1878, 111–113; assassinated, 141, 142
Garland, appointed to cabinet, 272
Gee, Major John H., of Salisbury, 46
General Amnesty Act (1872), 126
General Education Board, organized, 300
Gettysburg, reunion at, 257–260
Gilder, Richard Watson, editor of Scribner's, 221–223, 226, 227, 265, 266; his "Great Remembrance," 247; his understanding of South, 294–296
Gildersleeve, Basil L., on Negro problem, 292, 293
Gillette, William, 233
Gilman, D. C., 300
Gladden, Washington, advises forgiveness, 6, 13; on Negro vote, 278
Glass, Carter, on Negro vote, 286, 287
Godkin, Edwin L., 266; claims Lee unfit, 14; supports Grant, 95, 96; his criticism of pacification policy, 97–100; "under full sail of reform," 192; against Demo-